THE SCHWARTZ
STOCK MARKET HANDBOOK

THE SCHWARTZ STOCK MARKET HANDBOOK

1996 Edition

by
David Schwartz

Burleigh Publishing Company

© Burleigh Publishing Company 1995

Compiled and edited by David Schwartz
Published by Burleigh Publishing Company
Burleigh Hall, Burleigh, Stroud, Gloucestershire GL5 2PF
First published 1994
Second edition 1995

ISBN 0 9523961 5 7
ISSN 1358-9938

A CIP record for this book is available from the British Library

Produced by Trigon Press, Beckenham, Kent
Printed in England

CONTENTS

INTRODUCTION

The Schwartz Stock Market Handbook is a study of historical stock market trends. Our goal is to help investors to improve the odds of making profitable investment decisions by applying the lessons of the past to the future.

The current edition is designed to carry readers through 1996 on a month-by-month basis. An important adjunct to the Handbook is a free quarterly newsletter to give readers up-to-the-minute advice of what to expect from the stock market in the months ahead. Details on how to receive your free copy can be found on page xi.

Bigger and better

We made three major improvements to this edition:

▶ Many long-term investors are less interested in short-term windows of opportunity but are keen to discover multi-month and multi-year stock market opportunities. We have added lots of material to help forecast where prices are likely to go in the months and year ahead.

▶ We now include a *Monthly Investment Monitor* at the beginning of each month's chapter to help readers evaluate their portfolios and to maintain a record of key stock market indices to assist in future forecasting.

▶ Since Wall Street plays a large and increasingly important role in the UK stock market, we now provide information about America's stock market on a month-by-month basis as well.

Our conversations with readers suggest that some are failing to gain the full benefit from *The Schwartz Stock Market Handbook*. One group appears to have read it, agreed with some of the points, put it away, and promptly returned to their investment patterns of the past.

Others read each chapter after the fact to see whether the expected scenario actually materialised. We hate to ruin their good time but our forecasts are merely historically-derived probabilities. When we say prices rise eight out of 10 times after Condition X occurs, it also means they fall twice. By definition, all projections are periodically wrong.

Usage suggestion

The *Handbook* is designed to be a companion to all of your stock market decisions during 1996. We suspect it is very different from any other book about the stock market that you have ever encountered, and we recommend you read it differently as well. At the very minimum, start by reading the first few pages of each monthly chapter to give you an overview about the year ahead. Near the beginning of each month, re-read the appropriate chapter more carefully. Even if you don't study every monthly or quarterly trend, you should have a clear sense of how the month typically unfolds, whether the odds favour an up-move or a down-move, and which segments of the month are most likely to be strong or weak.

Important to re-read

Most important of all, whenever you contemplate a trade, you should re-read the relevant chapter, paying careful attention to the nuances as well as the big picture. This procedure will not put you on the winning side of every transaction, but over the long run, will shift the odds of being right a bit further in your favour.

About our data sources:

A 76 year-long monthly price trend index was built from

three sources: from 1919 to 1924, an index compiled by *British Banker Magazine*; from 1925 to March 1962, the *Investors Chronicle* Industrial Index which was periodically changed and up-dated; from April 1962 to the present, the FT-Non-financial Index (formerly the FT-'500') which also was periodically up-dated.

The *British Banker* and *Investors Chronicle* series' are both long out of print. They were located by researchers at Barclays deZoete Wedd Securities Limited. We are grateful to them, especially to Michael Hughes, Managing Director – Economics and Strategy for making this data available to *The Schwartz Stock Market Handbook* readers.

Prefer FT-Non-financial Index

We prefer the FT-Non-financial Index to the slightly broader FT-SE A All Shares Index for forecasting purposes. You can find it each day in the FT-SE Actuaries Share Indices chart in the *Financial Times*. On weekdays, it is on the back page of Section 2. On weekends, it is in the middle of Section 1.

All short-term (daily or partial month) price trends discussed in this book are derived from the FT Ordinary Share Index (or FT-30) which has been running since 1 July 1935. It is comprised of 30 leading, actively traded companies. Each has been deliberately selected because of size and frequency of share trading activity, to represent a cross-section of British industry. The FT-30 is not dominated by the recently privatised utilities, unlike some other indices, and is less interest-rate sensitive.

FT-30 for short-term trends

We agree that there are deficiencies associated with this index, not the least of which is that it is based on only 30 companies. Still, it is the only continuous daily index that has been published for 60 years and is the best tool available for comparing current short-term fluctuations with fluctuations stimulated by historical events. The FT-SE 100, in contrast, has been in existence for a little over one decade. On weekdays, you can find the FT Ordinary Share Index in the *Financial Times*, Section 2, three pages from the end, lower right hand corner. On weekends, Section 1, same position.

As you will see, this book contains many profit-enhancing trends to help you to maximise your investment performance in 1996. As you read and study them, keep in mind the three guiding principles that underly every historical price trend analysis:

▶ No one can forecast flawlessly where share prices are heading. Historically-based probabilities define the odds of an up or down move based on past performance trends. They increase the likelihood that investors make the right choice but do not guarantee success.

▶ Although historical price trends often provide strong clues about the direction of future share price moves, fresh economic or political news makes hash of these probabilities. Witness the market's reaction to a possible change of government, sudden increase in the inflation rate or to rumours of an interest rate change.

▶ Most important of all, knowledge of a probable event often causes investor behaviour to change (perhaps buying shares in advance to catch an expected up-move). The effect of these behaviour changes is to alter the underlying pattern that created the trend in the first place. Historical analysis is a never ending process. Investors must keep studying the market to keep abreast of changing patterns.

David Schwartz, Editor
June 1995

FREE QUARTERLY NEWSLETTER

Readers of *The Schwartz Stock Market Handbook* are invited to receive a free quarterly newsletter that we publish at the end of each quarter of the year – March, June, September, and December.

Each issue focuses on the three months ahead and contains our forecast of where the stock market is heading.

There are no gimmicks. It's absolutely free. To order, please submit a separate stamped, pre-addressed A4 sized envelope for each issue to:

Quarterly Newsletter
Schwartz Stock Market Handbook
Burleigh Publishing Company
Burleigh Hall, Burleigh
Stroud, Gloucestershire GL5 2PF

You may submit all four envelopes at once.

For readers who find it more convenient for us to address and provide postage for the newsletter, we will send to you the next four issues, air mailed when appropriate, for a total annual cost as follows:

United Kingdom	£3.00
Europe (including Eire)	£4.00
South Pacific and Far East	£7.00
Rest of world	£6.00

Be sure to print your name and mailing address clearly, using block letters. If you pay by credit card, please provide us with the card type, card number and expiry date.

DISCLAIMER

This book is essentially a review of past stock market trends. It is based upon an historical analysis of every closing price on the various share price indices available at the time this book was prepared.

Every statement we make about possible future price movements is a statistical projection derived from past trends. No one knows if any of these relationships will continue in the future. Our observations are not intended to be recommendations to buy or sell any particular stock or the market as a whole.

Statements about profits or losses associated with any buy or sell action are calculated before all fees and taxes of any kind.

Remember that the price of any stock market investment can go down as well as up. You can easily lose some or all of your investment. This is especially true of various derivatives which are very volatile.

Be sure to discuss the risk of any investment you are considering with a qualified adviser before making any investment decision.

CHAPTER ONE – OVERVIEW

£82,000 vs
£150 million

Prevailing wisdom advises investors to invest steadily for the long-run by buying and holding shares through thick and thin. You can't outguess the markets, so goes the theory, so keep fully invested to catch each up-surge whenever it comes.

At first glance, it is hard to fault the advice. Assuming someone invested £1,000 in the stock market in 1919, when modern stock market record-keeping began, and held on until the end of 1994, his or her portfolio would have grown to over £82,000, considerably better than the rate of inflation.

But here is another point of view to ponder. Imagine a second hypothetical investor who also held shares since 1919, but had the magical ability to move out of shares at the very beginning of every bear market, and jump back into shares at the very beginning of each bull market. His start-up investment of £1,000 would now be worth over £150 million, ignoring taxes and commissions. No joke.

If that same investor placed his funds into an interest-bearing savings account during bear market periods when he was not holding shares, assuming a modest 4% average annual interest rate for the 76 years covered by this survey, his £1,000 nest egg would have grown to over £400 million.

Do you think this analysis is unrealistic, amateurish or unattainable? We agree. No one can spot every bull market on day one, ride it to its peak, and step aside at the precise moment it reaches its high point.

But by the same token, do you still believe that investing for the long-run by steadily holding shares through thick and thin is the only stock market road to follow?

The goal of *The Schwartz Stock Market Handbook* is to help investors to manage their portfolios more effectively by guiding them through the year, month-by-month.

But some very important trends don't fit neatly into a specific segment of the year, and are best treated separately. A good example is the very pronounced tendency for broad, multi-month or multi-year advances, what many investors call bull markets, to run their course at a faster and faster speed.

Leisurely pace in first half of century

During the first half of this century, the typical long-term up-move ran for 72 months. Share prices rose by 145% during each advance, on average. The shortest advance ran for 55 months. With runs of this magnitude and length, investors had ample opportunity to ride a trend for several years, once it began, even if they didn't catch it at the very beginning.

Things began to change just after World War II. Stock market cycles shortened abruptly. The typical up-turn ran its course in 24 months during the third quarter of this century, one-third the typical pre-war length. The very longest ended in 1961 after a run of 38 months, shorter than *any* pre-war advance.

16 months is now the norm

The shortening process continues to this day. Since 1975, we have seen eight separate advances. The average length was 23 months, a figure helped by the 70-month up-turn that ended in 1987. If we eliminate this advance, which was atypical in many different ways, the remaining seven up-moves ran for just 16 months on average *(see Table 1.1)*. The longest ran for 21 months, *less* than the average of the previous quarter-century. The shortest of the seven ran for just 11 months.

The average increase in share prices during these seven recent rallies was 68%, less than half of the rate observed during the first half of this century. The average length of these recent rallies was less than one-quarter of the average pre-war length. In the current investment climate if you wait

Table 1.1   **TWENTIETH-CENTURY BULL MARKETS**

	Start of advance	Total gain	Length in months	Average gain	Average in months
1	Nov '21	119%	78		
2	June '32	124%	55	145%	72
3	July '40	192%	83		
4	Nov '49	35%	24		
5	July '52	110%	36		
6	Dec '56	27%	8		
7	Mar '58	186%	38	74%	24
8	Aug '62	34%	25		
9	Aug '65	20%	11		
10	Nov '66	102%	27		
11	June '70	75%	23		
12	Jan '75	164%	16		
13	Nov '76	87%	11		
14	Mar '78	46%	14		
15	Jan '80	43%	16		
16	Oct '81	359%	70	105%	23
17	Dec '87	52%	21		
18	Oct '90	38%	20		
19	Sept '92	49%	17		
20	July '94	?	?		

Table 1.1: Bull markets are running faster and faster. The record in the century's final quarter is helped by the atypical 70 month rally of 1981-1987. The other seven ran for 16 months on average and rose by 68%.

too long before committing funds, you run the risk of missing most of the up-turn.

Hard to spot a bull market

Compounding the problem is the difficulty in spotting the start of a bull market. Unfortunately, not every bull market begins with a Big Bang. As a case in point, think back to the events of 1994. A bull market ended at the beginning of February after a run of 17 months, near the average of the past few decades (excepting 1981–87). Prices then fell from February through June. A new bull market began in late-June. Many investors (and quite a few professionals as well) didn't recognise it for what it was during its first nine months. In retrospect, the reason is quite clear. The initial bull market 'rally' was minuscule in size.

▶ A solid price rise in July and August, 1994, ended with the stock market being slammed in September. Although many observers called the July/August rally a Suckers Rally and said 'told you so', a critical point was overlooked. The September decline ended before the June low was breached. In other words, the up-trend was still intact.

▶ There were additional gyrations during the final quarter of 1994. While many commentators correctly observed that the stock market was weak, one critical point was again overlooked. Prices actually rose during this period. The rise was tiny, less than 1%, but in broad terms the up-trend, now six months old, continued.

▶ Prices continued to drift during January and February of 1995. By the time the big spring 1995 rally began in mid-March, a very weak up-turn had been running for almost nine months.

When will it end?

We have no idea when this up-turn, the ninth of this quarter-century, will end. If it is still running at the end of 1995, it will be 18 months old. By June 1996, it will be a full fledged Old Timer. Given these facts, we hope you take a long look at Table 1.1 as you consider whether to take profits or commit fresh funds to shares in 1996. The possibility exists that Number Nine will be a long-running exception to the rule, just like the 1980s. But the recent historical record suggests low odds that 'this one will be different'.

Hard to spot bear markets

Spotting bear markets is even more difficult than spotting up-turns. In recent years, they have often caught investors by surprise by running for a short period of time and ending while many were still wondering if one had started yet.

Why is so difficult to decide whether we are in a bear market or not? First and foremost, you simply can't tell at the very beginning, based upon a month or two of falling prices. Price declines can occur at any time, including the middle of a wildly profitable bull market, so a two-month-long price drop often carries no special message. It is only after sufficient time passes that the general trend becomes clearer. Unfortunately, the stock market often drops so fast during bear markets that by the time investors know for sure that a down-turn has begun, it is too late to avoid most of the damage

Even the experts don't agree

Secondly: there is no single generally accepted definition of a bear market. Near the beginning of this century, an American financial writer, Charles Dow (of Dow-Jones fame), wrote about long downward price slides caused by broad economic ills, with prices dropping below the low point of the previous drop, and periodically interrupted by important rallies, none of which would penetrate the previous market peak or previous intermediate rally high. For much of the twentieth century, Dow's work under-pinned most bear market definitions.

Dow's definition no longer works, if it ever did. In 1987, shares peaked in mid-July and bottomed out just four months later. Even though billions were lost and investors remain traumatised to this day, Dow would have said there was no bear market for three reasons. It wasn't a long decline, prices never broke below the low point of the previous correction in September 1986 and there was no meaningful rally.

Big fall every four years

Since it is so difficult to find agreement about what is a bear market, we decided to attack the problem from another viewpoint and study every large drop in history, 14% or more, regardless of how the experts classify it. There are 20 members of this special club, which leads us to an important observation. Big falls occur frequently, once every four years or so, a lot more often than most investors would guess.

A striking point about these big falls is that 14 fell 20% or more. Ten exceeded 25%. In other words, once prices fall by 14%, as they did in the spring of 1994, the odds are high they will fall much more. The 14% decline in the first half of 1994 was a milder-than-normal decline.

As Table 1.2 reveals, the length and depth of a typical bear market is changing. From 1919 to 1950 there were four bear markets, roughly one every seven-and-a-half years. Each one typically ran for 35 months and fell 49%. The shortest was a 20-month smash in 1920–21, the longest a 49-month, 60% decline from 1928–1932, known for the rest of the century as the Great Depression.

Between 1950 and 1975, there were eight down-turns, compared with four in the previous 30 years, one every three years on average. The 1972–74 drop was an atypical horror, caused by a combination of events including global economic conditions and investor reaction to Labour's time at the helm. Putting that drop aside, the other seven typically ran their course in just 11 months and fell 24%.

Faster in recent years

In the past 20 years, we have witnessed eight additional bear markets. They are coming faster and faster. A bear phase now pops up every 2.5 years on average, and typically runs for around six months, quite a change from the 35-month long pre-war pace.

The average decrease in share prices during these eight recent declines was 20%, well under half the pre-war rate. The average six-month length was less than one-fifth the average pre-war length. In other words, as with recent bull

Table 1.2   **TWENTIETH-CENTURY BEAR MARKETS**

	Start of decline	Total loss	Length in months	Average loss	Average in months
1	Mar '20	47%	20		
2	May '28	60%	49	49%	35
3	Jan '37	55%	42		
4	June '47	32%	29		
5	Nov '51	26%	8		
6	July '55	26%	17		
7	Aug '57	21%	7		
8	May '61	22%	15	29%	14
9	Sept '64	16%	11		
10	July '66	20%	4		
11	Feb '69	34%	16		
12	May '72	69%	32		
13	May '76	28%	6		
14	Oct '77	14%	5		
15	May '79	19%	8		
16	May '81	18%	5	20%	6
17	Aug '87	34%	4		
18	Sept '89	20%	13		
19	June '92	16%	3		
20	Feb '94	14%	5		

Table 1.2: Bear markets are also running their course faster than ever. In the century's third quarter, the atypical 32-month drop of 1972–74 muddies the waters. The other seven ran for 11 months on average and fell by 23%.

markets, the stock market now moves much faster on the down-side as well.

In the current investment climate if you wait too long before stepping aside, you run the risk of being exposed to most of the down-turn. For investors who have grown accustomed to long, uninterrupted up-turns as in the 1980s, be warned: the 1980s was a rare event. This point has very serious implications for followers of the Buy-and-Hold theory of investing which became so popular in recent years.

No common elements

Are there any similarities between each of the 20 bear markets on our list? Not many. Some investors believe most bear markets start with a bang. Others think they usually sneak onto the scene, starting with a gentle slide. Both are right . . . sometimes. The historical record finds no single typical pattern.

Once the fall begins, losses are, on average, evenly distributed throughout the fall. You can't predict the length of the total fall or its depth by monitoring the extent of the first month's or first three month's decline. Some bear markets end with an explosive drop which exhausts all selling pressure, setting the stage for the next up-move. Others just peter out.

The Big One

One note of caution. Investors are becoming conditioned to short bear markets, and are increasingly willing to jump into shares after a brief drop, assuming they are near a low, even if they do not catch the precise bottom. Some analysts believe the stage is set for a lengthy old fashioned bear market with periodic rallies to suck investors back into shares, and further selling waves pulling values ever lower. Are they right? No one knows for sure. All we can say with confidence is that current bear market pattern has been the norm for half a century. Perhaps the seismologist's concern for The Big One lurking just around the corner should be extended to the stock market as well.

Given the increased speed with which the stock market moves, is it possible for investors to anticipate a broad up or down move early enough to profit from the knowledge? Fortunately, the answer is yes. Although it is devilishly difficult to get it right all the time, the stock market does provide some worthwhile clues.

Two-step Buy Signal

Here is a useful Buy Signal that often tips the start of a major up-move. It consists of two elements.

Step 1

The first is designed to identify broad price drops which usually precede long-term price rises. On the final trading day of each month, compare the FT-Non-financial Index with its corresponding score from one year earlier. Keep your eye peeled for a price drop of at least 10% below the year-earlier level. A fall of this size is more meaningful than you might guess. It means that the stock market fell down and stayed down for an extended period of time. By way of example, shares dropped by 14% in February–June 1994, yet were still above the level of the previous June.

In case you are wondering, we prefer to work with the FT-Non-financial Index over the FT-A-All Shares Index. It tends to be more sensitive. There are several instances when the Buy Signal flashed earlier, in some cases by several months, using the Non-financial instead of the All Shares.

Step 2

The second element of the calculation helps investors to avoid investing too early. Committing funds too fast can be a very expensive mistake. In February 1973, with prices down 12% from the previous February, the current/prior year ratio fell to .88, but shares continued to fall for the next 22 months until bottoming out in December 1974. Hence the need for Step 2, a safety net to keep from jumping into the stock market too soon

The Step 2 calculation is simply a comparison between the current month's closing price versus six months ago. Hold off investing any money until the current price rises above the level of six months ago. (It doesn't matter if the Step 1 ratio has risen above .90 by the time Step 2 flashes green.)

Not a perfect predictor

Although we like this market-timing tool, it is not flawless. Like everything else about the stock market, there are no 100% guarantees. As every experienced investor knows, following any stock market rule blindly is a questionable strategy. Please review each of the following failures carefully. We would rather run the risk of boring you with too much information on so important a point as this, than

9

glibly telling you the tool works 'most of the time'.

▶ Prior to 1950, there were several serious failures in the time period surrounding World War II. A Buy Signal flashed several times in late-1938 to mid-1939, but price advances were held back by the threat of war and of higher taxes needed to pay for it. Soon after another Buy Signal flashed in March 1940, strong German advances caused many investors to think the unthinkable – that we might lose the war – and prices fell sharply. A third Buy Signal flashed in April 1948 during a very painful post-war re-adjustment period. Prices finally turned up in November 1949, a year-and-a-half later.

▶ Since 1950, the signal has flashed 14 times, about three times per decade. Prices rose in the year ahead 12 times.

▶ Recent failure No 1: prices rose as expected for nine months after the 1965 signal. But the infamous 'July Measures' of 1966, which raised taxes, and introduced wage and price controls caught everyone by surprise and prices dropped sharply.

▶ Recent failure No 2: after several years of low inflation, a Buy Signal flashed in December 1969. Soon afterwards, large and unexpected price rises spooked investors. With headlines suddenly proclaiming wage increases of 20%, prices fell. Fortunately, the set-back was temporary. Shares rose by a whopping 39% in 1971.

▶ Recent failure No 3: the signal missed the entire 1979 rally triggered by Labour's expected defeat at the polls.

These failures make two points: *(1)* clearly, the signal is not infallible; *(2)* equally clear, the failures, so far, are associated with major economic or political events.

The signal last flashed in the spring of 1995. Barring some extraordinary event, we forecast rising prices for the months ahead.

Useful Sell Signal

Here is a Sell Signal that has tipped every large multi-year bear market since 1962 when the FT-Non-financial Index was first published. During this period, there have been four bear market falls of over 25%. This Sell Signal flashed near the beginning of each decline.

We call it the '50% Signal' because each time the FT-Non-financial Index rose at least 50% above the level reached 12 months ago, prices were at or near their bull market peak and it was time to sell.

It is extremely simple to use this Sell Signal. Merely remain invested until prices rise at least 50% ahead of the previous year, wait two months, and then sell. You would not have caught the precise top of every bull market but you would have been pretty close, selling your shares at the end of September 1987, just two weeks before the big crash, and in the spring of 1972, as shares began a two-year, stomach-churning decline of 69%, our worst bear market of the century.

The key problem with this signal, to date, is that it does not anticipate every fall, only the very biggest. For example, no Sell Signal flashed prior to the declines of 1989, 1992, or 1994.

We are working on other market timing signals and will report them to you in future editions of *The Schwartz Stock Market Handbook*.

Another good forecasting tool

For the present, we have discovered an interesting relationship between the Cyclical series, a collection of four indices, published each month by the Central Statistical Office to help interested organisations and individuals to monitor the state of the UK economy, and the stock market.

11

It is not widely known, but these four indices are excellent tools with which to forecast where share prices are heading in the year ahead. The four indices are:

▶ Longer Leading Index which forecasts turning points in the economy one year ahead;

▶ Shorter Leading Index which forecasts turning points six months ahead;

▶ Coincident Index which tracks the current economy;

▶ Lagging Index which follows the economy by one year.

The monthly indicators are released near the beginning of each month and are reported sporadically in the business media the following day. To get a full copy of each monthly release, telephone the Central Statistical Office in London at 0171 270 6363/6364. (We report on interesting trends involving these indicators in our quarterly newsletter, free to *Schwartz Stock Market Handbook* readers.)

Spot economy turns

For economic cycle forecasting purposes, exact scores are meaningless. The experts watch for changes in direction of the trend to help them to forecast economic conditions in the year ahead. The Indices are solely designed to forecast turning points in the economy. They cannot be used to measure the strength, longevity or even direction of the next phase of an economic cycle.

For example, a steady gradual rise on the Longer Leading Index is a signal that no trend change is expected one year ahead. A sharp increase sends the same message. In either case, the economy could be rapidly expanding or growing so weakly that it is on the verge of falling into recession. The index takes no notice. It merely signals more of the same – one year ahead.

By the same token, if the Longer Leading Index peaks

and begins to fall, it is a signal that the economy will weaken one year ahead. The steepness of the Index's decline or the height of the prior peak tells us nothing about the nature of the trend change due one year from now. The economy might be slipping into recession or merely be slowing to a lower rate of growth. The only conclusion that can be drawn from this index's down-turn is that the economy's rate of growth will change next year.

Despite their limitations as an economic forecasting tool, there are a large number of historical relationships involving the four indices that appear to do a fine job of forecasting where share prices will be heading in the next 12 months. A good starting point is with the Longer Leading Index.

Longer Lead Signal No 1

Since 1959, there have been 42 occasions when a monthly reading of under 100 on the Longer Leading Index was at least +0.73% above the previous month's signal. A move from 95.1 to 95.8 would fit the bill. Results like these typically precede an economic expansion. UK share prices rose 12 months later after 40 of those signals. Both failures resulted in a loss of under -5% in the year that followed so the cost of being wrong, as far as this signal is concerned, has not been too painful.[1]

Rose (40)

Fell (2)

Trend in next 12 months following a monthly reading under 100 on the Longer Leading Index that was at least +0.73% above the previous month's signal

---

[1]Reminder: All monthly calculations are based on the FT-Non-financial Index, formerly the FT-'500'.

13

Longer Lead Signal No 2

For readings of 100 to 105.9 on the Longer Leading Index, which often occur as the economy begins to expand, a larger monthly increase is needed to signal high odds of a stock market advance in the year ahead. Since 1959, there have been 24 occasions with a reading on the Longer Leading Index of 100.0 to 105.9 and a monthly increase of +0.97% or more. Share prices rose 22 times in the next 12 months (92%).

Rose (22)

Fell (2)

Trend in next 12 months following a monthly reading of 100 to 105.9 on the Longer Leading Index that was at least +0.97% above the previous month's signal

Longer Lead Signal No 3

When the Longer Leading Indicator rises to 106 or higher, the economic cycle is often quite mature. Investors are right to worry if it is time to take profits and prepare for a stock market down-turn. But if the monthly reading is at least +0.28% above the previous month, the odds favour holding on to shares a bit longer. There have been just 15 occasions that fit the bill since 1959. Prices stood higher in the year ahead after each of those signals.

Rose (15)

Fell (0)

Trend in next 12 months following a monthly reading 106 or higher on the Longer Leading Index that was at least +0.28% above the previous month's signal

Longer Lead Signal No 4

Here is a variation on the theme which also tips off good odds of rising prices in the year ahead. Since 1959, there have been 33 occasions when the Longer Leading Index was under 99.0 and had risen by at least +1.79% during a period of three consecutive months. A shift from 93.0 to 94.7 over three consecutive months would be large enough. Share prices rose 12 months later after 32 of those signals. There is some duplication with the previous signals but the three-month version catches some promising investment opportunities on its own.

Rose (32)

Fell (1)

Trend in next 12 months following a monthly reading under 99 on the Longer Leading Index that was at least +1.79% above three months ago

Longer Lead Signal No 5

Once the Longer Leading Indicator reaches between 99.0 and 102.9, a rise in the preceding three months of just +0.81% or higher is often associated with higher prices in the next 12 months. There have been 44 months that fit the bill. Prices rose in the next 12 months in 39 of those instances. While an 89% probability of success is pretty good when it comes to the stock market, the exceptions to the rule are worth noting.

▶ Late in 1975, after a year of wildly rising prices, the signal flashed two successive months. But the markets were so overextended that they plateaued despite the green light.

▶ In 1991, the signal flashed in three successive months and prices rose as expected until the summer of 1992. The impact of sterling's placement in the ERM at too high a level proved to be too great a burden for the economy and stock market prices fell.

15

Rose (39)

Fell (5)

Trend in next 12 months following a monthly reading of 99 to 102.9 on the Longer Leading Index that was at least +0.81% above three months ago

Longer Lead
Signal No 6

Since 1959, there were 56 readings on the Longer Leading Index of 103.0 or higher which were at least +0.47% above the level of three months earlier. An increase from 104.5 to 105.0 would fit the bill. Share prices rose in the year that followed after 47 of those signals. An 84% success rate is pretty good but the indicator is even better than it looks. Six of the nine failures occurred in 1987 when the green light flashed steadily from February to July. Unfortunately, the October crash proved too deep a hole out of which to climb within the next few months. Two other failures occurred late in 1975, after the stock market had rallied strongly from the lows reached at the end of the 1973–74 bear market.

Rose (47)

Fell (9)

Trend in next 12 months following a monthly reading of 103.0 or higher on the Longer Leading Index that was at least +0.47% above three months ago

Each of the tools reviewed thus far are based upon the actual score of the Longer Leading Index. But in some cases, the size of the increase to the Longer Leading Index over a three month period can tip off an impending stock market increase, regardless of the actual level of the indicator itself.

**Longer Lead
Signal No 7**

Since our records began, there have been 42 occasions when the Longer Leading Index rose strongly by +3.04% or more in a three month period. An increase from 101.2 to 104.3 or more would suffice. Prices rose in the next 12 months every single time.

Rose (42)

Fell (0)

Trend in next 12 months following a monthly reading on the Longer Leading Index that was at least +3.04% above three months ago

**Longer Lead
Signal No 8**

There were another 38 occasions when the Longer Leading Index rose by a smaller margin in the last three months (+0.37% to +3.03%) coupled with either a decline in share prices over the last 12 months or a tiny rise of +1.43% or less. Shares rose in the next 12 months after 37 of those signals.

Rose (37)

Fell (1)

Trend in next 12 months following a monthly reading on the Longer Leading Index of +0.37% to +3.03% above three months ago and a share price decline over the last 12 months or a tiny rise of up to +1.43%

By linking the Longer Leading Index with the Coincident Index, a number of additional profitable long-term trading opportunities can be identified.

**Longer and
Coincident
Signal No 1**

In the last 35 years, there have been 140 occasions when the Longer Leading Index was within a range of 95.7 to 103.9 and the Coincident Index was 92.5 to 102.3. In most cases, the economy was either near the beginning of an up-

17

turn or growing nicely but not excessively. Prices rose in the next 12 months after 130 of those occasions, a 93% success rate. There were just 10 declines.

Rose (130)

Fell (10)

Trend in next 12 months following a monthly reading of 95.7 to 103.9 on the Longer Leading Index *and* a monthly reading of 92.5 to 102.3 on the Coincident Index

Longer and Coincident Signal No 2

For investors who don't think 93% odds of success are good enough, here is a way to improve those odds. Sixty-one of the 140 signals were preceded with a stock market price decline in the most recent 12 months, or a rise in shares of up to +8.78%. Prices rose in the year ahead after 60 of those signals. The 61st was a small loss of just -1.51%

Rose (60)

Fell (1)

Trend in next 12 months following a monthly reading of 95.7 to 103.9 on the Longer Leading Index *and* a monthly reading of 92.5 to 102.3 on the Coincident Index *and* a share price decline over the last 12 months or a rise of up to +8.78%

The Shorter Leading Index, which is designed to anticipate turning points in the economy six months ahead, is another useful stock market forecasting tool. As one might expect low scores on this index often occur near the bottom of an economic cycle, a good sign for share price rises in the year ahead.

**Shorter Lead
Signal No 1**

Since 1959 to the present, there have been 34 occasions when the Shorter Leading Index stood at less than 95. Shares rose in the following 12 months in 32 of those occasions (94%). The two failures resulted in a loss of -5.64% and -3.13% in the 12 months ahead, so there was little financial pain associated with a failure at this low level.

Rose (32)

Fell (2)

Trend in next 12 months following a monthly reading of under 95.0 on the Shorter Leading Index

**Shorter Lead
Signal No 2**

There were 93 additional occasions when the Shorter Leading Index reached 95.0 to 99.9, and the stock market rose in the preceding 12 months by up to +72%. The record in the following 12 months was 84 up (90%) and nine down. A review of the nine failures is instructive for two reasons:

▶ The largest loss in the 12 months that followed a green light on this indicator was -11.97%. The other eight were less than 7%. In other words, there were relatively low levels of financial pain associated with a false signal.

▶ Four of the signals flashed between August 1961 and January 1962. But prices kept falling until August 1962, proving once again that no signal is completely infallible when it comes to the stock market. Three signals flashed in consecutive months (July–September 1991) but the stock market fell sharply the following summer as the effect of our membership in the ERM became increasingly apparent.

19

Rose (84)

Fell (9)

Trend in next 12 months following a monthly reading of 95.0 to 99.9 on the Shorter Leading Index *and* a share price rise over the last 12 months of up to +72%

Shorter and Coincident Signal No 1

Another way to use the Shorter Leading Index is in conjunction with the Coincident Index. If the shorter term indicator has fallen since last month, and the Coincident Index is at 100 or less, the odds are 90% that shares will rise in the year ahead.

Rose (45)

Fell (5)

Trend in next 12 months following a monthly decline on the Shorter Leading Index and a monthly reading of up to 100.0 on the Coincident Index

Shorter and Coincident Signal No 2

If the Shorter Leading Index has plateaued in the current month (in other words, the same reading as the previous month) or risen, and the Coincident Index is within a range of 92.5 to 97.7, the stock market will also probably rise in the year ahead. There have been 99 occasions when these two indicators were within the defined limits. Shares rose 90 times in the year ahead (91%).

Rose (90)

Fell (9)

Trend in next 12 months following an unchanged or increased Shorter Leading Index *and* a monthly reading of 92.5 to 97.7 on the Coincident Index

20

Shorter and
Coincident
Signal No 3

On the down-side, there have been 58 occasions since our records began with the short-term indicator rising above the previous month's score, and the Coincident Index reaching 101.3 or higher. This scenario typically occurs late in an economic up-turn. The stock market falls 60% of the time in the year ahead following such a signal and rises just 40%. Clearly, this indicator is of questionable usefulness since the odds of being wrong with any single forecast is quite high. Equally clear: once this signal flashes, it's time to invest cautiously and perhaps consider whether to start taking profits. It is the brave investor who commits fresh funds with no special thought about the future after this warning signal flashes.

Rose (23)

Fell (35)

Trend in next 12 months following an increase on Shorter Leading Index *and* a monthly reading of 101.3 or more on the Coincident Index

Lagging Signal

The Lagging Index usually runs about one year behind the actual economy. When it turns down, the economy has long since passed its turning point. Here is a way to use the Lagging Index to increase the odds of catching a stock market up-move in the 12 months ahead.

There have been 65 occasions since 1957 when the Lagging Index fell in the preceding month *and* the stock market either fell in the last 12 months or rose by no more than +2.77%. The record in the 12 months ahead was 63 up and two down, a 97% success rate. Better still, the two failures were losses of -6.66% and -0.93% so the chance of getting hurt badly is low even when the signal is wrong.

21

Rose (63)

Fell (2)

Trend in next 12 months following a monthly decline on the Lagging Index *and* a share price decline over the last 12 months or a rise of up to +2.77%

Improve the odds

Although there are never any guarantees when it comes to the stock market, signals like these can help to raise the odds of profit. If you had held shares during the past several decades in the 12 months that followed a 'green light' on one of these signals, you would have made money nine out of 10 times. Had you invested when no signal flashed its green light, you would have lost money more than half the time.

As you work with these signals, keep in mind that a forecast of rising prices in the next 12 months does not mean that prices will immediately begin to rise, or that they will reach their high point at the very end of the 12-month period. It often pays to wait once the buy signal flashes to make your purchase at a lower price. In other cases, it pays to sell well before the end of the twelfth month to maximise your gain.

TWO INVESTMENT OPTIONS

Many investors like the concept of moving in and out of shares when the odds of profiting are high or low, but also prefer to invest via a fund operated by professionals. Given the cost (initial charges are often around 5%), it is not practical for them to move periodically in and out of shares once the initial investment has been made.

Fortunately, there is a way to enjoy the best of both worlds, the benefits of professional management, and the ability to take advantage of seasonal windows of opportunity in an economical manner.

Unit-linked bond

One option is to invest in a unitised fund which is offered by many life insurance companies. Your investment is in a unit-linked bond. You control your capital, shifting into the equity-based fund of your choice (from among those offered by the management company with whom you work) when stock market conditions are good, and shifting back to an interest-bearing account when you decide market conditions are unpromising.

In most cases, the initial charge (that is, the difference between the 'bid' and 'offer' prices) is the same as the initial charge for other products offered by the company. The cost per transaction tends to be low. One major player in this segment of the industry charges just £20 per transfer, regardless of the size of the investment.

Two important points to remember: *(1)* sign up with a company that offers lots of investment choices so that you can invest in equities, gilts, emerging markets, America, Japan or what ever your choice; *(2)* the company should have a good track record; after all, what is the point of linking up with an institution that offers you little choice or delivers mediocre profits?

New fund concept

For those who like the concept of investing on a seasonal basis but prefer professionals to handle the entire job, we know of one fund that follows our philosophy, investing in equities when prospects are good and moving into cash when prospects are poor. The 'Sell In May' fund started at the beginning of 1994. It is early days but initial signs are good. They made 4.7% in 1994, better than all but four UK-based unit trusts during a period when the FT-A-All Shares Index fell. Two of the four unit trusts that out-performed them were 'bear funds' designed to rise in falling markets.

Note: We have no relationship with Sell In May. Before you invest with anyone, including Sell In May, use due diligence, common sense and remember that past performance does not guarantee future success. We will use this space in future editions to advise readers of other similar investment options as we learn of them.[2]

---

[2] Sell In May. For information, telephone: 0800 526 340

CHAPTER TWO – BUDGET DAY

Budget Day has a profound effect upon UK stock market price trends, both in the month that it occurs and in adjacent months.

March helped by Budget Day

March is a prime example of the power of the Budget to influence share prices. Prior to World War II, when Budgets were typically scheduled for April or May, March was a poor month for investors. During the 1930s and '40s, the March record was seven up and 13 down.

During the 1950s and '60s, Budgets were gradually advanced to April and the March price trend noticeably improved. Prices rose in 14 out of 20 years during this stretch. From the 1970s to the early 1990s, Budgets were pushed ahead still further into early and mid-March and the March price trend improved once again.

Price trends within the month of March have also been drastically influenced by Budget Day. History shows that these intra-month trends have changed in lock-step with Budget Day schedule changes. After 1970, when most Budgets were presented in early or mid-March, first-half prices rose seven out of ten times, twice as often as second-half prices. Prior to 1970, when Budgets typically were presented later in the month or in April, it was the second half of the month that rose in seven out of ten years, twice as often as the first half.

With Budgets now a late autumn phenomenon, we expect to see some significant trend changes on Budget Day itself, as well as in the several weeks on either side of it. To prepare for what is to come, here is what history reveals about the run-up to the Budget.

Four preceding weeks

From 1936 to the present, prices rose 66% of the time in the four weeks preceding Budget Day. If prices rise during this period, there is a 64% chance they will continue to rise in the four weeks that follow. If they fall in this period, there is just a 43% chance they will rise after Budget Day.[1]

These figures are interesting but of little practical use to an investor looking for a solid edge. After all, a 64% chance of success means there is also a substantial chance of failure in any single year.

But hidden in these figures is a provocative relationship that gives traders and investors alike, a significant edge. Very large price rises or price falls in the four-week run-up to Budget Day are often associated with price increases in the four weeks that follow. Look for a price rise of +6% or more, or a decline of at least -7%.

Here is the evidence. There have been 12 moves in the four-week run-up to Budget Day of at least +6% on the up-side or -7% on the down-side. Four weeks later? Prices were higher in 11 of those years.

Rose (11)

Fell (1)

Trend in four weeks that follow Budget Day if prices rise +6% or more, or drop -7% or more in preceding four weeks

In the remaining years with smaller pre-Budget swings, the odds of a post-Budget price rise are more or less 50:50.

Five preceding days

Unfortunately, the trend changes for the worse in the final five pre-budget trading days. Prices rise just 29% of the time during this period and fall 71%. This trend continues

---

[1]Reminder: All calculations in this chapter are based on the Ordinary Share Index, also known as the FT-30, from 1936 to 1994.

right up to the present day. In the last 10 years, prices rose just three times during this period.

Regardless of how this year turns out, it's clear that nervous investors generally use the run-up to Budget Day either to dump shares, or to stand aside until the Budget is presented. The culprit is probably the traditional content of most pre-Budget media coverage – full of reports of possible tax increases, benefit reductions, and lots of doom and gloom.

Budget Day

Fortunately, the size and direction of all price shifts in this five day pre-Budget period often tips off which way Budget Day prices will shift. History shows that if prices manage to rise in the week before Budget Day, the odds heavily favour a Budget Day price rise as well. Out of 19 years with a price rise in the five-day run-up to Budget Day, Budget Day prices fell just twice on the big day.

Rose (17)

Fell (2)

Budget Day trend if prices rise in preceding five days

Similarly, if prices fall by 3% or more in the five-day run-up, there is a very strong chance they will also rise on Budget Day. Out of seven occasions with a decline of 3% or more, Budget Day prices rose in six of those years.

Rose (6)

Fell (1)

Budget Day trend if prices drop -3% or more in preceding five days

Price rise likely

As far as Budget Day itself is concerned, do not be disheartened by the pre-budget media coverage. Negative news is what sells, so negative news is what gets delivered to the public. Regardless of the headlines, investors usually do well on Budget Day. Since 1936, share prices rose 72% of the time on Budget Day, held steady for 4% of the time and fell just 24% of the time.

When prices do rise, the average increase is +0.94%. When prices fall, the average decrease is -0.68%.

Budget Day gyrations are getting bigger. Since 1970, the average up-move is +1.36% and the average down-move -0.94%. Notice, though, the difference between the two averages is proportionately about the same as before.

The recent Budget Day trend continues to look good. Since 1984, the record has been nine up and two down *(see Figure 2.1)*.

Occasionally, the Chancellor's speech catches the stock market by surprise and prices react in a big way. In 1971, share prices rose by over 6% in response to the first Tory budget since 1964 as Chancellor Antony Barber reduced taxes and announced the eventual introduction of VAT. But in most years, key budget elements are tipped or leaked in advance, reducing the odds of the stock market being caught by surprise, and Budget Day shifts tend to be smaller.

Falls are
bad signs

When prices do fall on Budget Day, the problem is not just a single day's fall. It's what follows that should concern investors. History shows that if share prices do drop on Budget Day, the odds favour a further decline during the rest of budget week. Since 1938, there have been 10 occasions when share prices fell by at least -0.26% on Budget Day. Prices declined still further over the next three days in each of those years.

Figure 2.1   **BUDGET DAY GOOD NEWS**

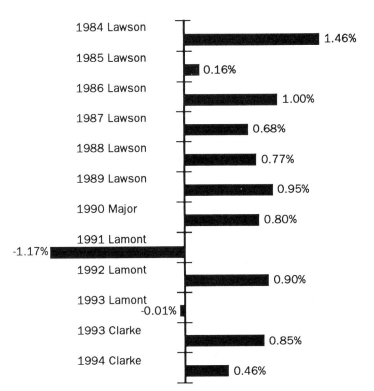

1984 Lawson — 1.46%
1985 Lawson — 0.16%
1986 Lawson — 1.00%
1987 Lawson — 0.68%
1988 Lawson — 0.77%
1989 Lawson — 0.95%
1990 Major — 0.80%
1991 Lamont — -1.17%
1992 Lamont — 0.90%
1993 Lamont — -0.01%
1993 Clarke — 0.85%
1994 Clarke — 0.46%

Figure 2.1: The recent Budget Day new has been quite good, except for 1991, Norman Lamont's first budget.

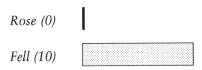

Rose (0)

Fell (10)

Trend of three days following Budget Day if Budget Day prices fall -0.26% or more

In most instances, the low point for the week was not even reached until Friday, although a few declines ended on

29

Wednesday or Thursday. At their lowest point, prices were down by an average of -2.61% from their already depressed Budget Day low. That's a whopping 86 points on an FT-SE 100 in the area of 3300.

The Big Question is not what happens on Budget Day but what the Budget Day shift tell us about future price trends. The direction of prices on Budget Day itself sends no usable signal to longer-term investors. Shares rise about the same amount of time in the four weeks that follow Budget Day in years with an up-move or a down-move on Budget Day itself. So don't try to make a snap prediction of where prices are heading after noting Tuesday night's closing prices. Knee-jerk reactions by stock market gun-slingers are great for the next morning's newspapers but are not reliable predictors of where prices are headed in the weeks ahead.

Three weeks ahead

There are better options available. One secret is to watch the price trend in the four week run-up to Budget Day, which was discussed earlier in this chapter.

Another trend to watch is the direction of prices in the three days that follow Budget Day. It is during this period that the stock market seems to sort out the implications of the Chancellor's speech and its effect on the economy. If prices shift moderately on the Wednesday to Friday that follow Budget Day, they will probably rise in the three weeks that follow. Be sure to watch the size of the price move, not just the direction.

If prices rise moderately in the first three post-Budget trading days, within a range of +1.4% to +2.6%, there is a very high likelihood that they will rise still further in the next three weeks. In eight out of nine years with share price increases in this range, they rose still higher three weeks later. The single exception was in October, 1945 in the midst of a nation-wide dock strike.

Rose (8)

Fell (1)

Trend in three weeks that follow Budget Day if prices rise
+1.4% to +2.6% in three days that follow Budget Day

In 22 other years that saw sharper or weaker three-day price rises, the record three weeks later was 10 up and 12 down. This kind of data doesn't definitely say what will happen this year, but it sends an important message for the long-run. If the three-day rise is too big or too small, the next three weeks are, on average, a losing proposition.

The same is true on the down-side. A medium-sized down-move in the three days following Budget Day is often associated with a solid up-move in the three weeks that follow. There have been 12 occasions with three-day falls between -1.47% and -3.02%. Prices rose in 11 of those years over the next three weeks.

Rose (11)

Fell (1)

Trend in three weeks that follow Budget Day if prices drop
-1.47% to -3.02% in three days that follow Budget Day

In the remaining 24 years with larger or weaker three-day drops, the record over the next three weeks was nine up and 15 down.

31

JANUARY INVESTMENT MONITOR

	LAST MONTH FINAL PRICE	END OF 1ST QUARTER		END OF 2ND QUARTER		END OF 3RD QUARTER		END OF 4TH QUARTER	
		PRICE	PERCENT CHANGE	PRICE	PERCENT CHANGE	PRICE	PERCENT CHANGE	PRICE	PERCENT CHANGE
FT-ORDINARY (FT-30)									
FT-SE 100									
FT-SE 250									
FT-NON-FINANCIAL (FT-500)									
FT-SE-A- ALL SHARES									
STANDARD & POORS COMPOSITE									
OTHER INDEX									
ENTER EACH SHARE, UNIT TRUST, ETC, BELOW									

CHAPTER THREE – JANUARY 1996

Slow start. Big finish

January is the year's best month for investors. There are no guarantees for 1996 of course, but shares rise in January in three out of four years.

Better yet, there are a number of historical trends that do a good job of forecasting which way January share prices will move. See page 38 for details. One trend that is sure to interest investors in 1996 is the tendency for the UK stock market to rise in years with a US Presidential election.

Despite the month's good overall record, it often starts off slowly. The odds of a profit are lowest in the first half of the month. But even in this relatively weak stretch, prices rise in most years, and the odds of a profit are especially good when the first quarter price trend drifts upward by a small amount. Shares usually rise in the final quarter of the month. They have fallen just twice in the last 20 years, one of the year's best segments.

As a new feature of the *Schwartz Stock Market Handbook*, investors are now provided with information to help forecast where shares will stand in the months ahead. Our research finds that a strong price advance in December and January is often followed with stock market declines in February and March. Mild price advances in November through January often signal that shares will rise strongly in the four months to follow, that is, to the end of May. See page 57 for further information.

Number one
month

January continues to be money-making time, the year's most profitable month. Between 1919 and 1994, January prices rose 75% of the time. The average price rise was +2.50%, equal to 83 points on an FT-SE 100 in the area of 3300.

No one knows why share prices rise so often in January. Some analysts guess that the large number of end-of-year company results and forecasts for the year ahead give investors more confidence to commit new funds. Others point to increased pension fund cash in-flows. Whatever the cause, the only money-losing decade for the January investor was back in the 1930s. Since then, the month has been consistently profitable. The constant January investor may not have profited every year, but did so on a decade-by-decade basis during the 1940s, '50s, '60s, '70s and '80s (see Table 3.1).

January's performance has been getting better in recent decades. In the 1960s, it was the number three-ranked month. In the 1970s, it moved up to number one. In the 1980s, it maintained its number one-ranked position, rising in nine out of 10 years, with an average monthly price rise of +5.52%.

Ignore recent
weakness

The 'January Juggernaut' looks to have slowed down as we entered the 1990s. The record through 1994 of three up (1991's profit was a miniscule +0.20%) and two down is poor by historic standards. Some investors may wonder if January has lost its magic. Our opinion is that the long-term trend has not changed. The recent bouts of weakness often occur near the beginning of the month, usually a temporary setback after a good December rally.

▶ In 1991, the FT-SE 100 fell 44 points in the first few trading days of the year to 2100 on 8 January. Prices then rose for the rest of the month, finishing up at 2170.

▶ In 1992, the previous year's December rally rolled on until 3 January when the FT- SE 100 reached 2504.

Table 3.1

JANUARY PRICE RISES AND DECLINES: 1919–1994

	Average January price change	Up	Down
1920–29	2.19%	8	2
1930–39	-0.29%	5	5
1940–49	1.85%	10	–
1950–59	0.91%	6	4
1960–69	2.17%	8	2
1970–79	5.55%	7	3
1980–89	5.52%	9	1
1990–94	0.62%	3	2
Average January price change	2.50%	57	19

UPDATE

Source: BZW and Datastream

Table 3.1: January investors last lost money during the 1930s. Since then, the month has been quite profitable. Investors did not profit every single year, but made money in every decade from the 1940s to 1980s. Even without 1975's extraordinary rise of +51.45%, January is a strong performer. The average price rise in the rest of the 1970s was +0.45%. Over the remaining 74 years, the average was +1.85%.

Prices then fell 37 points over the next few days, again reaching their low point on 8 January. The stock market rose sharply for the rest of the month, hitting 2571 by 31 January.

▶ In 1993, the FT-SE 100 reached 2862 on 4 January and then fell 124 points during the next 11 trading days. Prices began to rally on 20 January and regained all lost ground in the next 11 days.

▶ In 1994, the FT-SE 100 reached 3446 on 7 January and then fell 86 points in the next four trading days. Once the selling wave ended on 13 January, prices resumed their upward march and hit their all-time peak of 3520 on 2 February, 1994, a gain of almost 5% in just 14 trading days.

The balance of evidence suggests January has not lost its magic. Recent weakness usually occurred near the beginning of the month, not over the month as a whole. In contrast, the last series of poor Januarys was in the 1930s when prices fell three years in a row. The pattern in those years was exemplified by continued weakness throughout the whole month. In our opinion, favourable January trading conditions are 'alive and kicking'. Investors will not make money every year but will do so most of the time.

US Presidential cycle

The odds of a January profit are especially good in US Presidential election years like 1996. The effect of the US Presidential cycle on the UK stock market in January is striking. From 1968 to 1992, UK shares have risen seven election years in a row. The average level of profit is a whopping +6.15% per year. In the two years that follow, eg 1997 and 1998, the January record is quite poor *(see Table 3.2).*

Trend change?

On balance, the prospects for January are good. Unfortunately, when it comes to the stock market, there are no certainties. Trends do change. If January turns sour for investors, here are two factors which might play a role.

Expectation of Profit: We have written about the superb January record in earlier editions of the *Schwartz Stock Market Handbook* and in the national press. As more investors catch on and begin to alter their trading patterns to catch the expected January up-surge, the risk increases for some of the January rally to occur in December. Indeed, we may even be seeing signs of this already with rallies frequently occurring in the last half of December.

The stock market is, at its heart, an auction with the forces of supply and demand creating market value. A decrease in January demand because former 'January money' gets committed a bit earlier in December to catch the

Table 3.2

JANUARY RECORD DURING THE US PRESIDENTIAL CYCLE: 1967–1994

	Election Year	Year 2	Year 3	Year 4
Prices rose	7	4	4	6
Prices fell	–	3	3	1
Average price change	6.15%	2.48%	-0.01%	9.30%

Table 3.2: US Presidential election years have been good to UK investors. Unfortunately, the magic doesn't carry over to Year Two and Three of the cycle. But Year Four (next due in 1999) is also usually profitable. Note though that Year Four's high average January price change is influenced by 1975's +51.45% increase. Without it, the average Year Four increase is only +2.27%

expected rally is just the thing to cause a trend change in this fine investment month.

Budget: Another fly in the ointment is the recent shift to a late autumn Unified Budget. We don't yet know the long-term effect of this switch on January share prices, although history tells us stock market prices often rise in the weeks following Budget Day (see Chapter Two for specific Budget Day trends). Our fear is that January may become a Budget prisoner, recovering some of December's Budget-induced losses in poor Budget years, or giving back some December gains in years stimulated by good Budget news.

Watch the
first half

In the short-run, pay careful attention to the first half of the month where much of the recent weakness has clustered. The third and fourth quarters of the month continue to be profitable most of the time – especially the fourth quarter. In the last 20 years, fourth-quarter share prices fell just two times. The strong performance continued during the 1990s.

INCREASE YOUR PROFIT ODDS

Believe it or not, it is possible to do even better than average with a January investment. There are a number of historical trends that often tip which way share prices will shift in January. Obviously, there are no guarantees they will continue to work as well in the future but they have been quite useful up until now.

December signal   One signal that frequently forecasts a January price rise is a large increase in December, up by at least +4.18%. Strong up-moves of this magnitude have taken place 14 times since 1921. Shares continued to rise in January in 13 of those years (93%). The average January increase in years following a strong December up-move was +3.26%, around 108 points on an FT-SE 100 in the area of 3300.[1,2]

Rose (13)

Fell (1)

January's record after a December price rise of at least +4.18% (since 1921)

---

[1] Reminder: all monthly calculations are based on the FT-Non financial Index, formerly the FT-'500'. Unless otherwise stated, they are based on data from 1919–1994. All daily, quarterly and bi-monthly calculations are based on the Ordinary Share Index, also known as the FT-30. Unless otherwise stated, they are based on data from 1936–1994.

Both indices are usually found in the *Financial Times*: Non-financial Index, Monday to Friday, Section 2, back page; Saturday, buried in Section 1. Ordinary Share Index, Monday to Friday, Section 2, three pages from end; Saturday, Section 1, three pages from end.

[2] If you do not have price trends for the last 12 months readily available, we will provide them at no cost. Send a self-addressed, postage-paid envelope to:

Closing Price Offer
Burleigh Publishing company
Burleigh Hall
Burleigh, Stroud
Gloucestershire GL5 2PF

The single exception occurred in January 1990 as investors began to realise that 15% Base Rates were taking longer than expected to slow the economy, and that a very serious recession was developing.

Prior-12-month signal

As we pointed out in the 1995 edition of the *Schwartz Stock market Handbook,* one of the most accurate predictors of rising prices in January is a steadily rising price trend throughout the previous year. Look for (a) rising prices during the past month (December), past two months (1 November to 31 December), past three months, past six months and past 12 months, and (b) prices up by at least 2% in the last two months and three months. If the necessary conditions are met, there is an 89% likelihood that January prices will rise.

These conditions may seem onerous but, since 1920, have occurred 18 times. January prices rose in 16 of those years (89%). The average January share price increase in the 18 years with a strong prior year up-trend was +3.10%. This scenario occurred most recently in January 1994. Despite the fact that prices had rocketed up in the second half of the previous year, and were quite over-extended as the year began, prices rose by almost four percent. The stock market losses of 1994 first began in February.

UPDATE

Rose (16)

Fell (2)

January's record after steadily rising prices in the past 12 months (since 1920)

The two exceptions are instructive and provide further support for the rule. In 1959, January prices fell by a tiny -0.1%. In 1993, poor trading conditions at the beginning of the month were reversed with a late month rally that moved prices into positive territory on 1 February – one day late!

Six-month signal   A third trend to watch is the direction of prices during the preceding six months. If they move moderately, by no more than -0.85% on the down-side and +6.66% on the up-side, the odds of a January price increase improve considerably. Here's the evidence: since 1923, share prices shifted within this range in the six-month run-up to January on 22 occasions. January prices rose in 20 of those years (87%). The average annual price increase was +2.10%.

IMPROVEMENT

Rose (20)

Fell (2)

January's record after a price shift of -0.85% to +6.66% in the past six months (since 1923)

All other years   What about the remaining years in which the December Signal, 12-month Signal and the 6-month Signal did not apply? Since 1920, there were 37 such years. January share prices rose 23 times and fell 14 times. The average annual price increase was +2.40% but a large part of this increase was due to 1975's dramatic rise of +51.45%. If we eliminate this once-in-a-lifetime rally, the average increase for all other Januarys is +1.03%. In other words, in years with weaker prospects, you would still make money in January over the long-run, but much less of it, and on a more erratic basis.

Quarterly differences   Although January is a good month in which to invest, there are wide differences in profit potential associated with investments made during different segments of the month. To prove the point, January was divided into four quarters: January 1–8, 9–15, 16–23, and 24–31, and the price changes per quarter were analysed all the way back to 1936 *(see Table 3.3)*.

Table 3.3

PERCENTAGE PRICE CHANGE: JANUARY 1936–1994

	January 1–8	January 9–15	January 16–23	January 24–31
Average annual price change				
1936–39	0.15%	-0.29%	-0.76%	0.34%
1940–49	0.52%	0.49%	-0.39%	-0.01%
1950–59	0.20%	-0.25%	-0.22%	0.08%
1960–69	0.59%	-0.08%	0.27%	0.97%
1970–79	0.69%	1.39%	0.77%	1.96%
1980–89	1.76%	0.83%	2.09%	1.83%
1990–94	0.17%	-0.51%	0.30%	1.74%
Average quarterly price change	0.66%	0.34%	0.40%	0.99%
Number of years in which prices:				
rose	38	32	33	39
fell	21	27	26	20

Source: Datastream

Table 3.3: Over the long-term, the first and last quarters of the month have been the two most profitable segments. But in recent years, the third quarter's performance has improved. Since 1980, it has risen in 13 out of 15 years.

UPDATE

Trend change

Over the long-term, the first and last quarters of the month have been January's two most profitable segments. Both have been consistent money-makers. Investing in the two middle quarters produced less profit. But in recent years, third-quarter share price trends have been getting stronger and persistent weakness has emerged for short periods during the first half of the month.

Given the differences in profit potential between each quarter, and the recent trend changes, each segment will be examined separately.

FIRST QUARTER OF JANUARY – JANUARY 2ND TO 8TH

> The recent trend in the year's opening quarter is disappointing. Persistent weakness has occurred, often following a strong up-move in late December. And if prices do manage to hold their own, investors must contend with January's second quarter, traditionally a weak part of the month.
>
> There are no guarantees for 1996 of course, but the odds favour holding back any new investment, especially if a strong rally took place in the second half of December. But several pockets of profitability do exist. A mild price rise in the weeks preceding this quarter often tips off that prices will rise.

A long-term winner

Historically, the first quarter of the year has been quite profitable. Between 1936 to the present, prices have risen in 64% of all first quarters. A steady first-quarter investor made a profit in every single decade. Since records began, this part of the month has generated an average profit of +0.66% per year, equal to 22 points on an FT-SE 100 in the area of 3300.[2]

Recently weak

Although the long-term trend is good, don't get too complacent. The 1990s have started off poorly for first-quarter investors. Prices fell in three of the last four years. In the past, first-quarter weakness was often followed by further weakness in the rest of the month. But the current bout of weakness is different. Prices tend to be weak for a week or two, usually after a good December rally, and then resume their upward climb in the second half or the month. What is the cause? No one knows for sure. We hypothesize that profitable January trading conditions have become so widely known that investors who planned to commit new funds to the market around the turn of the year now jump

---

[2] Reminder: All daily, quarterly and bi-monthly price trends are based on the FT Ordinary Share index (FT-30) from 1936 to 1994 unless otherwise indicated

in a bit earlier to catch the expected rally. Such behaviour boosts shares in late December (precisely what has occurred recently) and hurts shares after the turn of the year due to a temporary reduction in demand.

UPDATE

One trend that has not changed is the tendency for share prices to rise on the first trading day of the year, regardless of whether the day falls on January 2, 3 or 4. In the 60 years between 1936 and 1995, share prices fell just 17 times (28%) on the year's first trading day.

Pre-Christmas signal

Although the odds are good that you will profit by holding shares on the year's opening trading day, you can load the dice in your favour to an even greater degree by monitoring the price trend on the final two trading days before Christmas. History shows that if share prices decline during this two-day stretch, they will probably also fall on the first trading day of the New Year, after investors forget the holiday spirit and settle down to some serious trading.

There have been 16 declines on the two pre-Christmas trading days since 1935. On 10 of those occasions, the first trading day of the New Year also fell (63%). In the remaining 44 years, prices fell just seven times (16%) on the first trading day after New Year's Day.

UPDATE

Pre-Xmas rise (16%)

Pre-Xmas fall (63%)

Likelihood of price drop on first trading day of New Year if prices rise or fall on two pre-Christmas days

Holiday length has no effect

Does the length of the New Year's holiday trading break have any effect on the market's likelihood of rising or falling? Not at all. The market rises the same percentage of the time, regardless of the length of the holiday.

It's not just the first trading day of the month that tends to be profitable. Analysis of daily share price trends over the long-run, shows that each day in the quarter is profitable at

43

least half the time. In fact, the second and the fourth are among the most profitable trading days of the entire month on an historical basis *(see Figure 3.1).*

INCREASE YOUR PROFIT ODDS

Here are some useful statistically-based rules of thumb to help you to maximise your trading profits in this first quarter of the year. While they will not work every year, they will improve your track record over the long-run.

December signal   It is not widely known but small shifts in December's monthly index are frequently associated with first-quarter price rises. Since our records began in 1936, there have been 12 years with a December shift within a range of -0.81% to +1.34%. Prices rose each time.

Rose (13)

Fell (1)

First-quarter record after a December price shift of -0.81% to +1.34%.

December
second-half
signal

The size of the price shift in the second half of December also does a good job of forecasting where first-quarter prices are heading. There have been 12 years when prices shifted moderately in the second half of December, by no more than -0.42% on the down-side and no more than +0.92% on the up-side. Prices rose in the first quarter of January in 11 of those years.

Rose (11)

Fell (1)

First-quarter record after a price shift of -0.42% to +0.92% in December's second half

Figure 3.1   **PERCENTAGE OF TIME PRICES RISE EACH TRADING DAY IN JANUARY'S FIRST QUARTER**

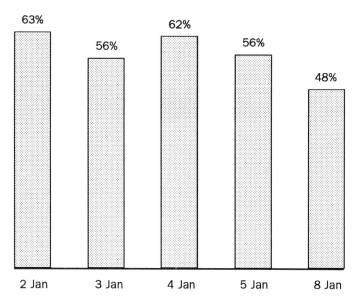

Figure 3.1: The likelihood of rising prices is high throughout the first quarter. 2 January is the most profitable day of the entire month. The weakest link is 8 January. (Market closed in 1996 on missing dates.)

December fourth-quarter signal

In the 1995 *Schwartz Stock Market Handbook*, we pointed out a correlation between the price trend in December's fourth quarter and the first quarter of January. Here's an improved up-date. If prices rise by a small amount in the fourth quarter of December, no more than +0.82%, a first-quarter increase usually follows. Since 1940, there have been 23 fourth-quarter price shifts within this range. January's first quarter rose in 20 of those years, most recently in the first quarter of 1994.

| IMPROVEMENT |

Rose (20)

Fell (3)

First-quarter record after a price rise of up to +0.82% in December's fourth quarter

---

SECOND QUARTER OF JANUARY – JANUARY 9TH TO 15TH

Be cautious if you are thinking of investing in the year's second quarter, especially on January 11th, the poorest day of the entire month. Over the long-run, it is the weakest quarter of the month. In recent years, the odds of making a profit have been roughly 50:50. Profit prospects are especially poor if shares have risen in the previous two quarters.

The second quarter has the questionable distinction of being January's worst-performing quarter. Although it is weak in a relative sense, share prices do rise slightly more often than they fall (54% of the time between 1936 and 1994) and produce an average annual profit of +0.34% per year.

No improvement in sight

At first glance, the performance of the second and third quarters looks to be quite similar. But the third-quarter profit trend has been improving and has become quite good to investors in recent years *(see Table 3.4)*. In contrast, the second-quarter trend remains unchanged. In the last 20 years, its record was nine up and 11 down. In the last 10 years, second-quarter prices rose just four times.

46

Table 3.4

PERCENTAGE PRICE CHANGE: 1985–1994

	January 1–8	January 9–15	January 16–23	January 24–31
Annual quarterly price change				
1985	1.98%	-0.97%	4.36%	-1.75%
1986	-0.67%	-1.26%	0.97%	3.62%
1987	6.93%	2.51%	1.35%	1.06%
1988	3.80%	0.79%	-1.09%	1.03%
1989	1.79%	2.59%	3.28%	6.68%
1990	1.48%	-2.47%	-3.02%	1.33%
1991	-2.20%	-1.01%	0.57%	4.19%
1992	-0.30%	2.90%	1.18%	1.69%
1993	-0.38%	-1.75%	0.64%	1.17%
1994	2.26%	-0.20%	2.16%	0.33%
Average quarterly price change				
1985–94	1.47%	0.11%	1.04%	1.93%
Number of years in which prices:				
rose	6	4	8	9
fell	4	6	2	1

Source: Datastream

Table 3.4: The second half of January is now the major source of profits. Without 1987, the first-quarter trend would be decidedly weaker.

UPDATE

Declines often follow rise in December's second half

Second-quarter prices are especially likely to fall in years following a big rally in December's second half. Since 1977, second-quarter prices have fallen in nine out of 13 years following a second-half price increase of at least +1.72%, 57 points on an FT-SE 100 in the area of 3300. Obviously, odds like this leave ample room for a second quarter up-move following a December second-half rally. By the same token, they should cause investors to think long and hard about committing new funds following a December rally of sufficient size.

Rose (4)

Fell (9)

Second-quarter record after a price rise of at least +1.72% in December's second half (since 1977)

During the bull market 1980s, January's second quarter produced a reasonably-sized average annual profit (+0.83% per year), causing some analysts to wonder if the basic underlying trend had improved. But be cautious in acting on this data. For one thing, in a decade that saw a consistent pattern of profitability for the entire month, during the greatest bull market of the century, the second quarter fell four times – in 1981, 1983, 1985 and 1986. It was ranked third or fourth in profitability for eight of the decade's 10 years. In addition, the +0.83% average annual profit was the weakest (by far) of the month's four quarters. During the 1990s, prices fell in four out of five years.

Mid-quarter blues

In timing your decision to buy or sell shares during this point of the month, note that most of the losses occur in the middle of the quarter, 10–12 January, which are the worst three trading days of the month. The 11th has been particularly poor in recent years. Since 1984, prices have risen once and fallen seven times (weekends account for the other days). Prices are most likely to rise at the very beginning and end of the quarter. So if you are thinking of buying or selling around mid-month, don't be afraid to adjust your timing by a day or two *(see Figure 3.2)*.

Increase Your Profit Odds

Despite this quarter's relatively weak performance, if you currently hold shares and are a long-term investor, in most years it would pay you to hold on to your position – given the good odds of a third- and fourth-quarter profit. But if you are contemplating making a purchase, you have,

Figure 3.2   **PERCENTAGE OF TIME PRICES RISE EACH TRADING DAY IN JANUARY'S SECOND QUARTER**

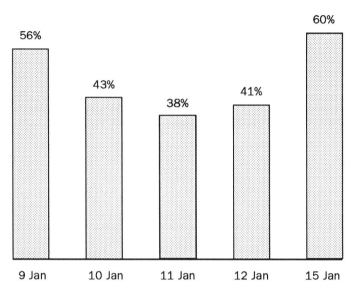

Figure 3.2: Prices tend to fall most often during the middle of the second quarter. The 11 January record has become worse in recent years, rising just once out of the last eight opportunities.

roughly, a 50:50 chance of profiting during this period. Fortunately, you can improve these odds by watching the direction of prices during January's first quarter.

Previous-two-quarter signal

As noted earlier, trading conditions are especially likely to be poor following a strong year-end rally. Here are some tools to help you to anticipate poor second quarters. Since 1956, there have been 12 occasions on which prices rose by at least +0.15% in the last quarter of December and rose by at least +1.05% in the first quarter of January. Second-quarter prices fell in 10 of those years.

Rose (2)

Fell (10)

Second-quarter record after a price rise of at least +0.15% in December's fourth quarter and price rise of at least +1.05% in the first quarter

This signal last flashed in 1994 and prices fell by a small amount in the second quarter, the only quarter of the month to show a loss.

First-quarter signal no 1

If first quarter prices fall by -0.38% to -3.20%, the odds suggest the second quarter will also fall. Here is the evidence: first-quarter prices have fallen within this range 12 times since 1939. Second quarter prices continued to fall in 10 of those years.

Rose (2)

Fell (10)

Second-quarter record after a price decline of -0.38% to -3.20% in the first quarter

First-quarter signal no 2

And on the up-side, there are 15 occasions on record when prices shifted by a small amount in January's first quarter, a loss no greater than -0.04% or a gain no greater than +0.97%. Each time, second-quarter prices rose.

Rose (15)

Fell (0)

Second-quarter record after a price shift of -0.04% to +0.97% in the first quarter

THIRD QUARTER OF JANUARY – JANUARY 16TH TO 23RD

The third quarter used to be mediocre. But since 1980, the profit trend has been quite impressive. Prices have risen in 13 of the last 15 years. Here is more good news: the quarter to follow has an even better record.

The only weak spot in the third quarter is on its final day, 23 January. Prices rise just 39% of the time.

Over the long-term, the third-quarter record is not particularly impressive. It is the 15th-best quarter of the year (out of 48).

End of quarter often weak

The source of the weakness is the end of the quarter. Prices have risen on just 39% of all January 23rds *(see Figure 3.3)*. The problem spills over to the beginning of the fourth quarter of the month, 24 January, when prices rise just 43% of the time.

Prior to the 1980s, a decade-by-decade analysis of third-quarter prices revealed a consistently poor investment climate. Investors lost money in the average year in the 1930s, '40s and '50s, and made a small amount in the 1960s by continuously investing during this segment of the month.

The 1970s continued to be a poor time to invest during the third quarter. The apparent +0.77% increase in average annual third-quarter prices during this decade was entirely due to 1975's impressive rally when third-quarter prices rose by +16.15%. If not for 1975, the 1970s would have generated an average annual quarterly loss of -0.94% for those who always invested in the third quarter.

Between 1936 and 1979, prices rose in the third quarter of January just 45% of the time.

Recent improvement

In 1980, a new third-quarter trend began. For the first time ever, the third quarter became January's most profitable segment. Share prices rose in nine of the decade's 10 years at an average annual rate of +2.09%, one of the best performances of the entire year. The 1990s' record of four up and

Figure 3.3   **PERCENTAGE OF TIME PRICES RISE EACH TRADING DAY IN JANUARY'S THIRD QUARTER**

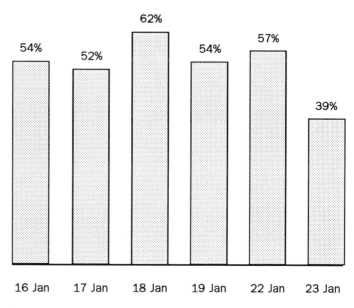

Figure 3.3: Prices tend to fall at the end of the third quarter.

one down suggests that the positive third-quarter trend continues. Even better, the quarter that follows is one of the best of the entire year, giving traders two consecutive periods of above-average profit potential. Note though, that 23 January continues to be a drain on the quarter's performance. We don't know why this is so, but the record since 1984 is three up and five down (weekends account for the missing days).

INCREASE YOUR PROFIT ODDS

First-half signal   Regardless of the overall third-quarter trend, there are several ways to improve the odds of making a profit. In last year's edition, we suggested that investors watch the price trend in the first half of January. Here's a refinement of the

First Half Rule that will increase the odds of making a profit. If prices are up in both the first *and* second quarters of the month, with a second quarter rise of no more than +2.76% in total, the third quarter usually rises. Out of 12 such occasions since 1949, third-quarter prices rose 10 times. And one of the two exceptions was a minuscule -0.07% decline in the third quarter of 1954.

IMPROVEMENT

Rose (10)

Fell (2)

Third-quarter record after a price rise in the first quarter (any amount) and second quarter of up to +2.76% (since 1949)

When it comes to the stock market, too much good news makes us nervous, especially when it suddenly appears after decades of mediocrity. With this in mind, we located an indicator associated with *falling* third quarter prices. Unfortunately, there are only nine observations on record, in part because it has not flashed since 1979.

December
second-half
signal

The signal to look for is a small price decline in the second half of December. When such an event occurs, the third-quarter price trend tends to disappoint, regardless of what happens in the first half of January. Either the early January rally peters out or the December down-trend drags on to this point in the month.

Here is the evidence: since 1938, there have been nine occasions with a small price drop in the second half of December, no greater than -2.10%. Third-quarter prices fell in seven of those years. Both exceptions saw very small price rises of about one-half of one percent. In other words, standing aside when this indicator flashed had little 'opportunity loss' even when the indicator was wrong.

Rose (2)

Fell (7)

Third-quarter record after a price drop in the second half of December of up to -2.10% (since 1938)

The year ahead   The price trend to this point of the New Year also serves as a useful early warning for the month as a whole. This is an important signal for those guided by the old City refrain 'As January goes, so goes the year'.

For investors who rely on the January price trend for insight into the direction of prices for the rest of the year, here's a tip to help you. There have been 11 occasions since records began when the first half of January and the third quarter both declined. On all 11 occasions, the full month finished lower. No matter how big the fourth-quarter price rise, it was never enough to compensate for the decline that had already occurred. Even more important, in eight of those 11 years, prices finished the year lower than they started.

So if you are contemplating a very long-term investment during the third quarter of the month, a smart course of action might be to sit tight until the situation is clarified, if the month has started off poorly.

FOURTH QUARTER OF JANUARY – JANUARY 24TH TO 31ST

> Here comes another fine money-making opportunity. In the last 20 years, prices rose 18 times, the best quarterly performance of the year.

Investors frequently profit during the fourth quarter of January. Between 1936–1994, prices rose 66% of the time. The average annual gain was +0.99%, second highest of all 48 quarters of the year. Only the last quarter of December, with an average annual profit of +1.02%, has out-performed it.

The fourth segment of the month failed to produce a profit in just one decade, the 1940s, when it lost -0.01% per year, equivalent to a mere one-third of a point on an FT-SE 100 in the area of 3300.

The recent fourth-quarter record has been unbelievably strong. Prices have risen in 18 of the last 20 years, and nine of the last 10, the year's best in both cases. Since 1990, prices have risen in all five years at an average of +1.74% per year.

24 January

Analysis of price trends on a day-by-day basis shows that the quarter starts off poorly, continuing the pattern of weakness observed at the very end of the third quarter. Prices rise just 43% of the time on 24 January (see Figure 3.4).

31 January

Prices are also relatively weak on the very last day of the quarter, 31 January. But further analysis shows that 31 January often is profitable when it lands on a Wednesday or Thursday, as it will in 1996. Prices rise two-thirds of the time on these two days.

INCREASE YOUR PROFIT ODDS

Third-quarter signal

Here is a price signal, operative since 1936, that seems to tip off a rising price trend during the fourth quarter. If prices rise in the third quarter by a small amount, within a range of +0.41% to +0.97%, they will probably also rise in the fourth quarter.

Figure 3.4   **PERCENTAGE OF TIME PRICES RISE EACH TRADING DAY IN JANUARY'S FOURTH QUARTER**

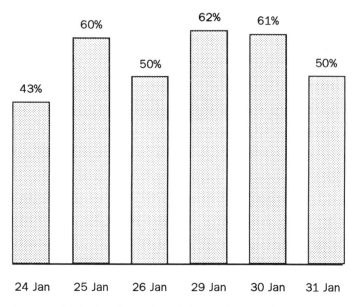

Figure 3.4: The fourth quarter of January is one of the year's best quarters. 24 January can be disappointing. But 31 January tends to be better than average when it lands on a Wednesday as in 1996.

Rose (9)

Fell (0)

Fourth-quarter record after a price rise of +0.41% to +0.97% in the third quarter

This signal last flashed in 1993 when a small third-quarter increase was followed by a fourth quarter price rise of +1.17%.

First-half signal

Another statistical relationship that signals an increased chance of higher prices in the fourth quarter is a rising price trend in the first half of January, followed by a decline in the third quarter. There have been 12 'up then down' occasions since 1945 and fourth-quarter prices have risen in 10 of them (83%). And in one of the two exceptional years, 1973, first half prices rose from 505.4 on the FT Ordinary Share index to 505.5, an insignificant increase of two one-hundredths of one percent.

Rose (10)

Fell (2)

Fourth-quarter record after a price rise in the first half and fall in the third quarter (since 1945)

LOOKING AHEAD

Trying to forecast a week or month ahead is hard enough to do. Looking further ahead to the rest of the year is even harder. Too many unforseen political and economic events, both domestic and international, easily confound even the most skillful and knowledgeable forecaster. Nevertheless, there are several historical trends involving January that have consistently tipped off the direction of prices in the months ahead.

Rising prices by 31 March

Take February and March for example. They tend to be unexceptional months, not steady money-makers. Over the 76 years for which we have data, prices rose 40 times and fell 36 times during this two-month stretch. February is ranked eighth in monthly profitability, tenth if 1975's extraordinary rally is omitted. March is ranked sixth. With a performance trend like this, it is particularly important to pick your time carefully if you plan to invest during this period. Fortunately, January price swings often tip off where shares are heading in the two months ahead, ending on 31 March.

Here is the evidence: there have been 14 years when January prices shifted by a tiny amount, no more than -0.10% on the down-side and no more than +1.10% on the up-side. This translates into a drop of up to three points on an FT-SE 100 in the area of 3300, or a gain of up to 37 points. Shares rose in February/March in 13 of those years. The sole exception was in 1970.

Rose (13)

Fell (1)

Price shift to 31 March after a January price shift of -0.10% to +1.10%

The signal last flashed in 1991, near the tail end of the 1990 bear market. A January price rise of just +0.20% was followed by a very large increase of over +15% in the next two months.

Falling prices by 31 March

On the other hand, if the stock market rallies strongly in December and January, producing a total two-month gain of +6.11% to +9.61%, history suggests low profit potential for February and March. There have been 11 occasions on record with a December/January price rise within this range. Prices were even lower by 31 March in 10 of those years. The average price decline was -3.74%. The single exception to the rule occurred in 1984.

Rose (1)

Fell (10)

Price shift to 31 March after a December/January price rise of +6.11% to +9.61%

Rising prices by
May 31

Looking further ahead to the end of May, the direction of prices in November to January provides a useful tip on where shares are heading. Throughout history, there have been 16 years with a small price rise between 1 November to 31 January, no more than +3.06%. In 15 of those years, prices rose still further in the next four months through to 31 May. The average increase was a quite healthy +8.74%. Be warned that the trend was rarely a straight line. In some years, prices peaked before 31 May then began to fall. In other years, even more money could have been made by waiting until the end of February or March before committing funds.

NEW

Rose (15)

Fell (1)

Price shift to 31 May after a November/January price rise of up to +3.06%

The single exception to the rule was back in 1945 when prices fell by an insignificant -0.60% in February to May, the equivalent of 20 points on an FT-SE 100 in the area of 3300. And even in this atypical year, prices rose by a small amount in each of the first three months, stumbled in May and recovered all losses in June.

AS JANUARY GOES, SO GOES THE YEAR

Old saws about the future direction of share prices are comforting to recite. But as investment guides, most are not to be trusted.

If you 'Sell in May and go away, and don't come back 'til St Leger's Day', you would miss being invested in the market during August, on average the year's third best investment month.

Do 'bull market bashes end with October crashes?' In fact, there have been more large increases in share prices during October than large decreases. Over the long-term, October has been profitable despite the headlines in 1929 and 1987.

One exception: 'As January goes, so goes the year' has withstood the test of time for most of this century. When January share prices rise, further rises often occur in the rest of the year. Falling January prices are often associated with further declines in the remaining 11 months of the year.

Be cautious

But be cautious as you read articles in the financial press about this frequently-publicised price signal. A lot of what is written is either misleading or out-and-out wrong. Here are two major problem areas.

▶ Some analysts include January's performance in their yearly total, thereby loading the dice in favour of their conclusion. Predicting a full year price rise after a January price rise of 8% provides an 8% head start toward being right. It may be great for your predictive accuracy but painful for the investor who commits new funds on 1 February, based upon that advice.

A better approach is to use the January price shift to forecast the direction of prices during the 11 months that follow.

▶ The relationship between January and the rest of the year is complex. It is not simply a case of January up – rest-of-year up, or January down – rest-of-year down, as some commentators seem to suggest.

It's true that big January price declines are invariably associated with further losses in the remainder of the year. If January's prices fall by -1.92% or more, there is only a 20% chance that prices will be higher on 31 December. This level is well below average. To put that figure into perspective,

Figure 3.5

CORRELATION BETWEEN JANUARY AND REST OF YEAR

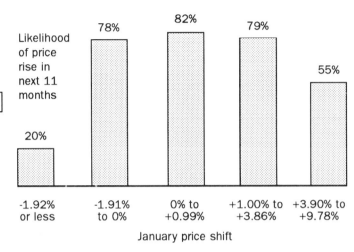

Figure 3.5: The best profit signal for the next 11 months is a January price shift within a range of -1.91% to +3.86%

over the long-run, prices rise 64% of the time in February to December.

Small gains or losses okay

But a small January loss is a good sign for investors, as is a small gain. Any January price move within a range of -1.91% to +3.86% is a strong signal that prices will rise in the rest of the year *(see Figure 3.5)*.

The trend changes for the worse if January prices rise any higher. The odds are a little over 50:50 that share prices will rise still further in the next 11 months if January prices rise +3.90% to +9.78%. (January, 1994 rose by +3.90% and the market turned down soon after.) Furthermore, the average level of profit for the 11 months that follows a big January price increase is just +1.45% per year, less than the level of interest provided by your neighbourhood Building Society.

There were only three years since 1919 with even larger January price rises. That is not enough data for us to make a proper forecast but we note that each of the three saw very strong further rises in the 11 months that followed.

FEBRUARY INVESTMENT MONITOR

	LAST MONTH FINAL PRICE	END OF 1ST QUARTER		END OF 2ND QUARTER		END OF 3RD QUARTER		END OF 4TH QUARTER	
		PRICE	PERCENT CHANGE	PRICE	PERCENT CHANGE	PRICE	PERCENT CHANGE	PRICE	PERCENT CHANGE
FT-ORDINARY (FT-30)									
FT-SE 100									
FT-SE 250									
FT-NON-FINANCIAL (FT-500)									
FT-SE-A ALL SHARES									
STANDARD & POORS COMPOSITE									
OTHER INDEX									
ENTER EACH SHARE, UNIT TRUST, ETC, BELOW									

CHAPTER FOUR – FEBRUARY 1996

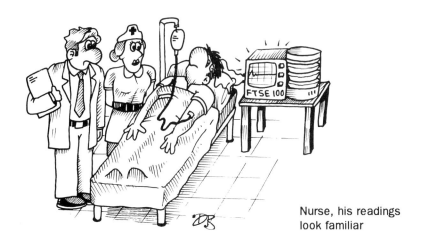

Nurse, his readings
look familiar

Compared with the typically strong stock market performance of December and January, February's trend is often quite disappointing to investors. Over the long-run, the February investor would have made more money by depositing his funds in an interest-bearing savings account. The chance of losing money is especially good after a strong January price rise.

Fortunately, the profit news is not totally bad. The odds of a profit are very good if prices rise by a small amount in the three-month run-up to February. And even in 'normal' years, most of February's weakness has historically occurred in the first three quarters of the month. The last quarter is often profitable.

While this month is not particularly known for its volatility, a declining price trend over the last 12 months is usually associated with 100-plus point swings on the FT-SE 100. There are several historic price trends which tip off in which direction this big swing will go.

Looking ahead, a small to medium February up-move is often associated with further gains in the next eight months to 31 October. See page 87 for additional details.

According to one City wag, there are just two kinds of market where February prices are especially likely to be weak – bull markets and bear markets!

This light-hearted advice is remarkably accurate. A review of all of February's closing prices since 1919 reveals a basic trend which has held firm for three-quarters of this century – investors who hold shares every February, for the entire month, are making a poor investment decision.

Weak trend

Although profits were earned in some years, the long-term February investor lost money in the 1930s, '40s, '50s, and '60s. The large average annual increase of the 1970s was almost entirely due to the explosive rally of 1975, which signalled the end of the 1973–74 bear market, when February gained +23.28%. In the 1980s' bull market, February performed better than its long-term average, as did most other months, producing an average annual monthly gain of +2.05%. But since October 1987, February has reverted to traditional form with a record of three ups and four downs (see Table 4.1).

Eighth-ranked

Between 1919 and 1994, February's prices rose just 49% of the time. In contrast, January's prices rose 75% of the time. In relative terms, that's 53% more often. During this period, the average February share price rise was just +0.26% per year, equal to nine points on an FT-SE 100 of 3300. A hypothetical investor who only invested in February, from 1919 to 1994, would have run up his £1,000 to just £1,101. If the rally of 1975 were eliminated from these computations, investors would have registered a loss after 75 years of steady investing. Historically, February is ranked eighth on monthly profitability. Without 1975, its rank would drop to tenth position.

No help from USA

In some months, the US Presidential election cycle helps UK stock market trading conditions. Unfortunately, February is not one of them. Share prices have risen just four times in the last 11 US Presidential election years. There is no getting away from it. Over the long-run, a February

Table 4.1

FEBRUARY PRICE RISES AND DECLINES: 1919–1994

	Average February price change	Up	Down
1920–29	1.06%	7	3
1930–39	-0.11%	4	6
1940–49	-1.93%	4	6
1950–59	-0.80%	6	4
1960–69	-1.05%	3	7
1970–79	2.40%	5	5
1980–89	2.05%	5	5
1990–94	1.30%	3	2
Average February price change	0.26%	37	39

Source: BZW and Datastream

Table 4.1: Historically, February has been a poor month in which to invest. Without 1975's rise of +23.28%, the 1970–79 average price rise was just +0.08%, equal to about three points on an FT-SE 100 of 3300 and the 75-year average would be in the red. The apparent improvement in the 1980s was a bull market phenomenon. Since the 1987 crash, the February record is three up and four down.

UPDATE

investor is better off placing his money into a savings account, gaining a higher average return on capital, with no risk to boot.

Three-year rule
As far as the future is concerned, we see no sign that the February trend will improve. The best-ever stretch of time for the February investor was back in 1922–5 when shares rose in value in four consecutive years. Since then there have been three occasions when prices rose three years in a row: 1944–6, 1979–81 and 1991–3. Each time, they fell the following year. In the most recent assault on the Three-Year rule, share prices rose to new peaks in December 1993 and January 1994 as commentators repeatedly warned that the stock market was over-extended and ripe for a fall. But prices kept rising until the start of February when they

suddenly ran out of steam with a -3.29% setback.

Incidentally, in the single exception to the Three-Year rule, the four-year up-turn of 1922–25, February share prices rose by just +0.51% in 1925. It seems safe to assume that any long-term change in the February trend will be associated with a successful attack on the Three-Year rule. Until then, invest in February with caution.

Why are share prices so disappointing in February? No one knows with any certainty. Obviously, no market can continue to rise forever. Prices must rest or occasionally react against a rising up-trend in even the best bull market. But why does it happen so consistently in February? Why not in January? Why not in December? The most likely reason is that the of start-of-year money flows and up-to-the-minute company statements which often power a January price advance peter out in February, causing shares to give back some of their January gains.

Final quarter is profitable

Despite the poor overall trend, there are a number of ways to profit with a February investment. Take, for example, the pattern of profit and loss during different parts of the month. Over the long-term, virtually all of February's profits have been realised in the last week of the month which rises 59% of the time. The last week of the month has been either first or second-ranked from the 1930s to the 1970s. It is the sixth-best quarter of the entire year. Since 1984, the third quarter trend has also been quite strong, creating a back-to-back pocket of profitability *(see Figure 4.1)*.

Watch out in first half

Unfortunately, the price trend for the first half of the month continues to disappoint. At first glance, this profit picture seems to have changed in the 1980s when fourth-quarter profits were surpassed by the first and second quarters. In fact, what happened was that the first and second quarters disproportionately improved during the 1980s bull market. After the 1987 crash, the long-term strength of the fourth quarter again became apparent.

INCREASE YOUR PROFIT ODDS

January signal

One way to beat the odds in February is to identify specific years when share prices are especially likely to rise or decline. One trend worth watching is the size of the January advance. History shows that strong January advances are often followed by partial February pull-backs, in other words declines that are *smaller* than the preceding advance. Here is the evidence: since records began in 1919, there have been 11 occasions when January's prices have strongly risen by +4.52% to +8.33%. February shares fell in 10 of those years. Nine of the falls were partial retractions of the January rise. There was only one occasion, over 30 years ago, when a strong January rise was followed by a February advance.[1]

NEW

Rose (1)

Fell (10)

February record if January prices rose by +4.52% to +8.33%

This information has value for investors who are looking to avoid February losses as well as those who wish to move into shares after a healthy January advance. Since the odds favour a partial pull-back, any price drop which eats up much of the January advance can be regarded as being near February's low point and serve as a useful 'buy signal'.

January second-half signal

Another way to anticipate falling share prices in February is to watch the averages during the second half of

---

[1] Reminder: All monthly calculations are based on the FT-Non-financial Index, formerly the FT-'500'; unless otherwise stated, they are based on data from 1919–1994. All daily, quarterly, and bi-monthly calculations are based on the Ordinary Share Index, also known as the FT-30; unless otherwise stated, they are based on data from 1936–1994

Figure 4.1 **ODDS OF A FEBRUARY PRICE RISE: 1936–1994**

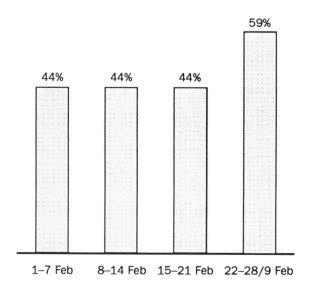

Figure 4.1: Prices rise in the fourth quarter more often than in other quarters. The average annual profit of +0.79% is also much higher than the first (+0.03%), second (-0.24%) or third (-0.29%) quarters.

January. There have been 20 second halves with price drops of up to -3.30%. February prices fell 16 times.

Rose (4)

Fell (16)

February record after prices fell by up to -3.30% in January's second half (since 1936)

Past-12-months signal

On the up-side, one signal which, historically, has done a good job of anticipating rising prices in February is the price trend in the previous year. If prices shift within each of the following limits, the odds of a February profit is quite high.

Previous 12 months:	price shift between -4.40% to +13.63%
Previous 6 months:	price shift between -2.21% to +11.79%
Previous 3 months:	price rise (any amount)
Previous month:	price rise to +9.78%

Since 1920, there have been 14 years with appropriate price shifts within each one of these four ranges in the run-up to February. February prices rose in 13 of those years. The single exception was back in 1929.

Rose (13)

Fell (1)

February record if prices shift within defined limits (since 1920)

The average annual February profit in these 14 years was a quite healthy +2.36%. But one word of warning. Watch the size of the past 12-month up-move very carefully. If prices rise by more than +13.63%, the odds of a decline in February are 50:50. An excessively large rise in the previous 12 months was last observed in 1994. Shares fell in February by over three percent, the start of the 1994 mini-bear market.

Past-three-month signal

It also pays to keep an eye on the direction of prices in November to January. There have been 10 instances where prices rose in the past three months between +1.72% and +3.07%. February prices rose in all 10 years. The average annual increase was +3.17%.

Rose (10)

Fell (0)

February record after a price rise of +1.72% to +3.07% in
November to January

UPDATE

Volatility

If we eliminate duplication within these last two up-trends,
there were 18 years that were flagged by at least one of
them. February prices rose 17 times. In the remaining 57
years between 1920 and 1994, February's record was simply terrible. Prices fell 65% of the time (20 up and 37 down).

Although its long-term record is poor, February prices
are not particularly volatile. Shifts of ±3.03% or more (at
least 100 points on an FT-SE 100 of 3300) are about average compared with other months. But if prices have dropped
in the past 12 months by at least -3.68%, be on the alert for
very volatile trading conditions.

Since 1920, there have been 22 years in which share
prices declined by at least -3.68% in the 12 months preceding February. February's prices rose or fell by at least 3% in
18 of those years. And two of the four smaller moves were
near misses. With moves of this magnitude, it is important
to know the direction of the shift so that you can either step
aside or commit more funds for a short-term investment. In
addition to the forecasting tools described earlier, the stock
market provides one other clue – the direction of prices in
the first quarter of February.

Since 1936, there were 17 Big Move signals (past 12
months down by -3.68% or worse). In 14 of those years, the
direction of price shifts in the first quarter was followed by
further shifts in the same direction during the rest of the
month. It's not a perfect answer since part of the move has
already occurred. But knowing that three-quarters of a Big
Move is still to come is far better than having no information at all.

FIRST QUARTER OF FEBRUARY – FEBRUARY 1ST TO 7TH

Over the long-run, share prices rise in the first quarter just **44%** of the time. The trend improved during the 1980s but it was simply a bull market phenomenon. Since the 1987 crash, the first-quarter record has reverted to form, three up and four down.

The second quarter which follows also has a poor profit record making these two quarters a difficult time within which to make money consistently with shares.

The price trend during the second half of January often tips whether prices will rise or fall during the first quarter of the month.

It's hard to turn a profit in February by steadily holding shares year-in and year-out. Profiting in the first quarter of the month is even more difficult.

The general investment climate is poor. The average increase in share prices during the first quarter is just +0.03% per year, equal to about one point on a 3300 FT-SE 100. If we eliminate all profits associated with 1975, an annual investment in February's first quarter would produce a loss. Profits seem to have improved since 1980 but this is a function of the bull market which saw many segments of the year perform better than their long-term average. Since the 1987 crash, the first-quarter record has reverted to form – three up and four down *(see Table 4.2)*.

Long-term money loser

If you plan to purchase any shares during this quarter of the month, keep in mind that the first two days are the most profitable. The three trading days that follow lose money in most years. The clear implication to investors: if you are planning to invest new funds from the 5th onward, in most years it would pay you to keep your money in a bank; if you are planning to sell, the odds favour holding on for the first two days of the quarter. Following this strategy will not

Table 4.2   **PERCENTAGE PRICE CHANGE: FEBRUARY 1936–1994**

	February 1–7	February 8–14	February 15–21	February 22–28(9)
Average annual price change				
1936–39	0.30%	-0.43%	0.07%	1.51%
1940–49	-0.74%	-1.17%	-0.30%	0.39%
1950–59	0.81%	-0.83%	-0.73%	-0.02%
1960–69	-0.32%	0.15%	-0.88%	-0.25%
1970–79	-0.56%	-0.43%	0.03%	3.05%
1980–89	0.94%	0.97%	-0.02%	0.62%
1990–94	-0.18%	0.09%	0.31%	0.59%
Average quarterly price change	0.03%	-0.24%	-0.29%	0.79%
Number of years in which prices:				
rose	26	26	26	35
fell	29	33	32	23
remained unchanged	4	–	1	1

Source: Datastream

Table 4.2: Most February profits are gained in the fourth quarter. Without 1975, the average quarterly price change would be: first quarter: -0.12%; second quarter: -0.37%; third quarter: -0.21%; fourth quarter: +0.53%. Historically, the best strategy was to stand aside until the end of the month. But since 1984, the third quarter has also performed well. Most 1980s third-quarter trading losses occurred in the first four years of the decade.

UPDATE

increase your profits each and every year but will shade things a bit more in your favour over the long-run *(see Figure 4.2).*

Figure 4.2

PERCENTAGE OF TIME PRICES RISE EACH TRADING DAY IN FEBRUARY'S FIRST QUARTER

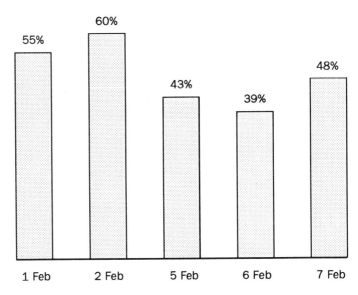

Figure 4.2: The first two days are the best days of the quarter. If you are planning to sell shares around this point of the year, the odds suggest holding on during these two days.

INCREASE YOUR PROFIT ODDS

January signal   Despite the generally poor trading conditions, it is possible to profit in this difficult time period by investing selectively. One key period to watch is the direction that prices move during the month of January. Since 1965, each time January's prices rose by +3.65% to +8.33%, they fell in the first quarter of February. This signal flashed most recently in 1994 when a strong January rise was promptly followed with a decline of -1.64% in February's opening quarter.

UPDATE

Rose (0)

Fell (10)

First-quarter record after a price rise of +3.65% to +8.33% in
January (since 1965)

January second-
half signal No 1

Another period to watch is the direction of prices in the last
half of January. Since 1969, the price of an average share
either fell in the last half of January or rose by no more than
+1.02% in 10 different years. Prices continued to disappoint
in the first quarter of February in all 10 years. Betting
against the market (for example buying Puts) or simply
pulling out completely, would have been a profitable course
of action to take during these 10 years.

IMPROVEMENT

Rose (0)

Fell (10)

First-quarter record after a price decline in January's second
half, or a rise of up to +1.02% (since 1969)

January second-
half signal No 2

On the other hand, if second half prices increase by +1.27%
to +2.63%, there is a very good chance of a price rise in the
first quarter of February.

UPDATE

Rose (10)

Fell (1)

First-quarter record after a price rise of +1.27% to +2.63% in
January's second half

January third-quarter signal

There is a strange correlation between the third quarter of January and February's first quarter. It seems that a drop in prices during January's third quarter is often followed by a price decline in the first quarter of February, regardless of how prices move in January's fourth quarter. Apparently, market forces and money flows during January's fourth quarter (one of the best quarters of the entire year) are sufficiently powerful to overwhelm the negative trend for a short period of time. But, as soon as the fourth quarter ends, the negative trend comes back into effect at the beginning of February.

Since 1960, prices fell in January's third quarter by -0.87% or more in 10 different years. Prices continued to decline in each of these years in the first quarter of February, regardless of how they moved in January's fourth quarter.

Rose (0)

Fell (10)

First-quarter record after a price fall of -0.87% or more in January's third quarter (since 1960)

SECOND QUARTER OF FEBRUARY – FEBRUARY 8TH TO 14TH

> Here comes another segment of the year with poor profit potential. You might make money in any single year but over the long-run, you will lose money more often than you will make it.
>
> Be especially cautious on 12 February. Prices often fall when the 12th lands on a Monday, as it will do in 1996.

February's second quarter is another tough period in which to make money in the stock market. Prices fall 56% of the time and generate an average annual loss of -0.24%.

The investment climate seems to have improved in the 1980s. Prices rose six times, fell four times, and increased at an average rate of +0.97%. But here again, the improvement was a temporary bull market phenomenon. The trend since 1987 has reverted to form with a record of two up and five down *(see Table 4.3)*.

As you execute your trades, keep in mind that the very best trading day in this quarter is February 13 when prices rise 54% of the time *(see Figure 4.3)*. During the last 20 years, prices have been especially strong on this day, rising in 11 out of 15 years (Saturdays and Sundays account for the missing days).

Watch out on 12 February

Unfortunately history also reveals a persistent weakness in share prices on the second Monday of February. The 12th of the month has landed on a Monday eight times since 1936. Prices rose twice. Before dismissing this as an interesting, but statistically untrustworthy observation because of the low number of observations, consider this: The 13th also landed on a Monday in eight years and rose just once. And the 14th rose on a Monday in just one year out of nine. In general, daily prices rise 48% of the time during the month of February. They rise 38% of the time on February Mondays. Within this context, a 16% rate of increase for Monday, the 12th, 13th and 14th seems excessively low.

Table 4.3   **PERCENTAGE PRICE CHANGE: 1985–1994**

	February 1–7	February 8–14	February 15–21	February 22–28(9)
Annual quarterly price change				
1985	0.31%	-0.45%	0.02%	-0.39%
1986	2.30%	2.62%	3.05%	1.70%
1987	4.71%	0.80%	3.02%	2.09%
1988	-3.39%	-0.15%	-0.17%	3.39%
1989	1.22%	-1.17%	1.25%	-2.71%
1990	-2.03%	-0.21%	-2.12%	-0.13%
1991	3.43%	3.49%	1.49%	3.58%
1992	-2.58%	0.30%	1.64%	0.01%
1993	1.90%	-1.40%	0.60%	0.35%
1994	-1.64%	-1.75%	-0.05%	-0.84%
Average quarterly price change				
1985–94	0.42%	0.21%	0.87%	0.71%
Number of years in which prices:				
rose	6	4	7	6
fell	4	6	3	4

Source: Datastream

Table 4.3: The first- and second-quarter trend improved during the 1980s. Alas, it was a bull market phenomenon. Since the 1987 crash, both quarters returned to traditional, less profitable trading patterns.

UPDATE

Here is the record for every Monday, 12, 13, and 14 February since 1970:

	One-day price shift		One day price shift
14 Feb 1972	-1.73%	14 Feb 1983	-0.27%
12 Feb 1973	-0.13%	13 Feb 1984	-0.30%
14 Feb 1977	-3.98%	13 Feb 1989	-1.36%
13 Feb 1978	-0.23%	12 Feb 1990	-1.10%
12 Feb 1979	-1.02%	14 Feb 1994	-0.32%

Figure 4.3   **PERCENTAGE OF TIME PRICES RISE EACH TRADING DAY IN FEBRUARY'S SECOND QUARTER**

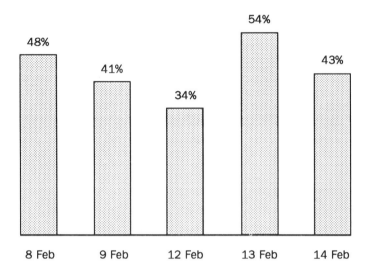

Figure 4.3: 12 February is the worst day of the quarter. Prices are especially likely to fall when 12 February lands on a Monday.

In case you haven't noticed, 12 February lands on a Monday in 1996.

St Valentine's Day

Incidentally, 14 February, St Valentine's Day, is disappointing to investors, even when it does not land on a Monday. On average, prices rise just 43% of the time. If you have ever wondered why Cupid is always shooting arrows at people, perhaps it is because he's a frustrated investor!

INCREASE YOUR PROFIT ODDS

Fortunately, the stock market sends several key signals to help nimble investors to profit or to avoid losses during these very difficult trading conditions.

January/February first-quarter signal

Here is a new signal for readers of the *Schwartz Stock Market Handbook*. There have been 19 years with a large January up-move, at least +1.52%, followed by a price drop in February's first quarter. Prices continued to fall in the second quarter in 15 of those years.

Rose (4)

Fell (15)

Second-quarter record after a January price rise of at least +1.52% and a price decline in February's first quarter

If a large January price rise is followed by a *small* February first-quarter decline, no more than -1.64%, the odds of a second-quarter decline are even higher. There have been 10 occasions with a large January price rise, followed by a small first-quarter decline. Prices fell in February's second quarter in nine of those years. The signal last flashed in 1994. After a strong January rally, the stock market reached its all-time peak on 2 February. By the end of the first quarter, shares had fallen by a small amount, and second quarter prices fell by an additional -1.75%.

Rose (1)

Fell (9)

Second-quarter record after a January price rise of at least +1.52% and a price drop of up to -1.64% in February's first quarter

First-quarter signal

Another price signal to watch is the direction of prices in February's first quarter, regardless of what happened in January. If they fall slightly, by -0.29% to -1.01%, share prices will probably also drop in the second quarter. Out of 11 declines of this magnitude in the first quarter, second-quarter prices dropped 10 times. The average decline was -0.98% per year, about 32 points on an FT-SE 100 in the area of 3300. This trend partially duplicates the previous signal but it also flags some second-quarter declines on its own.

Rose (1)

Fell (10)

Second-quarter record after a price fall of -0.29% to -1.01% in the first quarter

January third-quarter signal

A third signal to watch for is a flat price trend in January's third quarter. By 'flat', we mean any small shift within a range of -0.52% to +0.43%. Between 1936–1994, there were 14 years with small third-quarter price shifts within this range. February's second quarter fell in 12 of those years (86% of the time) and generated an average loss of -1.51% per year.

Rose (2)

Fell (12)

Second-quarter record after a price shift of -0.52% to +0.43% in January's third quarter

If we eliminate duplication within the last three trends, there are 22 years that are flagged by at least one of them. Second-quarter prices fell 19 times. In the remaining 37 years since 1936, the second-quarter record was up 23 and down 14. You wouldn't make money every year but simply avoiding share ownership when warned would lead to a small average annual profit during the years that you did invest.

THIRD QUARTER OF FEBRUARY – FEBRUARY 15TH TO 21ST

> A mediocre period for many decades, things recently hotted up for the third-quarter investor. Since 1984, the record has been quite good – eight up and three down. And the quarter to follow also offers high profit potential.
>
> History suggests that a weak trend in the preceding weeks is often associated with further price declines during this quarter. A small rise in the second quarter is often followed with further price increases.

The third quarter of February has been a money-loser since the 1940s. The typical share price fell 54% of the time between 1936 and 1994, with an average decline of -0.29%. Even during the early 1980s when other so-so segments of the year turned a profit, the third quarter was a money-loser.

Trend change

But the trend has improved in recent years. Since 1984, the third-quarter record is eight up and three down. Two of the falls were quite tiny, the equivalent of 12 points on a 3300 FT-SE, in 1985 and again in 1994. What is going on? No one knows for sure. It may be that investors are coming to realise profits are likely in the final quarter of the month and are moving into shares to catch the expected up-turn. What ever the cause, it is an event we shall monitor with great interest.

15 February

The best day of the quarter is the 15th. Shares also seem to do especially well on mid-month Thursdays. Since 1936, prices rise 70% of the time whenever 14–17 February lands on a Thursday. No guarantees of course, but 15 February lands on a Thursday in 1996 so the odds favour an up-move.

21 February

Unfortunately, the price trend soon weakens. The 21st is one of the weakest days of the entire year. Prices rise just 29% of the time *(see Figure 4.4).*

Figure 4.4   **PERCENTAGE OF TIME PRICES RISE EACH TRADING DAY IN FEBRUARY'S THIRD QUARTER**

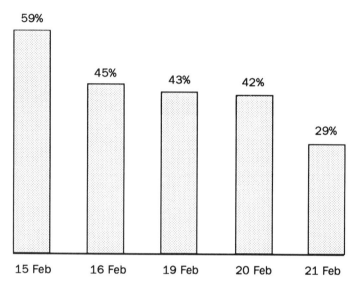

Figure 4.4: Share prices often rise on 15 February, especially if it lands on a Thursday, so the odds favour investors in 1996. But the trend soon deteriorates. 21 February is one of the worst trading days of the entire year.

INCREASE YOUR PROFIT ODDS

February first-
half signal

If you choose to bet on a rising market during this quarter of the month, here is a price trend that consistently forecasts rising prices – a small shift in prices during the first half of the month. If prices shift slightly in the first half, by -0.14% to +1.15%, there is a 91% chance that third-quarter prices will also rise. The single exception to the rule occurred in 1967.

Rose (10)

Fell (1)

Third-quarter record after a price shift of -0.14% to +1.15% in first half

Second-quarter signal

Here is a new relationship that seems to have begun in 1984, just as the profit odds improved for this quarter of the month. We use the word 'seems' deliberately. It's too early to call it a definite trend but we note the following events with great interest. Prices have risen in the second quarter five times since 1984. Third-quarter prices rose each time. During the other six years of this period, the third-quarter record is three up and three down.

If you choose to bet on a falling market, here are some pointers to help you to increase the probability of profiting:

First-half signal

▶ Keep on the look out for weak prices in the first half of February. If the first quarter rises by no more than +0.61%, or falls by any amount, and the second quarter falls by -0.74% to -2.62%, the third quarter is especially likely to fall. The average annual decline during these years is -1.63%. This signal last flashed in 1994 and third-quarter prices fell on cue.

Rose (0)

UPDATE

Fell (11)

Third-quarter record after a price shift of +0.61% or less in first quarter and a decline of -0.74% to -2.62% in second quarter

January second-half/February first-half signal

▶ An even better early warning signal is a weak price trend in January's second half and February's first half. If prices decline in February's first half and either rise

83

by no more than +0.33% or decline in January's second half, the odds favour a decline in the third quarter. Between 1936 and 1994, there were 19 years that matched this profile. The third quarter of February declined in 18 of those years (95%). The single exception was back in 1947. The average decline was -1.41% per year.

Rose (1)

Fell (18)

Third-quarter record after a price shift of +0.33% or less in January's second half and a decline in February's first half

FOURTH QUARTER OF FEBRUARY – FEBRUARY 22ND TO 29TH

Prices usually rise in this quarter, especially during leap years. No one knows why but since 1956, prices have risen in every single leap year, 10 times in a row.

The fourth quarter is February's best segment. Prices rise 59% of the time. It is February's only quarterly segment that rises in most years. Between 1936 and 1994, the average an-nual gain was +0.79%.

28 February looks good

The best day of the month is 28 February – prices rise 64% of the time. So if you are planning to sell shares late in the month, the odds favour holding on until the very end of the month *(see Figure 4.5)*.

In most years, 28 February is a very safe day in which to hold shares. In addition to the high percentage of time that

Figure 4.5

PERCENTAGE OF TIME PRICES RISE EACH TRADING DAY IN FEBRUARY'S FOURTH QUARTER

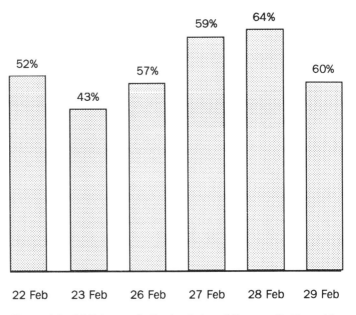

Figure 4.5: 28 February is the best day of the month. The odds are especially good if it lands on a Wednesday as in 1996. If you plan to sell shares near the end of the month, holding on until the very end will move profits a bit more in your favour in most years.

prices rise, it is one of the few days in the entire year in which prices have *never* fallen by over 1%.

For some unknown reason, the final Wednesday of the month does well in most years, whether the date is 25, 26, 27 or 28 February. Since our records began in 1936, February's final Wednesday rose 24 times and fell six times (20%). Happily, 28 February lands on a Wednesday in 1996.

23 February

In contrast, 23 February is the quarter's weakest link. Prices have risen just 43% of the time since 1936. And the recent trend shows no sign of improvement. In the last 10 years, the 23 February record is two up and five down.

INCREASE YOUR PROFIT ODDS

Second/third-quarter signal

If you want to improve the odds of making a profit during the fourth quarter, watch the behaviour of prices in the two preceding quarters. Between 1936 and 1994 there were 15 occasions when share prices rose by at least +1.69% in total in the second and third quarters. Prices continued to rise in the fourth quarter in 13 of those years (87%). The average increase was +2.52%.

Rose (13)

Fell (2)

Fourth-quarter record after a price rise of at least +1.69% in the second and third quarters

First-half signal

There is also an interesting relationship between the first half of February and the fourth quarter, regardless of which direction prices move in the third quarter. Solid moves, either up or down, are associated with fourth-quarter price increases. But a neutral trend that ends close to where the first half started is often associated with fourth-quarter price declines. Here is the evidence: since 1936, first-half prices rose by at least +1.15% 18 times. Fourth-quarter prices also rose in 16 of those years (89%). The average annual increase was +2.24%.

Rose (16)

Fell (2)

Fourth-quarter record after a price rise of at least +1.15% in the first half

During this same period, there were 13 additional years with a first half decline of -2.29% to -5.10%. Fourth-quarter prices rose in 11 of those years.

Rose (11)

Fell (2)

Fourth-quarter record after a price drop of -2.29% to -5.10% in the first half

There were an additional 24 years with a smaller first-half price shift, no more than +1.14% on the up-side and -2.28% on the down-side. Fourth-quarter prices rose just seven times (29%).

Prices leap in leap year

Here's one final statistical relationship to help you to make money in February which is particularly appropriate to call to your attention in 1996. We offer no rationale to explain why it works. But it does work. Since 1956, there have been 10 leap years. Fourth-quarter prices have risen in every single one of them. The average annual price increase was +1.62%. During the other 29 years since 1956, fourth-quarter prices have risen just 45% of the time.

Surprisingly, 29 February itself is not consistently profitable. Since 1956, its record is three up and four down (the missing three days fell on weekends) with an average daily loss of -0.26%.

LOOKING AHEAD

The February price trend shows an uncanny ability to forecast where prices are heading eight months ahead, that is, to the end of October.

Rising prices by 31 October

Since 1923, there have been 23 years with a February price rise of up to +3.29% or a tiny fall, no greater than -0.55%. In 22 of those years, prices rose in the eight months to October 31. The average increase was +8.8%. This signal last flashed in 1993. A February price rise of just under 2% was followed with an additional +9.19% gain by the end of October.

As you use this data, remember that prices do not necessarily peak on 31 October. It is theoretically possible for prices to peak on 31 March, drift downward for the next seven months, yet show a profit for the eight-month period.

A single exception to the rule occurred in 1957 and even then, the February up-move was followed with rising prices in March, April, May and June, stimulated by falling Bank Rates and an expanding economy. The party came to an end with a July Bank Rate rise to 7%, the highest level in four decades. Equities fell sharply from their early summer peak for the next four months.

Rose (22)

Fell (1)

Trend to 31 October after a February price shift of -0.55% to +3.29%

When February prices move outside of the -0.55% to +3.29% range, the chance of a profit between 1 March and 31 October is much less. Out of 53 years with a bigger February price swing, the record to 31 October was 30 up (57%) and 23 down.

Rising prices by 31 December

If prices rise in the six-month period between 1 September and 28/29 February by +4.08% to +20.47%, the odds are very good that prices will rise still higher in the 10 months ahead, that is, through the rest of the year to 31 December. Since 1925, there have been 30 years with a September– February price rise within the designated range. In 27 of those years, prices rose still further in the next 10 months.

Rose (27)

Fell (3)

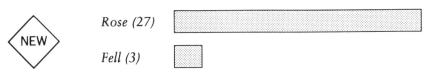

Trend to 31 December after a September–February price shift
of +4.08% to +20.47% (since 1925)

**Falling prices
by 30 April**

Here is a relationship that does a good job of flagging price declines in the near future. If prices fall by a small amount, no more than -2.99% in the three months from 1 December to 28/29 February, the odds are high that further declines will occur in the next two months. There have been 14 years with a small price drop in the December–February time period. Prices fell even lower by 30 April in 12 of those years. One of the two exceptions was a tiny +0.60% rise in 1935.

Rose (2)

Fell (12)

Trend to 30 April after a December–February price drop of
up to -2.99%

MARCH INVESTMENT MONITOR

	LAST MONTH FINAL PRICE	END OF 1ST QUARTER		END OF 2ND QUARTER		END OF 3RD QUARTER		END OF 4TH QUARTER	
		PRICE	PERCENT CHANGE	PRICE	PERCENT CHANGE	PRICE	PERCENT CHANGE	PRICE	PERCENT CHANGE
FT-ORDINARY (FT-30)									
FT-SE 100									
FT-SE 250									
FT-NON-FINANCIAL (FT-500)									
FT-SE-A- ALL SHARES									
STANDARD & POORS COMPOSITE									
OTHER INDEX									
ENTER EACH SHARE, UNIT TRUST, ETC, BELOW									

CHAPTER FIVE – MARCH 1996

The March story is heavily influenced by the former Spring Budget.

Up until the 1940s, when Spring Budgets were a late-April or May event, March was a money-loser in most years. The trend began to improve as Budget schedules were steadily advanced. By the 1980s, with Budget Day typically landing in mid-March, shares rose in value in eight out of 10 years.

Spring Budgets are now a thing of the past. We think the March trend will revert to the historic lacklustre levels last seen in the 1940s.

The pattern of price shifts within the month is also likely to change. In the 1940s to 1960s when many Budgets landed in April, first-half prices rose just 32% of the time. Once Budgets began to appear in early and mid-March, the first-half profit picture dramatically improved. Now that Spring Budgets are gone, our working hypothesis is that share price trends for the first half of March will return to the pattern of the past, frequently losing money.

The second half's price trend is also likely to change. When Budgets were an April event, second half prices rose 68% of the time. But in recent decades, its performance slipped badly with prices rising just 37% of the time as shares gave back some of their Budget-induced first half advance. We expect to see some improvement from these recent dismal levels.

Looking ahead, a small price shift in the first three months of the year does a good job of forecasting where prices are headed in the nine months ahead. See page 112 for further details.

Investors who held shares every March made a small profit over the long-run. Between 1919 and 1994, March prices rose 55% of the time. The average price rise was just 0.69%, equal to 23 points on an FT-SE 100 in the area of 3300. Historically, March has been the sixth-best month to invest in shares *(see Table 5.1)*. A 1919 investment of £1,000, held in shares each March and in cash for the other 11 months of the year, would now be worth just £1,536 after 76 years of steady investing.

Budget Day affects March

Budget Day seems to play a role in March's long-term performance *(see Figure 5.1)*. From 1919–43, the first 25 years of our historical record, March prices rose just 10 times. During this money-losing period, 21 out of 25 budgets were presented in late April. In the next 25 year period, from 1944–1968, Budget Day was often scheduled in early/mid-April, and March prices rose 15 times. From 1969–93, 19 Budgets were presented in March and the month's typical profits improved once again, despite 1974 when March was slammed by a -19.55% drop following a surprise Labour victory, the worst monthly drop in the entire 1973–4 bear market, and the third-worst month of all time. Only October 1987 (-26.32%) and June 1940 (-22.10%), when investors feared we might lose the war, were worse.

1944 was a fitting response

There is no way to prove conclusively that Budget Day caused this long-term trend. There are too many other issues that also influence share price trends. However, we believe it is not a coincidence that the Budget Day trend and the March profit trend are so similar. For this reason, we find it very fitting that prices fell by -5.79% in 1994, the first spring without a Spring Budget. We don't expect big drops like this every year. The 1994 drop was triggered by concerns over further interest rate rises on both sides of the Atlantic. But as a symbol of the 'new' March, the decline was very appropriate.

Table 5.1

MARCH PRICE RISES AND DECLINES: 1919–1994

	Average March price change	Up	Down
1920–29	0.59%	4	6
1930–39	-0.40%	4	6
1940–49	-0.62%	3	7
1950–59	0.40%	7	3
1960–69	2.25%	7	3
1970–79	0.38%	6	4
1980–89	2.11%	8	2
1990–94	-1.28%	2	3
Average March price change	0.69%	42	34

Source: BZW and Datastream

Table 5.1: The March record has steadily improved since the 1940s. Prices even rose in the 1970s despite the disaster in 1974 when prices fell -19.55% in response to Labour's surprise win.

UPDATE

A few readers may be tempted to draw some unwarranted conclusions about March because of its performance during the 1980s when it turned in its best-ever decade (as did other months). Prices rose in eight out of 10 years. The average monthly price rise was +2.11%. As this fine performance was heavily influenced by the bull market as well as the shift to March Budgets, we caution readers not to extrapolate this trend into the future.

Intra-month changes

Budget Day affected the point in the month when most profits are accumulated, as well as the month's overall performance. Prior to 1970, second-half prices rose 68% of the time as against 32% in the first half. Since then, as the tendency for Budget Days to be presented in the first half of March became more pronounced, the profit pattern abruptly changed. Second-half prices rose just 37% of the time, producing an average annual loss of -0.74%. The second

93

Figure 5.1:   **NUMBER OF TIMES MARCH PRICES ROSE: 1919–1993**

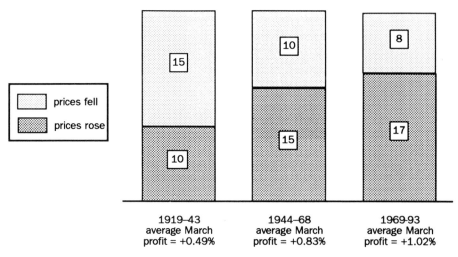

<table>
<tr><td>1919–43
average March
profit = +0.49%</td><td>1944–68
average March
profit = +0.83%</td><td>1969-93
average March
profit = +1.02%</td></tr>
</table>

Figure 5.1: March prices rose more frequently in successive 25-year periods. So did profitability. The average annual profit of +0.75% in 1969–93 would have been even higher if not for 1974.

half became a time period to avoid unless you were betting on the down-side.

Meanwhile, the strength formerly associated with the second half has shifted to the first half. First-half prices have risen 71% of the time since 1970 compared to 32% pre-1970. The average profit from 1970–1993 rose to +1.38% *(see Figure 5.2)*.

How will March prices behave now that Spring Budgets are a thing of the past? No one knows for sure. The answer will become clear in two or three decades from now. For the present, consider this:

▶ From 1919 to 1943, when most Budgets were presented in late April, and March business news contained little

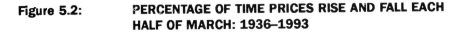
Figure 5.2:   **PERCENTAGE OF TIME PRICES RISE AND FALL EACH HALF OF MARCH: 1936–1993**

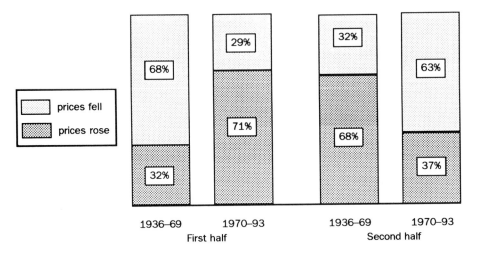

Figure 5.2: The shift to a mid-March budget in the 1970s had a strong and immediate effect on the pattern of profits in the first-versus-second half of the month. The first half of March became the most profitable part of the month.

coverage of the up-coming Budget, March was a mediocre month. Daily and weekly records are not available for most of this period so we can not calculate the relative strength of each half of the month.

▶ From 1944 to 1968, when Budgets were often present-ed in the first half of April, the second half of March was much more profitable than the first half. Although the third and fourth quarters rose the same amount of time during this period, the fourth quarter, one week closer to Budget Day and to the beginning of the new tax year, tended to generate bigger increases.

▶ During the 1980s, a period of tax cuts and generally well-received Budgets, most Budgets were presented around the middle of March. The first and second quarters of the month became March's most profitable segments.

First half to get worse

Our hypothesis is for a return to poor March trading conditions, now that Budget Day no longer affects March prices. The weak prospects for the first half are clearly indicated in Figure 5.3 which shows just how poorly the first and second quarters used to perform (particularly the second quarter) before most Budgets were presented in March.

Second half may improve

The second-half trend is more difficult to forecast. Budgets will no longer help second half prices as they did in the pre-1970s period. By the same token, there will be less down-side pressure for prices to give back some of their first-half gains as in the 1970s and '80s. Our best guess is second half prices will rise somewhere between the levels achieved pre- and post-1970, perhaps about half the time, with the fourth quarter out-performing the third because of its closer proximity to the start of the new fiscal year. Time will tell.

INCREASE YOUR PROFIT ODDS[1]

As with other months, historical price trends help to identify specific years when March prices are especially likely to rise or decline. Unfortunately, the effect of the Budget Day shift adds an unknown dimension to these forecasts. Nevertheless, here are several trends which, historically,

---

[1] Reminder: All monthly calculations are based on the FT-Non-financial Index, formerly the FT-'500'; unless otherwise stated, they are based on data from 1919–1994. All daily, quarterly, and bi-monthly calculations are based on the Ordinary Share Index, also known as the FT-30; unless otherwise stated, they are based on data from 1936–1994

Figure 5.3:   **PERCENTAGE OF TIME PRICES RISE EACH QUARTER OF MARCH: 1936–1993**

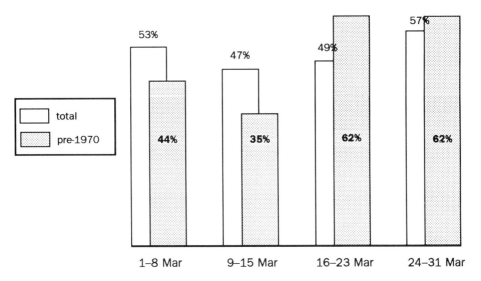

Figure 5.3: The first half of March used to be quite painful to investors, especially the second quarter. Prices fell in two out of three years. The trend improved with the advent of March budgets. Look out for possible trouble now that March budgets are a thing of the past.

have done a good job of anticipating the direction of March price shifts and which we believe are not dependent on Budget Day. We will not know for certain if our hypothesis is correct for several more years

Past-12-months signal

The direction of prices during the preceding 1 March to 28 February has traditionally been a good predictor of March prices. Big rises in the preceding 12 months are often associated with a March profit. Since records began, there have been 12 years in which prices rose between +22.49% to +35.45% in the previous 12 months. March shares rose each time. Since this trend was operative prior to the 1970s, as well as more recently, we believe it is still operative today.

	Rose (12)

IMPROVEMENT

Fell (0)

March record after a price rise of +22.49% to +35.45% in the 12 preceding months

Past-three-month signal No 1

Another signal to look for is the price trend in December to February. A small price decline in this three-month period is often associated with further declines in March. A large decline is often associated with rising March prices. The magic number for which to watch is a decline of about -3%. Smaller than that is a danger signal.

Here is the evidence: there have been 12 instances where prices fell in the past three months within a range of -3.30% and -13.71%. March prices rose in 10 of those years. The two exceptions were in 1952 and 1974.

Rose (10)

Fell (2)

March record after a price fall of -3.30% to -13.71% in the three preceding months

Past-three-month signal No 2

There were 13 other years with smaller price declines during December to February, within a range of -0.39% to -2.99%. The March record during these 13 years was up twice and down 11 times. The last exception was in 1981.

Rose (2)

Fell (11)

March record after a price fall of -0.39% to -2.99% in the three preceding months

98

February fourth-quarter signal

The direction of prices in the fourth quarter of February often tips off the direction of March price shifts. A small fourth-quarter rise, within a range of +0.44% to +1.70%, often signals an increase in March share prices. Since 1936, there have been 11 quarterly shifts of that size. March prices rose in nine of those years with an average annual increase of +2.86%.

Rose (9)

Fell (2)

March record after a price rise of +0.44% to +1.70% in February's fourth quarter

FIRST QUARTER OF MARCH – MARCH 1ST TO 8TH

Profit prospects for the first quarter are poor.

The best years for the first-quarter investor were in the 1980s when prices rose eight out of 10 times, helped by an early or mid-March Budget. But in the 1930s to 1960s, when later Budgets provided little help to the first quarter investor, prices usually fell.

Our working hypothesis is that first quarter price trends will follow the patterns of the past, now that Spring Budgets have been terminated. Profits might be made in any single year but not on a steady or systematic basis.

To increase the odds of a first quarter profit, watch the size of the February price shift. A small shift, up or down, is often associated with a profit in this quarter.

Like the month as a whole, investors gained very little by steadily investing every first quarter of March. After 59 years, the first quarter produced a record of 31 up, 28 down and a +0.07% level of price increase, the equivalent of less than three points a year on a 3300 FT-SE 100.

Helped by a March Budget

A decade-by-decade analysis finds small losses during the 1930s and '40s, when Budgets were often presented in late April, and tiny profits in the 1950s and '60s, when Budgets were often presented in early or mid-April. Once Budgets were moved to March, there was a marked improvement in the first-quarter trend. The relatively large average annual decline of -1.06% in the 1970s was largely due to a -12.67% decline in the 1974 bear market. Prices rose throughout the remainder of the decade and continued to do so in the 1980s with increases in eight out of 10 years and an average annual gain of +1.33% *(see Table 5.2)*.

Future not as rosy

With March Budgets a thing of the past, we fear a return to poor trading conditions during this quarter of the month. Our view of the future is quite visible in Figure 5.4 which shows daily price changes for the quarter over the long-run. Without the stimulus provided by the strong performance of the last two decades, the daily trend for first-quarter share prices is decidedly mediocre. Prior to 1974, prices fell on the majority of all days except one.

4 March

History suggests the chance of an up-move on 4 March is lower than usual in 1996. Since 1936, 4 and 5 March have both done poorly when they landed on a Monday, with a record of one up and 13 down. 4 March lands on a Monday in 1996.

Table 5.2

PERCENTAGE PRICE CHANGE: MARCH 1936–1994

	March 1–8	March 9–15	March 16–23	March 24–31
Average annual price change				
1936–39	-0.57%	-2.89%	0.24%	-0.96%
1940–49	-0.40%	-0.63%	0.12%	0.43%
1950–59	0.02%	-0.76%	0.67%	0.61%
1960–69	0.19%	0.39%	0.51%	0.82%
1970–79	-1.06%	1.92%	-1.02%	0.19%
1980–89	1.33%	0.72%	0.21%	-0.71%
1990–94	1.17%	-0.30%	-1.18%	-0.71%
Average quarterly price change	0.07%	0.06%	0.00%	0.10%
Number of years in which prices:				
rose	31	28	29	33
fell	28	30	29	25
remained unchanged	–	1	1	1

Source: Datastream

Table 5.2: The first- and second-quarter profit trend improved with the shift to a March budget. The first-quarter improvement is disguised by the drop of -12.67% in 1974. Both quarters could weaken now that March budgets are a thing of the past.

UPDATE

INCREASE YOUR PROFIT ODDS

February signal

The chronic Budget Day shifts of the past makes trend-spotting especially hazardous during this part of the year. But three trends have been in effect since before World War II, pre-dating the effects of March Budget Days: one of them is the direction of prices during the month of February. If they fluctuate by a small amount, from -1.35% to +1.15%, it is likely that first-quarter prices will rise. Since 1936, there have been 13 years with a small February move within this range. First-quarter prices rose in 11 of them (85%).

101

Figure 5.4:   **PERCENTAGE OF TIME PRICES RISE EACH TRADING DAY IN MARCH'S FIRST QUARTER**

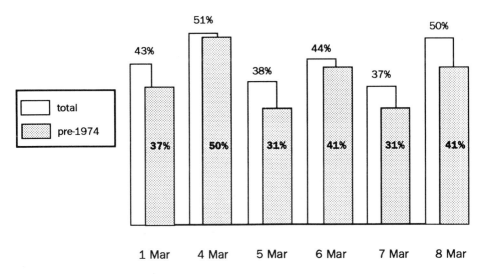

Figure 5.4: Prior to 1974, prices fell most of the time in the first quarter. When 4 or 5 March lands on a Monday, the odds of a profit are especially poor

Rose (11)

Fell (2)

First-quarter record after a price shift of -1.35% to +1.15% in February

February fourth-quarter signal No 1	The direction that prices move in February's fourth quarter also helps investors to anticipate the first-quarter trend. If prices decline in February's fourth quarter within a range of -0.97% to -2.71%, the chances are good they will rise strongly in the first quarter of March. Between 1936 and 1994, February's fourth quarter declined 13 times within

this range. March's first quarter rose in 11 of those years (85%) at an average annual rate of +1.24%.

IMPROVEMENT

Rose (11)

Fell (2)

First-quarter record after a price fall of -0.97% to -2.71% in February's fourth quarter

February fourth-quarter signal No 2

Just as a small decline in February's fourth quarter often forecasts a price rise in the first quarter, a small rise often signals a first-quarter decline. Out of 10 years with small February fourth-quarter price rises in the range of +0.42% to +1.34%, March prices fell nine times, at an average annual rate of -1.57%.

Rose (1)

Fell (9)

First-quarter record after a price rise of +0.42% to +1.34% in February's fourth quarter

SECOND QUARTER OF MARCH – MARCH 9TH TO 15TH

Be careful.

Like the first quarter, the best years for second quarter investors were in the 1980s when prices rose in most years. But back in the 1930s to 1960s, when Budgets were much later in the spring and had little effect on the second quarter, prices rose in just one year out of three.

Now that Spring Budgets are gone, we fear a return to the poor trading conditions of the past.

Budget Day
correlation

Second-quarter prices rose 47% of the time between 1936 and 1994. The average annual price change was +0.06%. Neither figure is very different from first-quarter results.

As in the first quarter, the long-term trend is correlated with the budget presentation schedule. From 1936 to 1959, when most Budget Days were in April, the second-quarter record was dismal: six up, 17 down, one quarter unchanged and an average loss of -1.06% per year.

During the next three decades, the price trend strengthened. The 1960s saw an average annual increase of +0.39%. Prices rose eight times in the 1970s at an average rate of +1.92%, equal to 63 points on a 3300 FT-SE 100. The last 10 years saw six price rises and an average share price increase of +0.54% per year *(see Table 5.3)*.

The daily price trend shows a similar pattern. The likelihood of a price rise on any day within the second quarter was decidedly lower in the 'old days' before March Budget Days became commonplace. Back then, prices were especially likely to fall on 11 and 13 March *(see Figure 5.5)*.

Table 5.3

PERCENTAGE PRICE CHANGE: 1985–1994

	March 1–8	March 9–15	March 16–23	March 24–31
Annual quarterly price change				
1985	0.71%	1.46%	-1.01%	-2.83%
1986	2.46%	3.97%	3.78%	-1.57%
1987	0.10%	-1.09%	1.74%	-2.13%
1988	1.97%	0.87%	-0.72%	-5.01%
1989	4.51%	1.73%	-3.19%	0.56%
1990	0.39%	-0.49%	1.72%	-1.53%
1991	2.51%	1.27%	-1.99%	0.51%
1992	-0.73%	-1.67%	-1.29%	0.21%
1993	3.85%	-1.03%	-1.39%	-0.57%
1994	-0.20%	0.40%	-2.93%	-2.19%
Average quarterly price change				
1985–94	1.56%	0.54%	-0.53%	-1.45%
Number of years in which prices:				
rose	8	6	3	3
fell	2	4	7	7

Source: Datastream

Table 5.3: The first and second quarters were extremely profitable in recent years. The third-quarter trend has been very weak since the 1987 crash. Prices have fallen in six of the past seven years.

| UPDATE |

INCREASE YOUR PROFIT ODDS

First-quarter
signal No 1

To help improve the odds of avoiding a poor second quarter, watch for a small decline in share prices during the first quarter. Since 1936, first-quarter prices fell by -0.52% to -1.08% in nine years. Second-quarter prices continued to decline each time.

Figure 5.5:   **PERCENTAGE OF TIME PRICES RISE EACH TRADING DAY IN MARCH'S SECOND QUARTER**

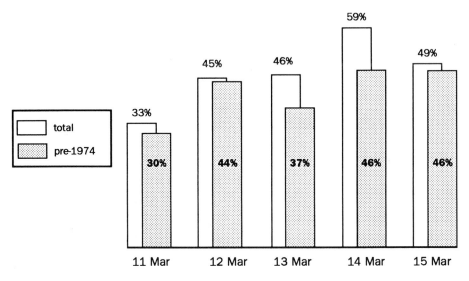

Figure 5.5: Prior to 1974, the price trend was noticeably weaker throughout the second quarter.

Rose (0)

Fell (9)

Second-quarter record after a price fall of -0.52% to -1.08% in the first quarter (since 1936)

First-quarter signal No 2

Another trend which correlates the first and second quarter emerged in 1978. Since then, the first quarter rose by at least +0.71% 11 times and the second quarter followed 10 times. The single exception was in 1993 when the FT-SE 100 rose 89 points in the first quarter, an increase of over 3%, and the second quarter gave back some of that gain. We fear that Budget Day may have had a role in causing this relationship, and will watch the situation carefully to ensure this relationship continues to be operative in the future.

Rose (10)

Fell (1)

Second-quarter record after a price rise of at least +0.71% in the first quarter (since 1978)

THIRD QUARTER OF MARCH – MARCH 16TH TO 23RD

The recent third-quarter trend has been poor, an effect of the move toward earlier Spring Budgets. Now that Spring Budgets are gone, we expect the third-quarter trend to improve.

Budget shifts hurt performance

Unlike the first two quarters, whose recent performance has improved because of Budget Day shifts, the record for pre-1970s third quarters looks better than the more recent record. Here again, Budget Day played a role.

During the 1930s and '40s, a constant third-quarter investor would have made money by being fully invested during the third quarter of March. During the 1950s and '60s, prices rose in 13 years and fell six times (there was one no change year), one of the best records of the entire year in those decades.

Things changed in the 1970s, the first losing decade on record. At first glance, the problem looks to be caused by the events of 1975. After an extraordinary rally during January and February of that year, the trend plateaued for the first two quarters of March and then dropped -11.47% in the third quarter, a temporary and long-overdue correction.

But the rest of the decade wasn't that good either. Although the remaining nine years showed an average annual third-quarter profit of +0.14%, the record was three up and six down.

The trend did strengthen in the bull market 1980s, but since the October 1987 crash, the record has been quite weak: one up and six down – one of the worst quarterly performances of the entire year – quite a change from the 1950s and '60s. In fact, over the last 20 years, from 1975 to 1994, the third-quarter record of seven up and 13 down is second worst (tied with three others) of the year.

Improved
conditions
ahead

Now that Budget Day has been shifted to November, we see a chance that the performance trend for March's third quarter will improve. However, we do not expect the improvement to rival the strength of the 1950s and '60s, as those years were aided by an approaching budget. We shall watch the situation carefully. For the moment, be careful.

18 March

Analysis of price trends on a day-by-day basis reveals that the odds of a profit were especially high on 18 and 21 March, prior to 1974, a good sign for the present *(see Figure 5.6)*. Unfortunately, the profit prospects for March 18 are below average in 1996. Since our daily records began in 1936, 17 or 18 March have landed on a Monday in 16 different years. Prices rose in just three of those years. In 1996, 18 March lands on a Monday.

INCREASE YOUR PROFIT ODDS

First-half signal

Here is an interesting trend that used to be associated with third quarter price rises. It ran for over three decades but stopped working after 1970, around the time that the Budget was moved to mid-March.

Between 1936 to 1970, prices fell in the first half of

Figure 5.6: **PERCENTAGE OF TIME PRICES RISE EACH TRADING DAY IN MARCH'S THIRD QUARTER**

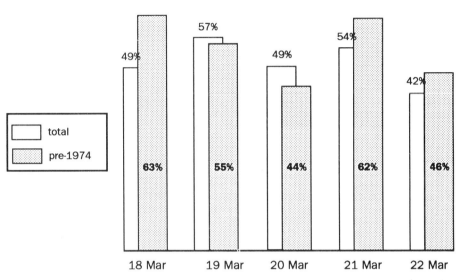

Figure 5.6: It is difficult to make money consistently during the third quarter. The odds of a profit are low when 18 March lands on a Monday, as it will in 1996.

March 13 times by -1.33% or more. Third-quarter prices rose in 10 of those years. We don't know if this relationship will re-start now that Spring Budgets are gone. We will watch with great interest.

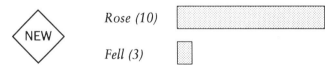

Rose (10)

Fell (3)

Third-quarter record after a price drop of at least -1.33% in the first half (1936-1970)

Fourth Quarter of March – March 24th to 31st

> The fourth-quarter price trend has been poor in recent years but should improve now that Spring Budgets are a thing of the past.

The fourth quarter used to be a good time to hold shares. From 1940 to 1969, when the quarter was helped by a soon-to-arrive April Budget, prices rose 70% of the time. The average annual increase in share prices during this stretch was +0.62%.

Budget shifts hurt fourth quarter

Unfortunately, the trend began to change in the 1970s with a weaker average annual profit of +0.19%. The trend weakened still further during the 1980s. Prices fell six times including 1984, 1985, 1986 and 1987, the heart of the best bull market of the century. (In each of these four years, March as a whole was quite profitable.)

The last minute rush into PEPs has not helped share prices. Since their 1987 introduction, the record is three up and four down, with each up-move relatively small and each down-move relatively large.

29 March

Analysis of day-to-day trends finds that prices used to rise in most years and we anticipate some improvement from recent weaker levels. However, the profit odds are low on 29 March. Our reason for drawing this conclusion? Since 1985, prices have risen just 25% of the time on 29–31 March *(see Figure 5.7)*.

Increase your profit odds

We forecast an improvement, now that Spring Budgets are gone, but not to the levels of the 1950s and 1960s which were aided by an approaching Budget. Here is a statistical correlation that may help investors to predict profitable fourth quarters.

Figure 5.7:   **PERCENTAGE OF TIME PRICES RISE EACH TRADING DAY IN MARCH'S FOURTH QUARTER**

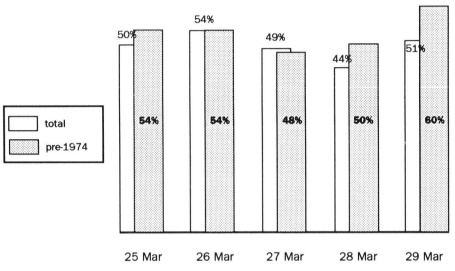

Figure 5.7: Prior to 1974, fourth-quarter prices frequently rose, especially on 29 March. The trend was helped by the approach of Budget Day. But the profit trend then weakened as Budget Days were shifted to mid-March. In the last 10 years, 29–31 March rose just 25% of the time.

Third-quarter signal	Between 1936 and 1971, third-quarter prices shifted by a small amount 10 times, no more than -0.78% on the down-side and +0.56% on the up-side. Fourth-quarter prices rose all 10 times. Since the mid-1970s shift to a mid-March Budget, this price signal stopped working. We shall wait to see if it comes alive again now that March Budgets are a thing of the past.

Rose (10)

Fell (0)

Fourth-quarter record after a price shift of -0.78% to +0.56% in the third quarter (1936–71)

LOOKING AHEAD

Rising prices by 31 December No 1

The price trend over the first three months offers investors two interesting clues about where shares are heading in the next nine months, that is, up to 31 December.

Since 1941, there have been 24 years with a small price shift in the first three months of the year, no more than -1.96% on the down-side and no more than +5.77% on the up-side. Prices rose still further by the end of the year in 23 of those years. The average increase was over 14%. The sole exception was in 1966 when a small first quarter increase was followed by rising prices until July when an announcement of higher taxes caught the markets by surprise. Prices fell over 20% in the next two months, and then plateaued for the rest of the year.

Rose (23)

Fell (1)

Trend to 31 December after a price shift of -1.96% to +5.77% in the first three months of the year (since 1941)

Rising prices by 31 December No 2

Since 1932, there have been 19 years with a March price rise of +1.77% to +9.66%. Prices rose still higher in the nine months that followed, until year-end, 18 times. The average increase was almost 13%. The sole exception occurred in 1961.

Rose (18)

Fell (1)

Trend to 31 December after a March price rise of +1.77% to +9.66% (since 1932)

Poor odds

Since 1941, there were 35 years touched by one or both of these signals. Prices rose still higher in the next nine months in 33 of those years. In the remaining 29 years during this period of time, the record for the next nine months was four up and 16 down. It would take a brave soul to hold shares in 1996 if neither of the March signals flashes.

APRIL INVESTMENT MONITOR

	LAST MONTH FINAL PRICE	END OF 1ST QUARTER		END OF 2ND QUARTER		END OF 3RD QUARTER		END OF 4TH QUARTER	
		PRICE	PERCENT CHANGE	PRICE	PERCENT CHANGE	PRICE	PERCENT CHANGE	PRICE	PERCENT CHANGE
FT-ORDINARY (FT-30)									
FT-SE 100									
FT-SE 250									
FT-NON-FINANCIAL (FT-500)									
FT-SE-A ALL SHARES									
STANDARD & POORS COMPOSITE									
OTHER INDEX									
ENTER EACH SHARE, UNIT TRUST, ETC, BELOW									

CHAPTER SIX – APRIL 1996

Appearances can fool you

Historically, April has been extremely profitable. Prices fell just six times from 1940–1990. Three factors were associated with this profit trend: start-of-fiscal-year money flows, Budget Day and investor expectation of profit.

Sadly, things have changed.

Spring Budgets are now a thing of the past. In the perverse world of investing, the expectation of profit often causes a loss as investors change their behaviour to catch an expected profit. But the third factor, start-of-year money flows, is still helping to drive April prices up.

We forecast that April will continue to be profitable although not to the degree it had been in the past. The odds of an April up-move are even better than normal if prices rise in the first three months of the year. This trend was in effect from the 1920s when Budgets were a May event to the 1980s when they frequently landed in early March so we don't think the Budget shift will change things.

Regardless of how the total month moves, the first and third quarters have been frequent money-losers in recent years.

Watch April's closing price for insight into the direction that shares will shift in the next five months through 30 September. See page 134 for more information.

April is the year's second-best month over the long-run. A hypothetical £1,000 April investment in 1919 (moved into cash in the other 11 months) would have grown to £4,083 by 1994.

Last half-century superb

The last decade in which April investors lost money was in the 1930s. In the next 50 years, prices rose 44 times and fell just six times. During this period, April's worst performance was in the 1940s when it was fourth-best month and produced an average annual profit of +1.70%. In the four decades that followed, it was ranked either number one or two. Prices rose in eight or nine out of 10 years in the 1950s, '60s and '70s. In the 1980s prices rose in all 10 years, a rare event that has occurred just one other time (January 1940 – 49). Is it any surprise that many investors began to think April is the closest thing to a one-way bet that the stock market offers? *(see Table 6.1)*

Recently weak

Unfortunately, the price trend has weakened in the 1990s. The record so far: three up and two down. Some investors may think it is too early to forecast a trend change. We are more pessimistic. In our opinion, the glorious April trend is a thing of the past. From now on, prices will behave as they do in other, more normal months – some ups and some downs. We offer two reasons to support this conclusion: the shift to a late November unified Budget Day and investors' expectation of April profits.

Budgets

The April success story is, like March, heavily influenced by the Spring Budget. This influence is especially visible when each April price shift is correlated with its corresponding Spring Budget date.

In the 1920s and '30s, when 15 of 20 Budgets were presented on 16 April or later, April's prices rose just half the time. It was seventh-ranked in the '20s and ninth-ranked in the '30s. Prices fell each year, on average, in both decades. In the 1940s to '80s, when most Budgets were presented in March to mid-April, the April price trend considerably improved. Furthermore, as Figure 6.1 shows, the earlier that

Table 6.1

APRIL PRICE RISES AND DECLINES: 1919–1994

	Average April price change	Up	Down/ no change
1920–29	-0.50%	4	6
1930–39	-0.93%	5	5
1940–49	1.70%	8	2
1950–59	4.17%	9	1
1960–69	2.21%	8	2
1970–79	4.81%	9	1
1980–89	3.31%	10	–
1990–94	0.79%	3	2
Average April price change	1.98%	56	20

Source: BZW and Datastream

Table 6.1: Prior to the 1940s, April was just an average performer. The climate then noticeably improved. In the last five decades, April investments were highly profitable. Prices rose in at least eight out of every 10 years. The Spring Budget probably provided some of the stimulus. Unfortunately, so far the 1990s price trend is noticeably weaker and, to make matters worse, the Spring Budget has been shifted to November.

UPDATE

Budget Day arrived, the higher the profit.

Spring Budgets are now a thing of the past. Where does this leave April? No one knows for sure. But the historical evidence suggests that April's superb performance has been significantly helped by the Spring Budget and that its future performance will now change.

Expectation

A second factor to consider is the expectation of profit which is rampant in April. Investors have come to expect a profitable stretch during this segment of the year and make their investment decisions accordingly. This expectation of profit will cause the trend to change because stock markets simply cannot follow the same trend forever, even if an underlying stimulus continues to be in force. Human nature eventually causes change as investors become aware of a

Figure 6.1: **AVERAGE MONTHLY PERFORMANCE: 1960–1993**

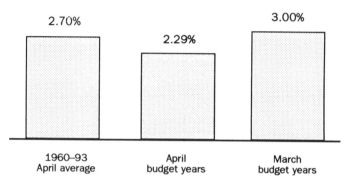

Figure 6.1: Profits were one-third higher in years following a March budget (1975 was excluded because the +16.23% increase was part of the enormous rally signalling the end of the 1973–74 Bear Market).

likely event, and try to take advantage of this knowledge. (If you thought you knew which way prices were likely to move tomorrow, wouldn't you act on that information?)

▶ Perhaps money is committed to the market earlier, thereby reducing the concentrated flow which drove up prices in the first place.

▶ Perhaps money leaves the market a bit earlier, knowing a weak stretch is likely to occur soon, thereby removing the concentrated selling pressure that formerly drove down prices or causing the decline to happen a little earlier.

No one knows how the April trend will run in the future. Our hypothesis is that it will not be as strongly positive as in the past. But it will still be profitable, a function of start-of-year money flows which will drive prices up in most years. Will our forecast prove to be accurate? Time will tell.

INCREASE YOUR PROFIT ODDS

In view of the uncertainty surrounding April, historic price trends that forecast which way April prices are most likely to move are especially valuable. Here are several trends which have done a good job in the past of anticipating April price shifts. Each has been in effect for many decades, and is based on price shifts over the past several months or the past year, not on what just happened in March (which could be budget-related).[1]

Past-12-months signal No 1

One useful trend is the direction of prices in the past 12 months, April 1st to March 31st. A sharp up-move often tips rising April prices. Since 1923, there have been 20 years when prices rose in the preceding 12 months by +19.26% or more. April share prices rose 19 times. The single exception was back in 1960.

Rose (19)

Fell (1)

April record after a price rise of at least +19.26% in past 12 months (since 1923)

Past-12-months signal No 2

Another trend associated with rising April prices is a decline in the last 12 months of -4.93% to -12.53%. Since 1948, in 14 years with a price decline within this range, April prices rose every time.

---

[1] Reminder: All monthly calculations are based on the FT-Non-financial Index, formerly the FT-'500'; unless otherwise stated, they are based on data from 1919–1994. All daily, quarterly, and bi-monthly calculations are based on the Ordinary Share Index, also known as the FT-30; unless otherwise stated, they are based on data from 1936–1994

Rose (14)

Fell (0)

April record after a price fall of -4.93% to -12.53% in past 12 months (since 1948)

Past-three-months signal

A third trend to watch is the direction of prices in the year's first quarter. Since 1922, prices rose in this three-month period by at least +4.38% on 29 separate occasions. April's prices rose in 27 of those years (93%).

Rose (27)

Fell (2)

April record after a price rise of at least +4.38% in past three months (since 1922)

The April trend has been so strong for so many years that it is hard to find enough 'down' months to develop 'down indicators'. But here is one trend that has been running since 1924 which is associated with a higher than usual chance of an April price decline.

Past-seven-months signal

There have been 10 years with a poor trend in the last seven months, a loss of up to -9.69%, and a shift in March of +1.28% to -5.64%. April share prices fell in eight of those years.

Rose (2)

Fell (8)

April record after a price drop of up to -9.69% in past seven months and a March price shift of +1.28% to -5.64% (since 1924)

120

FIRST QUARTER OF APRIL – APRIL 1ST TO 8TH

> This quarter used to be very profitable but has weakened in recent years. Last minute PEP money has not helped to improve the price trend.
>
> A small price shift (up as well as down) in the last quarter of March is often associated with an up-move in this segment of April.

Over the years, each quarter of April has been quite profitable *(see Table 6.2)*. The best performer of all was the first quarter. Prices rose 64% of the time during this quarter, generating an average annual profit of +0.80%, one of the best quarterly performances for the entire year. First-quarter share prices increased in value in every single decade on record, with the best trading days of the quarter occurring up to 5 April, the end of the tax year *(see Figure 6.2)*. Prices rise less often at the tail end of the quarter. Happily, the stock market is closed for the Easter break during this weaker period in 1996.

3 April

Prices are especially likely to rise on 2 and 3 April when they land on a Wednesday or Thursday. Since 1936, shares rose 26 out of the 33 times (79%) that 2–3 April landed in mid week. In 1996, 3 April lands on a Wednesday.

Recently weak

Unfortunately, the trend has changed recently. During the 1980s, in the midst of a fabulously profitable bull market, first-quarter prices rose just three times. The trend changed around the time that Spring Budgets were moved up to mid-March. Many of the losses were small so the decade still showed an average annual gain – of just +0.13%. The 1990s record? More of the same with two up and three down.

To put things into perspective, in the last 10 years, 1985–1994, first-quarter prices have risen just three times, one of the worst performances of the year *(see Table 6.3)*. It is quite rare for such a drastic trend change to occur,

Table 6.2   **PERCENTAGE PRICE CHANGE: APRIL 1936–1994**

	April 1–8	April 9–15	April 16–23	April 24–30
Average annual price change				
1936–39	1.59%	-0.34%	-0.26%	-1.01%
1940–49	0.54%	0.04%	0.38%	0.56%
1950–59	1.96%	1.20%	0.88%	-0.45%
1960–69	0.67%	0.28%	0.63%	0.79%
1970–79	1.08%	0.76%	1.96%	0.80%
1980–89	0.13%	0.62%	0.76%	2.18%
1990–94	-0.54%	2.75%	-0.77%	-0.42%
Average quarterly price change	0.80%	0.70%	0.70%	0.55%
Number of years in which prices:				
rose	38	37	35	39
fell	20	20	23	20
remained unchanged	1	2	1	–

Source: Datastream

Table 6.2: Each of April's four quarters has been quite profitable over the long-run. But the first-quarter and third-quarter trends have noticeably weakened since 1980, around the time Budget Day was moved to March. (The third quarter figure is distorted by a large increase in 1981.) The second quarter continues to be strong, perhaps due to its role as the opening quarter of the new tax year.

UPDATE

causing the same segment of the month to be on a 'Best' list and 'Worst' list at the same time.

No help from PEPs

The 1987 introduction of PEPs has not helped this final quarter of the year. The common assumption is that lots of PEP money pours into shares at the very last minute to beat the end-of-year tax deadline, driving up share prices. The theory is not supported by the facts. First-quarter prices have fallen in four out of the last six years.

Figure 6.2   **PERCENTAGE OF TIME PRICES RISE EACH TRADING DAY IN APRIL'S FIRST QUARTER**

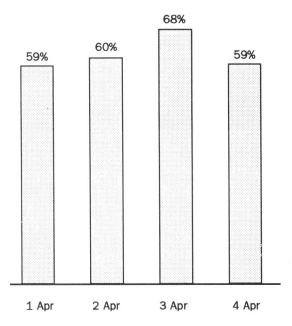

Figure 6.2: Over the long-term, the first few trading days of the quarter (end of the tax year) are the most profitable. If you do purchase any shares, the odds favour completing your transaction at the very beginning of the quarter.

Will the move from a mid-March budget allow prices to regain their former profitability? Or has the shift to November added additional down-side pressure to the price trend? Only time will tell.

For the present, investors should be very cautious during this part of the month. Assuming prices continue their pattern of recent weakness, why jump in at the beginning of the month if you can buy at a better price by waiting a few days? And sadly, the budget-date switch undermines many of the historical trends that once helped to forecast the direction of first-quarter share price shifts. We think the best strategy is to stand aside.

123

Table 6.3: **YEAR'S BEST AND WORST QUARTER IN LAST 10 YEARS: 1985–1994**

	Number of increases		Number of increases
	Best		*Worst*
January 4th quarter	9	June 4th quarter	2
January 3rd quarter	8	March 3rd quarter	3
April 2nd quarter	8	March 4th quarter	3
August 3rd quarter	8	April 1st quarter	3
August 4th quarter	8	April 3rd quarter	3
December 3rd quarter	8	September 2nd quarter	3
Several	7	September 3rd quarter	3
		October 4th quarter	3

Source: Datastream

Table 6.3: It's hard to believe but it's true. One of the best months in history has two entries on a list of the year's worst quarters. The first and third quarters have become points in the year in which it is best to stand aside.

UPDATE

INCREASE YOUR PROFIT ODDS

For readers who disagree and think the patterns of the past will continue, or who think unique trading conditions will make this year an exception to the rule, here is a new trend that possibly could help.

March third/fourth-quarter signal

There have been 20 occasions when prices rose in the third quarter of March by any amount, and drifted in the fourth quarter, within a range of -1.00% to +2.42%. Prices rose in the first quarter of April in each of these years. The average increase was +1.44%.

NEW

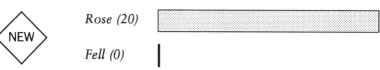

Rose (20)

Fell (0)

First-quarter record after a March third-quarter rise and fourth-quarter price shift between -1.00% to +2.42%

What makes us particularly keen on this indicator is that it was in effect back when the first quarter preceded Budget Day, and more recently when it followed Budget Day by several weeks.

March fourth-quarter signal

Here is a related indicator. Although it overlaps the March Third Quarter/Fourth Quarter indicator in some years, it often flashes independently. Since 1936, there were 28 years when prices shifted by a small margin of -1.35% to +0.72% in March's fourth quarter. April first-quarter prices rose in 24 of those years (86%). Each exception occurred after the introduction of mid-March Budgets which is no longer an issue as far as April investors are concerned *(see Table 6.4)*.

Assuming first-quarter price ebbs and flows return to the patterns of the past, now that March Budgets have been eliminated, this trend could be useful.

Table 6.4: **APRIL FIRST QUARTER / MARCH FOURTH QUARTER CORRELATION**

| | First quarter | | Typical date |
	Up	Down	of Budget
1936–39	3	–	late April
1940–49	7	–	various points in April
1950–59	5	–	mid April
1960–69	3	–	mid April
1970–79	4	–	late March & early April
1980–89	1	2	mid March
1990–93	1	2	mid March
Total	24	4	

Table 6.4: Direction of April first-quarter prices after March fourth-quarter price shift of -1.35% to +0.72%.

125

SECOND QUARTER OF APRIL – APRIL 9TH TO 15TH

The odds of a profit in the first quarter of the new fiscal year are very high.

Shares rose 63% of the time in the year's opening fiscal quarter between 1936 and 1994. Prices increased by +0.70% per year, on average. Unlike the first quarter, the recent trend remains strong. The average annual increase in the 1970s was +0.76% (six out of 10 years increased, one no change). The average annual increase for the 1980s was +0.62% (seven out of 10 years increased) *(see Table 6.5)*.

Year's best

The record since the 1987 crash is seven out of seven increases for the first full quarter of the new year, tied with one other quarter as the year's best during this recent stretch of time. We are intrigued by this strong performance given the weakness of the adjacent first and third quarters during the same period of time. Each is, recently, among the year's very worst performers. A possible explanation: the start of a new tax year releases a short-lived flood of new money, providing a brief boost to prices.

Analysis of trading conditions on a day-by-day basis finds that prices are strong throughout the quarter except for 12 April which rises just 42% of the time. But this weakness is largely due to its performance in the 1930s to '60s. In the last 20 years, 12 April has performed as strongly as the other days of the period – profitable in most years *(see Figure 6.3)*.

11 April

Here is some more good news. The odds of a profit on 11April are better than average in 1996. Since our records began, 10 and 11 April have landed on a Thursday 16 times. Prices rose on 12 of those occasions (75%). 11 April lands on a Thursday in 1996.

126

Table 6.5

PERCENTAGE PRICE CHANGE: 1985—1994

	April 1–8	April 9–15	April 16–23	April 24–30
Annual quarterly price change				
1985	-0.19%	1.51%	-1.78%	1.23%
1986	-0.14%	-1.25%	-0.64%	2.42%
1987	-1.17%	-2.79%	2.65%	3.65%
1988	1.93%	0.16%	-0.29%	2.29%
1989	-1.46%	0.48%	0.56%	2.93%
1990	-1.61%	0.05%	-2.77%	-2.31%
1991	2.31%	0.23%	-1.89%	-0.62%
1992	-2.56%	10.69%	-0.50%	1.50%
1993	-2.01%	1.15%	1.57%	-0.85%
1994	1.15%	1.61%	-0.25%	0.20%
Average quarterly price change				
1985–94	-0.38%	1.18%	-0.33%	1.04%
Number of years in which prices:				
rose	3	8	3	7
fell	7	2	7	3

UPDATE

Source: Datastream

Table 6.5: First- and third-quarter prices have fallen in most recent years. The second quarter (the fiscal year's opening quarter) and the fourth quarter continue to be profitable. Prices have been especially strong in the second quarter since the 1987 crash, with a record of seven up and none down.

INCREASE YOUR PROFIT ODDS

On balance, if you are thinking of selling shares during this quarter, the odds favour holding on until its end. However, a newly-developing price trend may be of interest to readers who wish to make a second-quarter transaction.

Figure 6.3: **PERCENTAGE OF TIME PRICES RISE EACH TRADING DAY IN APRIL'S SECOND QUARTER**

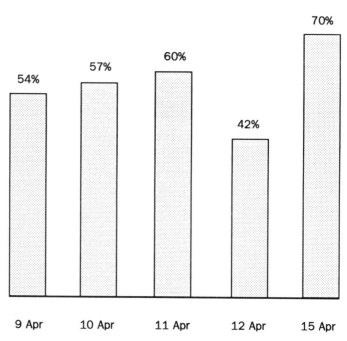

Figure 6.3: Most second-quarter trading days tend to be profitable. The record of the single loser, 12 April, has improved in the past 20 years. Its recent record is comparable to the other days in this quarter.

First-quarter signal

In last year's edition of the *Schwartz Stock Market Handbook*, we pointed out that since 1980, every second-quarter loss has been tipped by a small price drop of -0.14% to -1.44% in the first quarter. All other second quarters have been profitable. 1994 followed the norm. A first-quarter price increase was followed by another increase in the second quarter.

Correlation between price shifts in April's first and second quarters: 1980–1994

	Second quarter	
First-quarter shift	Up	Down
-0.13% or better	6	–
-0.14% to -1.44%	2	3
-1.45% or worse	4	–

The data suggest that mild weakness in the last quarter of the year is a stimulus for more of the same as the new year begins. But if bigger losses are incurred in the year's final quarter, perhaps triggered by tax-related considerations, the decks are cleared for a good start to the new year. On the up-side, investors who sense good trading conditions around the start of the new year tip their hand by bidding up shares in the last week of the old year.

This trend is based on a period of just 15 years. Treat it as a hypothesis, not a confirmed relationship. Likewise, our description of the underlying cause are guesses, not informed statements of fact.

Despite the favourable trading conditions, it is not a particularly good point at which to commit new funds because of the high probability of a third-quarter price drop.

Third Quarter of April – April 16th to 23rd

The third quarter profit trend used to be very good. Sadly, the trend has weakened in recent years. But prices often rise if the stock market is weak in the run-up to the third quarter.

Like April's first quarter, the third quarter was traditionally quite good to investors, producing an average yearly profit in every decade on record. Between 1936 and 1994, third-quarter prices rose 59% of the time. The average annual profit was +0.70%.

Recently weak

Also like the first quarter, things may be changing for the worse. The 1980s price trend was a warning signal. The beginning of the decade produced all of this quarter's profits (1981, +6.41%; 1982, +4.09%). Even though a strong bull market dominated the decade, and the full month consistently generated high profits, prices rose in only two of the decade's remaining eight years. Note that the March Budget was presented at least four weeks earlier during this period, reducing the odds that short-term budget effects were exerting pressure on third-quarter prices.

In the last 10 years, third-quarter prices have risen just three times, one of the worst performances of the entire year. Unfortunately, with a good probability of a fourth-quarter profit, investors have no incentive to sell shares at the beginning of this quarter. By the same token, there is no incentive to commit additional money either.

19 April

Analysis of daily price records finds that trading conditions are best at the beginning of the quarter with the likelihood of a price rise peaking on 19 April when prices rise 65% of the time *(see Figure 6.4)*.

Figure 6.4   **PERCENTAGE OF TIME PRICES RISE EACH TRADING DAY IN APRIL'S THIRD QUARTER**

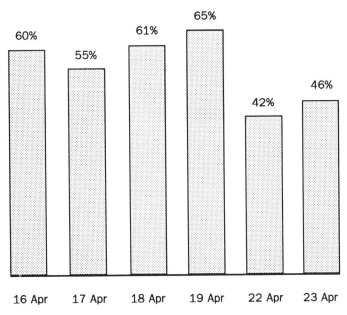

Figure 6.4: Trading conditions are quite good at the beginning of the quarter, but weakened in the last two days.

There are two mini trends affecting April 17 and 22 that are operating in 1996:

17 April   ▶ Prices rise on most mid-month Wednesdays. Since our records began, prices have risen 20 out of 25 times (80%) when 15–17 April has landed on a Wednesday. When these three days land on other weekdays, prices rise 56% of the time. In 1996, 17 April lands on a Wednesday.

22 April   ▶ Prices often fall when 21 or 22 April lands on a Monday. The record since 1936 is two up and 12 down. 22 April lands on a Monday in 1996.

INCREASE YOUR PROFIT ODDS

We are distrustful of many historical trends because of the possible influence of the spring Budget. But two relationships may still be worth watching.

Second-quarter signal

One involves the second-quarter price trend. If prices decline, they often rise in the third quarter. Since 1942, there have been 15 occasions when share prices declined in the second quarter. The third quarter bounced back with an increase in 13 of them (87%). During this period, Budget Day advanced from late April, through early April to mid-March, suggesting the trend is not (just) Budget Day-related. The signal last flashed in 1987 when Budget Day was on 17 March. April's second-quarter fall of -2.79% was followed with a +2.65% increase in the third quarter.

Rose (13)

Fell (2)

Third-quarter record after a second-quarter price decline (since 1942)

First-half signal

Another signal, very new, seems to be rearing its head. Since 1976, a rise of at least +1.32% in April's first half has been associated with a decline in the third quarter in 10 out of 11 occurrences. As with other trends that appear during this part of the year, we are unsure of the effect of Budget Day and shall watch the situation carefully. Initial signs are good. The signal last flashed in 1994 when a first-half price rise of +2.78% was followed by a small third-quarter decline.

Rose (1)

UPDATE

Fell (10)

Third-quarter record after a first half price rise of at least +1.32% (since 1976)

FOURTH QUARTER OF APRIL – APRIL 24TH TO 30TH

> The long-term trend is positive and, unlike the third quarter, there are no signs of recent weakness during this segment of the month. The profit odds are even better following a small price rise during the third quarter.

Prices rise 66% of the time during the fourth quarter of April, the third-best quarter of the year. Between 1936 and 1994, the average annual increase in share prices was +0.55%.

Recent trend looking good

The only full decade in which the fourth segment of the month failed to produce a profit was in the 1950s when it dropped at a rate of -0.45% per year.

Unlike the first and third quarters of the month, no sign of weakness has been detected in the fourth quarter during the 1980s. Prices rose in all 10 years at a superb average annual rate of +2.18%, the best level of profit for any quarter in April since records began.

Surprisingly for such a profitable segment, the odds of profiting on any single day are about 50:50 over the long run. But during the last 20 years, the trends for 26, 29 and 30 April have improved. Each has been profitable in two out of three years *(see Figure 6.5)*.

INCREASE YOUR PROFIT ODDS

Third-quarter signal

Here's a statistical relationship to help investors pin-point profitable fourth quarters. If prices rise in the third quarter, the odds are high that fourth-quarter prices will also rise. The trend has been quite hot since 1959. The shift to a mid-March Budget has had no affect on this price signal.

Here is the evidence: since 1959, there were 18 years when the third quarter rose up to +6.41%. The fourth quarter rose in 16 of them (89%), with an average gain of +1.78%.

Figure 6.5:   **PERCENTAGE OF TIME PRICES RISE EACH TRADING DAY IN APRIL'S FOURTH QUARTER**

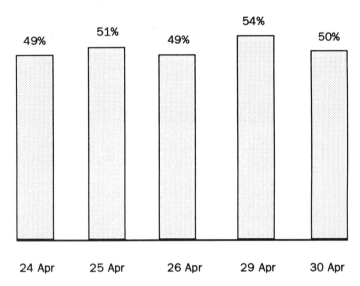

24 Apr	25 Apr	26 Apr	29 Apr	30 Apr

Figure 6.5: Over the long-run, the odds of a profit on any single day is just 50:50. But in the last few decades, prices rose on the last three days two-thirds of the time.

Rose (16)

Fell (2)

Fourth-quarter record after a third quarter price rise of up to +6.41% (since 1959)

LOOKING AHEAD

The next few months have a horrid reputation. One of the first things a novice investor learns is 'Sell in May and go away'. We don't subscribe to this simplistic rule of thumb as a steady investment approach, as subsequent chapters will demonstrate. But there are times when shares do fall in value between May and September. Fortunately, the price trend for the year to date often tips how prices will shift during the next five months, to 30 September.

Falling prices by 30 September

Since 1936, there have been 13 years when prices fell in the first four months of the year within a range of -3.68% to -12.99%. Shares fell still further by 30 September in 12 of those years. The sole exception occurred in 1970 when they rose by just over 5% in the five months to 30 September.

Rose (1)

Fell (12)

Trend to September 30 after a January to April price drop of -3.68% to -12.99% (since 1936)

Rising prices by 31 October

During this same period, there were 12 other years with a price rise in the first four months of the years within a range of +3.66% to +8.08%. Prices rose still higher in the next six months to 31 October in each of those 12 years.

Rose (12)

Fell (0)

Trend to October 31 after a January to April price rise of +3.66% to +8.08% (since 1936)

When using either of these forecasting tools, keep in mind that the lowest point may have been reached before 30 September and the highest point before 31 October.

MAY INVESTMENT MONITOR

	LAST MONTH FINAL PRICE	END OF 1ST QUARTER		END OF 2ND QUARTER		END OF 3RD QUARTER		END OF 4TH QUARTER	
		PRICE	PERCENT CHANGE	PRICE	PERCENT CHANGE	PRICE	PERCENT CHANGE	PRICE	PERCENT CHANGE
FT-ORDINARY (FT-30)									
FT-SE 100									
FT-SE 250									
FT-NON-FINANCIAL (FT-500)									
FT-SE-A ALL SHARES									
STANDARD & POORS COMPOSITE									
OTHER INDEX									
ENTER EACH SHARE, UNIT TRUST, ETC, BELOW									

CHAPTER SEVEN – MAY 1996

Don't be too quick to believe the old adage to 'Sell in May and go away. Don't come back 'til St. Leger's Day'. May can be quite profitable if you pick your year carefully.

Although May is only the eleventh-best investment month and shares fall -0.52% on average, prices rise in half of all Mays. It is far from the year's best month, but by the same token, not the horror that many investors believe it to be. The real problem in May are Big Hits – declines of at least 5% which occur every five or six years. They tend to occur more often in May (and June) than in other months.

Fortunately, the stock market often provides clues which tip off when a Big Hit is likely. The clues don't work flawlessly, but they reduce the odds of being caught by surprise. One of the most useful indicators is the size of the price shift over the past 12 months. A Big Hit has never occurred if prices have risen moderately in the past 12 months (see page 141).

Another fact not widely known is that the first quarter of the month is profitable in most years. When losses do occur, they most often occur in the second to fourth quarters.

Looking ahead, the price trend over the past six months often gives good insight into prospects for the remainder of the year (see page 158).

According to conventional wisdom, May is a poor month in which to hold shares – and has been for three-quarters of this century.

At first glance, the argument against a May investment in shares is quite persuasive. May investors have lost money in every single decade on record except for the 1950s. From 1919 to 1994, prices fell at a yearly average of -0.52%, equal to 17 points on a 3300 FT-SE 100 *(see Table 7.1)*. Only June produces poorer results. A May investor who started with £1,000 in 1919, shifting into cash for the other 11 months of the year, would now be worth just £613. Is it any wonder that conventional wisdom advises investors to 'Sell in May and go away. Don't come back 'til St Leger's Day'?

Conventional
wisdom is
wrong

In last year's edition of the *Schwartz Stock Market Handbook*, we told readers not to listen. Our exact words were 'Conventional wisdom is wrong'. The book was still on the printing press when in May 1994 prices fell by -5.15%, a victim of fears of still another US interest rate increase. We hate to tempt fate again, but we stand by our analysis. May is safer than many investors suspect. Before you back away from shares too far, consider these seven facts:

First quarter is
profitable

Most May losses occur in the second to the fourth segments of the month. The first quarter tends to be profitable. Prices rise 59% of the time. The average annual profit is +0.38%. That's equal to 13 points on a 3300 FT-SE 100 *(see Figure 7.1)*. It's a perfectly safe time in which to own shares. Yes, you will lose money in some years but over the long run, the profits will outweigh the losses by a wide margin. So even if the May-bashers are right, in most years it does not pay to move out of shares on 1 May.

Global forces

We live in a global economy. Narrow national interests are increasingly undermined by international forces. This is especially true in the stock market. Organisations like the European Community and the World Trade Organisation

Table 7.1　　　**MAY PRICE RISES AND DECLINES: 1919–1994**

	Average May price change	Up	Down/ no change
1920–29	-0.73%	5	5
1930–39	-1.45%	3	7
1940–49	-0.63%	7	3
1950–59	0.52%	6	4
1960–69	-1.35%	3	7
1970–79	-1.37%	5	5
1980–89	-0.88%	4	5
1990–94	1.71%	4	1

UPDATE

Source: BZW and Datastream

Average May price change	-0.52%	38	38

Table 7.1: The price of the average share has fallen in every decade but one since the 1920s. Bit Hits of -5% or worse are the source of May's problems. Prices usually fall by a large amount once or twice a decade. The rest of the decade tends to be profitable. If you can avoid the Big Hits, a May investment can be quite profitable over the long-run.

---

have a large and rapidly growing effect on the profits of our local businesses. The competence or lack of demonstrated by foreign governments in America, Japan, Germany, etc, plays a huge role in our local economy and our stock market. Witness the wild gyration in share prices here when some distant international event takes place.

Foreign investors　　Foreign funds account for a constantly growing share of UK investment capital. Decisions by these foreign investors to buy or sell are often stimulated by conditions at the source of their funds – their local market, not ours.

'Smart money'　　Multi-billion pound hedge funds, specifically set up to exploit short-term speculative opportunities, jump in and out of the world's stock markets at the flick of a computer button. Assuming May prices did drop with sufficient pre-

Figure 7.1:   **PROFITABILITY OF MAY'S FOUR QUARTERS**

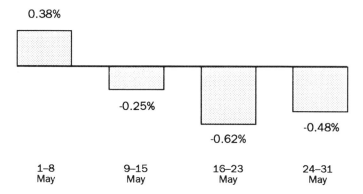

Figure 7.1: The first quarter is profitable in most years. The trend soon deteriorates. The third-quarter price trend is a horror. Prices drop 61% of the time, the year's worst quarterly performance. The size of the average annual price drop is -0.62%, equal to 20 points on a 3300 FT-SE 100.

dictability to interest these investors, the weight of money would quickly change the underlying trend. For example: if 'smart money' knew May prices would drop, they would sell short or purchase Puts at the end of April to catch the May drop. Prices would then fall in late April because of this selling pressure (whereas, at present, late April prices usually don't fall) and rise in May in the absence of heavy selling, or as speculators rush to cover their short positions.

Budget Day

History tells us that Budget Days are usually good for investors. Let us assume, for the sake of discussion, that some past spring Budget rallies were followed by a partial retraction against the up-turn in May. If so, the switch to a November date eliminates this source of May weakness.

Big Hits are the problem

Despite the scare headlines, May share prices rise 50% of the time. The real problem in May: share prices take a very bad 'hit' every few years, large enough to affect the average performance for the whole decade. There have been 15 years with price declines of 5% or more.[1] They seem to occur once every five or six years. On this dimension, May has the dubious distinction of being ranked Number One.

Recent record looks good

If you are still not convinced that 'Sell in May' is bad advice, consider this: from 1989 to 1993 prices rose in five consecutive years. This was the first time since records began in 1919 that May prices rose five times in a row. It doesn't mean that prices will always rise in May. But it certainly contradicts the theory that May is a loser to be avoided consistently. Furthermore, the Big Hit of 1994 was externally caused. The FT-SE 100 was a few points up on the month as late as May 20 when US interest rate rise fears hit the market. Prices fell 161 points in five trading days.

The key issue to address in this difficult investment month is how to avoid occasional profit-wrecking Big Hits. If there were a way of avoiding Big Hit years, May investors would profit handsomely. They would still encounter some losing years but the winners would more than compensate for those 'normal' sized losers. Is there such a way? In a word, yes.

INCREASE YOUR PROFIT ODDS

How to avoid Big Hits

The best way to avoid Big Hit years is to monitor the size of the April price change. If April prices shift by a small amount, declining by less than -1.66% or rising by no more than +2.81%, there is a low likelihood of a Big Hit in May. There have been 34 years in which April prices either rose or fell within this range. There was one Big Hit in all those years, the drop of 1994 (see Figure 7.2).

UPDATE

---

[1] Reminder: All monthly calculations are based on the FT-Non-financial Index, formerly the FT-'500'; unless otherwise stated, they are based on data from 1919–1994. All daily, quarterly, and bi-monthly calculations are based on the Ordinary Share Index, also known as the FT-30; unless otherwise stated, they are based on data from 1936–1994.

Figure 7.2: **PERCENTAGE OF TIME PRICES FALL BY 5% OR MORE IN MAY**

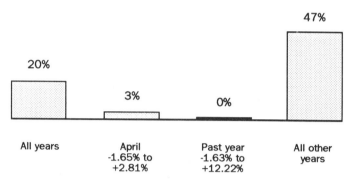

Figure 7.2: Big Hits occur every five or six years on average. They usually don't occur in years with small price fluctuations in the previous month, or in the past 12 months. But in an 'all other' year – look out. There were 14 Big Hits in 30 'all other' years.

Another way to avoid Big Hits is to watch the price trend in the preceding 12 months. May prices never declined by 5% or more if prices in the past 12 months moved within a range of -1.63% to +12.22%. There have been 20 years in which prices either rose or fell within this range. There were no 5% plus May price declines in any of these years. Obviously, important fresh economic or political news could throw May prices into a tail-spin, regardless of what either historical trend suggests, but the odds of this happening are low unless the news catches the markets by surprise.

UPDATE

Eliminating duplication between these two trends, there were 46 years when prices in the past month or past 12 months moved within the designated ranges. One Big Hit occurred in all of these years. In the remaining 30 years on record, a Big Hit occurred 14 times – almost a 50% 'success' rate. And two of the misses were very near misses.

Aside from avoiding Big Hit years, you can also increase

profits by identifying specific years when May prices are especially likely to rise. Short sellers or Put buyers can also profit by identifying years with a high likelihood of May price drops. Here are two trends which, historically, have done a good job of anticipating the direction of May price shifts.

March/April signal

There have been 15 years in which share prices satisfied two conditions: (a) they rose in March and April by at least +1.33% in total, and (b) they rose in April within a range of +0.70% to +2.81%. May prices rose each time.

Rose (15)

Fell (0)

May record after a March/April price rise of at least +1.33% and an April rise of +0.70% to +2.81%

April signal

On the other hand if prices rise too high in April, May prices often suffer. There have been nine years when April's prices increased between +5.59% to +8.31%. The May record in those years is zero up and nine down.

Rose (0)

Fell (9)

May record after an April price rise of +5.59% to +8.31%

Four-month signal

Another way to flag a month with a high probability of declining is to look for sharply falling prices in the first four months of the year. There have been 10 years on record with a decline of -5.28% to -12.66% in January to April. May shares fell nine times. Six were Big Hits. The single exception was in 1973 when shares rose by one-tenth of a percent.

143

NEW	Rose (1)
	Fell (9)

May record after a January to April price drop of -5.28% to -12.66%

FIRST QUARTER OF MAY – MAY 1ST TO 8TH

Here comes the most profitable quarter of the month. Prices rise 59% of the time. The odds of a profit in the first quarter are especially high if shares shift by a small amount during the month of April.

Money-maker

Although May can be a poor investment month, the first quarter is a consistent money-maker. A first-quarter investment in each year since 1936 produced an average annual profit of +0.38%. Presumably the final phase of April's rally spills over to this segment of May.

In contrast, the rest of the month typically produces an average loss: second quarter, -0.25%; third quarter, -0.62%; fourth quarter, -0.48% *(see Table 7.2)*.

1–3 May

Prices are usually strong at the very beginning of the month. They rise on 1–3 May, in more than six out of 10 years and are the best three back-to-back trading days of the entire month. Since 1984, prices on 1 and 2 May have risen 11 out of 13 times. If you are planning to sell shares at this point of the year, waiting a few days will be a profit-maker more often than a profit-loser *(see Figure 7.3)*.

144

Table 7.2

PERCENTAGE PRICE CHANGE: MAY 1936–1994

	May 1–8	May 9–15	May 16–23	May 24–31
Average annual price change				
1936–39	1.51%	-1.08%	-1.11%	-0.24%
1940–49	0.46%	0.00%	-0.84%	-0.64%
1950–59	0.75%	-0.23%	0.14%	0.61%
1960–69	-0.35%	-0.04%	-1.35%	-0.59%
1970–79	0.64%	-0.35%	-0.46%	-1.84%
1980–89	-0.39%	-0.28%	-1.26%	-0.06%
1990–94	1.10%	-0.35%	0.08%	-0.41%
Average quarterly price change	0.38%	-0.25%	-0.62%	-0.48%
Number of years in which prices:				
rose	35	32	23	28
fell	24	27	36	31

Source: Datastream

Table 7.2: The first-quarter investor often profits. But the second-quarter investor loses money in the long-run despite the fact that prices rise in most second quarters. The declines in down years are bigger than the profits in up years. The third quarter is a long-term money-loser, the worst or next-to-worst quarter of the month in every decade through the 1980s. The fourth quarter also tends to be a loser although the direction of prices in the run-up to it often provides good clues to its profitability.

UPDATE

INCREASE YOUR PROFIT ODDS

April second-half signal No 1

The odds of a first-quarter profit can be improved by watching for a price rise in the third quarter of April (by any amount) and the fourth quarter by up to +1.53%. There have been 16 occasions when the April price trend followed this pattern. Prices rose in May's first quarter 14 times (88%). The average increase was +0.86%. This signal last failed to deliver in 1952.

Figure 7.3: **PERCENTAGE OF TIME PRICES RISE EACH TRADING DAY IN MAY'S FIRST QUARTER**

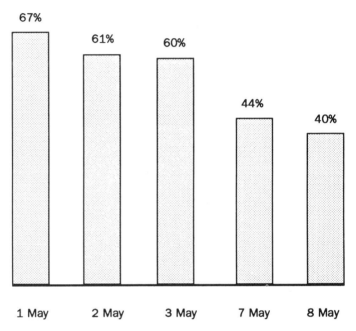

Figure 7.3: 1–3 May are the best three back-to-back trading days of the month. In most years, it would pay not to sell any shares until the end of this period.

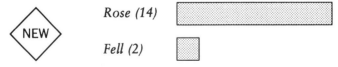

Rose (14)

Fell (2)

First-quarter record after an April third quarter price rise (any amount) and a fourth-quarter rise of up to +1.53%

April signal   Another signal that tips better than average odds of an up-move in the first quarter is a small price shift during April. If prices move within a range of -1.29% to +2.81%, the odds of a first-quarter profit are high. Since 1936, there were 23 April shifts within this range. First-quarter prices rose 19 times (83%), at an average annual rate of +0.95%. This signal has failed once each decade in the 1960s, '70s and '80s. It last failed in 1994.

Rose (19)

Fell (4)

UPDATE

First-quarter record after an April price shift of -1.29% to +2.81%

April second-half signal No 2

Although prices often rise during the first quarter, they do decline on occasion. A decline of any size in April's third quarter, or a tiny rise (no more than +0.20%), followed by an increase in the fourth quarter, or a tiny fall (no more than -0.04%), often tips off that prices will drop in May's first quarter. Since 1947, there were 13 years when prices declined in the third quarter of April (or rose very slightly) and rose in the fourth quarter (or declined very slightly). May first-quarter prices fell in 11 of them (85%). This signal last flashed in 1994 and first quarter prices fell by almost 1%.

Rose (2)

Fell (11)

UPDATE

First-quarter record after a third-quarter shift of +0.20% or lower and fourth-quarter shift of -0.04% or higher (since 1947)

Second Quarter of May – May 8th to 15th

The second quarter is a loser over the long-run despite the fact that prices rise in most years. Big Hit years are the problem.

The direction of price shifts in the first quarter often sends a useful tip about where second-quarter prices are heading.

Recent record unchanged

The second quarter of May has cost investors money in every decade on record except for the 1940s when prices broke exactly even. The trend did not even improve during the 1980s' bull market decade when prices rose just five times and generated an average annual loss of -0.28%. Prices continue to disappoint right up to the present. The record since the 1987 crash is three up and four down with a small average loss of -0.16% *(see Table 7.3)*.

Daily share price trends tend to be disappointing at the beginning of the quarter. But the trend steadily improves from its low point on 9 May to its high point on 15 May which rises in most years *(see Figure 7.4)*.

Increase your profit odds

April/May first-quarter signal No 1

The best way to profit in this quarter of May is to bet against the market. Increase the odds of being right by watching the direction of first-quarter prices. There have been 14 occasions since 1936 when April's prices rose in a range of +2.83% to +8.31%, and were followed by a fall in May's first quarter. Second-quarter prices continued to decline in 11 of those years (79%). The average second-quarter decline during those 14 years was -1.31%, equal to 43 points on an FT-SE 100 in the area of 3300.

Table 7.3   **PERCENTAGE PRICE CHANGE: 1985–1994**

	May 1–8	May 9–15	May 16–23	May 24–31
Annual quarterly price change				
1985	1.76%	3.42%	-1.18%	-0.76%
1986	-4.16%	-2.57%	2.21%	-0.77%
1987	2.90%	1.98%	-0.29%	1.51%
1988	-0.26%	-0.80%	-1.47%	1.41%
1989	0.70%	1.39%	0.01%	-1.77%
1990	3.42%	1.26%	4.53%	2.49%
1991	1.56%	-2.92%	1.00%	0.61%
1992	2.96%	-1.00%	1.72%	-1.66%
1993	-1.44%	1.32%	-1.40%	0.80%
1994	-0.99%	-0.40%	-0.46%	-4.29%
Average quarterly price change				
1985–1994	0.64%	0.17%	0.47%	-0.24%
Number of years in which prices:				
rose	6	5	5	5
fell	4	5	5	5

Source: Datastream

Table 7.3: Recent trends continue to demonstrate that you can profit in May by avoiding Big Hit years.

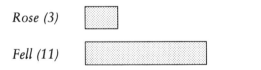

Rose (3)

Fell (11)

Second-quarter record after an April price rise of +2.83% to +8.31% and a fall in May's first quarter

April/May first-quarter signal No 2

Just as a rising April trend, followed by a price decline in May's first-quarter, signals that second-quarter prices are likely to fall, rising April prices followed by a price rise in the

Figure 7.4: **PERCENTAGE OF TIME PRICES RISE EACH TRADING DAY IN MAY'S SECOND QUARTER**

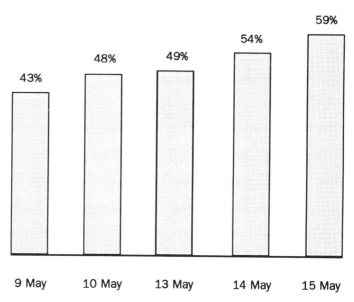

Figure 7.4: The chance of a price rise gradually increases as the quarter unfolds. Nevertheless, the odds favour standing aside during this segment of the month unless a unique situation arises. The quarter that follows is a long-term loser.

first quarter of May is a signal that second-quarter prices will rise. There have been 21 years when April prices rose by no more than +5.48% and first-quarter prices rose by +0.62% to +4.00%. Second-quarter prices continued to rise in 18 of those years (86%). The average increase was +0.93%.

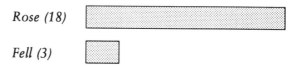

Rose (18)

Fell (3)

Second-quarter record after an April price rise of up to +5.48% and a rise in May's first quarter of +0.62% to +4.00%

Here are two new second-quarter trends, still in the process of development, that look promising.

Last-three-quarters signal

Since 1970, when Spring Budgets were advanced to mid-March, and were 'out of the way' as far as their effect on late-April and May price fluctuations, an up-trend that ran for three consecutive quarters was often followed with a further price increase in May's second quarter. It is early days for this indicator but here is the evidence to date.

There have been seven years since 1970 with shares rising in the third and fourth quarters of April and the first quarter of May. Shares rose in the second quarter in six of those years. The single exception was a tiny -0.17% decline in 1974, a horrid bear market year.

Rose (6)

Fell (1)

Second-quarter record after a price rise in April's third and fourth quarters, and May's first quarter (since 1970)

April third-quarter/May first-quarter signal

Another developing trend is the tendency for second-quarter prices to fall if they have fallen in the third quarter of April and the first quarter of May. Twin falls have occurred nine times since 1970 and second-quarter prices fell seven times. The two exceptions were small increases of +0.09% in 1973 and +0.25% in 1980. Why does this relationship ignore April's fourth quarter? We don't know.

Here too, we shall watch carefully to see if this relationship develops into a fully-fledged trend.

Rose (2)

Fell (7)

Second-quarter record after a price rise in April's third quarter and May's first quarter (since 1970)

THIRD QUARTER OF MAY – MAY 16TH TO 23RD

Here comes the worst quarter of the entire year. You might profit this year but over the long-run, a steady third-quarter investment is a money-losing proposition.

Big swings in April are often associated with price declines in the third quarter, regardless of which way prices shifted in the first half of May.

And if prices decline in the first two quarters of May, history suggests the decline will continue into this quarter.

Money-losing time

Investors lost money by investing during the third quarter during the 1930s, '40s, '60s, '70s, and '80s. The only time a profit was made, and a small one at that, was back in the 1950s.

Between 1936 and 1994, the third quarter of May rose just 39% of the time, the worst performance of any quarter of the year, and generated an average loss of -0.62%, second-worst of the year. Even during the 1980s, prices fell seven times. The only way to profit consistently in this quarter is to bet on falling prices.

Recent trend unchanged

From 1989 to 1992, prices increased in four consecutive years, for the first time ever. The previous best was three ups in a row back in 1958–1960. We wondered if this was a preliminary sign that the trend was improving. No such luck. The up-trend record was broken in 1993 with a -1.40% decline in share prices, and again in 1994 with a -0.46% drop. On balance, the evidence is clear. If you want to invest during this segment of the year, use extreme caution. Although you might make a profit by holding shares in any single year, the odds strongly favour standing on the sidelines or betting against the market.

16 May

There are no pockets of strength during the quarter. Analysis of daily price trends finds that each day rises less than half the time *(see Figure 7.5)*. But one trend may help

Figure 7.5 **PERCENTAGE OF TIME PRICES RISE EACH TRADING DAY IN MAY'S THIRD QUARTER**

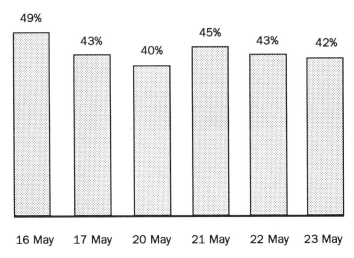

Figure 7.5: Another poor segment of the month. It most years, it makes sense to stand aside.

investors in 1996, the tendency for prices to rise on mid-month Thursdays. Since 1936, prices have risen on Thursday 16 May and Thursday 17 May in 12 out of 16 years (75%). During the other four days of the week, the 15th and 16th rise just 37% of the time. In 1996, 16 May lands on a Thursday.

INCREASE YOUR PROFIT ODDS

April signal

If you plan to bet on the down-side, there are several ways to maximise your return. Here is a newly discovered relationship between the month of April and the third quarter of May. Since 1936, April prices rose +2.83% to +8.81% 25 times. Third-quarter prices fell in 21 of those years regardless of what happened in the first half of May.

What we like about this trend, despite our inability to explain why the first and second quarters have no role in the relationship, is that it has been running steadily for six decades including the 1970s and '80s, through all of Budget Day's many schedule changes.

Rose (4)

Fell (21)

Third-quarter record after an April price rise of +2.83% to +8.81%

April second-half signal

We also find that a price surge in the second half of April is often associated with a decline in the second half of May. There have been 27 years with a price rise of +1.50% or more in the second half of April. Either the third quarter or the fourth quarter of May, or both, fell in 26 of those years. So be alert for a price drop at this point in the month following a strong second half of April. And if the decline doesn't occur by the end of this quarter, be doubly cautious in the fourth quarter.

Rose (1)

Fell (26)

Odds of a decline in the third or fourth quarter after a price rise of +1.50% or more in April's second half

May first-half signal

Another way to maximise your gain by betting on the downside is to monitor first- and second-quarter prices. If prices fall in the first quarter or rise a little bit (no more than +0.94%), and they fall in the second quarter, the odds of a third-quarter decline increase. Since 1936, there have been 20 occasions with first- and second-quarter price trends within the designated limits. In 17 of these years (85%), prices continued to decline in the third quarter. The average third-quarter loss was -1.69%, equal to 55 points on a 3300 FT-SE 100. The signal last flashed in 1994 and third quarter prices fell as expected.

UPDATE

Rose (3)

Fell (17)

Third-quarter record after a first-quarter price shift of +0.94% or less and a second-quarter fall

FOURTH QUARTER OF MAY – MAY 24TH TO 31ST

It is easy to lose money during this quarter of the month, one of the year's worst. But in years with a steady up-turn in the first three quarters of May, the odds of a fourth-quarter profit are pretty high.

In some respects, the fourth quarter of May is a re-run of the third quarter. Investors consistently lose money by investing during the fourth quarter. The only decade on record in which profits were made was the 1950s.

29 May

Between 1936 and 1994, the fourth quarter of May rose 47% of the time and generated an average loss of -0.48%, the fourth-worst record of the year. Analysis of daily price trends shows a steady pattern of declines with the exception of 29 May which rises in most years *(see Figure 7.6)*.

155

Figure 7.6: **PERCENTAGE OF TIME PRICES RISE EACH TRADING DAY IN MAY'S FOURTH QUARTER**

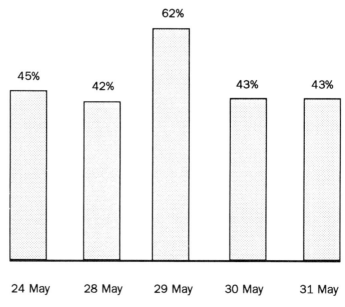

Figure 7.6: Another losing stretch in the long-run. 29 May is the best day of the quarter. But it is the only winning day.

INCREASE YOUR PROFIT ODDS

Third-quarter signal

But unlike the third quarter, smart investors can profit on the up-side as well as the down-side. Maximise gains by monitoring third-quarter prices. Our historical review found nine occasions when third-quarter prices fell by -3.10% to -4.73%. Fourth quarter continued to fall in eight of those years. The signal last failed in 1945. Since then, it has correctly flagged a fourth quarter decline six times in a row.

Rose (1)

IMPROVEMENT

Fell (8)

Fourth-quarter record after a third-quarter fall of -3.10% to -4.73%,

Second-/third-quarter signal

Another down-side indicator is the trend in the second and third quarters of May. If the price of an average share falls in both quarters, with the second-quarter fall in a range of -0.86% to -4.32%, fourth-quarter prices will probably fall. Since 1938, out of nine moves within this range, fourth-quarter prices fell every time. There is some overlap with the Third Quarter Indicator but this one also tips some declines on its own.

Rose (0)

Fell (9)

Fourth-quarter record after a second-quarter fall of -0.86% to -4.32% and a third-quarter fall (since 1938)

Last-three-quarters signal

It's also possible to profit on the up-side during this segment of May. Watch for a steady up-trend in the first three quarters of the month. There have been 11 years since 1936 when prices rose in the first, second and third quarters of the month. Fourth-quarter prices rose in nine of those years.

Rose (9)

Fell (2)

Fourth-quarter record after a rise in the first, second, and third quarters

The two exceptions to the rule are instructive. In 1989, prices rose in the third quarter by just +0.01%, thereby qualifying but by just a whisker. Clearly, a real third-quarter rise is needed to push fourth-quarter prices up. And, at the other extreme, in 1975, an April price rise of +16.23% was followed by +1.19%, +1.33% and +5.81% in the first three quarters of May. The markets simply ran out of steam in the short-run because of the enormous rally that had just taken place.

Reminder: A price surge in the second half of April of at least +1.50% has occurred 27 times. In all but one of those years, prices fell in the third and/or fourth quarters of May. So if a strong April run-up is followed by rising prices in May's third quarter, consider it to be a strong warning that prices are due to fall in this quarter.

LOOKING AHEAD

To help you to gauge the odds of a price rise or fall in the months ahead, you should pay careful attention to the price trend over the last several months.

Rising prices by 28 February

If prices have risen between 1 December and 31 May by up to +13.96%, it is a clear signal that shares will rise still further in the nine months to follow. Since 1925, there have been 29 years on record with a six-month price rise within this range. By nine months later, February 28 of the following year, prices had risen still higher 26 times.

Rose (26)

Fell (3)

Trend to 28 February after a December–May price rise of up to +13.96% (since 1925)

On the down-side, a price decline in the five month period from January to May within a range of -3.45% to -12.42% is a strong signal that prices will fall even lower by 31 December.

Falling prices by 31 December

There have been 14 occasions since 1929 when prices fell within the defined range in the first five months of the year. By year-end, shares were even lower in 12 of those years. The two exceptions were +5.27% in 1962 and a miniscule +1.17% increase in 1994. The 1994 exception was particularly instructive. Prices had steadily fallen throughout the spring in response to fears of rising interest rates. In the final week of May, the FT-SE 100 fell over 150 points in response to fears of still another rate rise, bringing prices down to near their 1994 bear market bottom. Despite this low point, the best shares could do was climb +1.17% by year-end.

Rose (2)

Fell (12)

Trend to 31 December after a January–May price decline of -3.45% to -12.42% (since 1929)

159

JUNE INVESTMENT MONITOR

	LAST MONTH FINAL PRICE	END OF 1ST QUARTER PRICE	PERCENT CHANGE	END OF 2ND QUARTER PRICE	PERCENT CHANGE	END OF 3RD QUARTER PRICE	PERCENT CHANGE	END OF 4TH QUARTER PRICE	PERCENT CHANGE
FT-ORDINARY (FT-30)									
FT-SE 100									
FT-SE 250									
FT-NON-FINANCIAL (FT-500)									
FT-SE-A ALL SHARES									
STANDARD & POORS COMPOSITE									
OTHER INDEX									

ENTER EACH SHARE, UNIT TRUST, ETC, BELOW

Chapter Eight – June 1996

Here comes the year's worst month. You may make money in some years but over the long-run, a June investor is a money-loser.

As in May, the major problem to avoid is Big Hits, months when prices decline by 5% or more. The trick is to avoid shares in months when the odds of a Big Hit are high, and hold shares when the odds of a Big Hit are low. In low-probability months, prices rise two-thirds of the time and the odds of a profit over the long-run are quite good.

Fortunately, dangerous months with a high probability of suffering a Big Hit are usually well sign-posted. They seem most likely to occur when the stock market is overheated or when the price trend is very weak. Several specific warning signs are listed on page 163.

There are wide differences in the chance of a profit during various segments of the month. The first quarter is often the most profitable. Prices have risen in three out of four years over the past two decades. The remaining three quarters are frequent money-losers with the third and fourth quarters performing especially poorly in recent years.

Looking to the year ahead, a small price rise in June is frequently associated with further price rises in the 12 months that follow (see page 184).

Long-term
disaster

The best way for investors to finish up with a small fortune in June is to start with a large one. It is the year's worst month. A £1,000 June investment, from 1919 to 1994, would have shrunk to £539. During this period, prices fell at an average rate of -0.68%, equal to 22 points on a 3300 FT-SE 100.

This poor record is not just a recent trend. Going back through history, it was 12th-ranked in 1919–43, the first 25 years of our historical record. The trend seemingly improved in the 1980s. Prices rose +1.81% per year with a record of seven up and three down. But the rise was more a function of broad trading conditions affecting all months, rather than an improvement in June's relative strength, as June was ranked eighth-best month during this period *(see Table 8.1)*.

Recent record
poor

As far as the 1990s is concerned, the record is two up and three down. The average loss of -2.02% over the past five years places June, once again, in twelfth place on the monthly profit rankings for the current decade.

Given this dismal record, it may surprise you to learn that, like May, June prices rise in slightly more than half of all years. Also, like May, the first quarter of the month tends to be profitable. The losses occur in the second to fourth segments of the month.

Big Hits

The major problem for the June investor is the imbalance between the size of up- versus down-moves. Since records began, there have been 14 declines of -5% or more versus just four increases of that magnitude. A Big Hit seems to pop up every five or six years on average. Simply put, the pain provided by losing years is greater then the pleasure provided by winning years.

Anticipate
Big Hits

If there were a way of avoiding Big Hit years, long-term June investors would profit handsomely. They would still encounter some losing years but the winners would more than compensate for those 'normal' sized losers. Our historical record shows that Big Hit years are well sign-posted in

Table 8.1

JUNE PRICE RISES AND DECLINES: 1919–1994

	Average June price change	Up	Down/ no change
1920–29	-1.39%	4	6
1930–39	0.79%	6	4
1940–49	-2.93%	5	5
1950–59	1.45%	7	3
1960–69	-1.20%	4	6
1970–79	-2.79%	3	7
1980–89	1.81%	7	3
1990–94	-2.02%	2	3
Average June price change	-0.68%	39	37

UPDATE

Source: BZW and Datastream

Table 8.1: June is the year's worst month for investors despite the fact that share prices rise more than 50% of the time. The key problem is that big drops of 5% or more occur every five or six years on average. Fortunately, there are ways to pin-point when Big Hits are most likely to occur.

the run-up to June. Big Hits have never appeared if any single one of these conditions has occurred.[1]

Time frame	Trend	Number of years	Number of Big Hits
December–May	0.00% to +11.57%	27	0
March–May	+1.50% to +4.81%	14	0
April–May	+5.13% to +10.57%	17	0
May	+2.43% to +6.01%	15	0

[1] Reminder: All monthly calculations are based on the FT-Non-financial Index, formerly the FT-'500'; unless otherwise stated, they are based on data from 1919–1994. All daily, quarterly, and bi-monthly calculations are based on the Ordinary Share Index, also known as the FT-30; unless otherwise stated, they are based on data from 1936–1994.

In using these signals, resist the temptation to round off to the nearest whole percent. Fractions of a percent count. Take the May rule for example: there were two years close to but just below the 'safety zone': a +2.04% May increase in 1985 and a +2.00% increase in 1992. June prices fell by -6.72% and -7.58% in those two years. Imagine your pain if you modified the rule and held shares in those two years because you considered any May increase in the area of 2% to be a safe signal.

Good odds if no Big Hit expected

There is a good deal of overlap between these safety zones. In total, there have been 41 years touched by at least one of them. A Big Hit has not occurred in any of them. Prices have fallen in just 14 of those years or 34% of the time – so you would have made money most of the time. The typical profit in these 41 'safe' years is +1.08%, equal to about 36 points on a FT-SE 100 in the area of 3300. Could a Big Hit occur in the future in a so-called safe year? Of course. But it hasn't happened yet *(see Figure 8.1)*.

There is a single common element that links each 'safe' year. Up until now, Big Hits do not seem to occur when share prices are rising at a comfortable rate. The odds of one occurring increase when markets rise too strongly and become overheated, rise very weakly, or fall in the run-up to June.

UPDATE

In the 35 years outside of these safety ranges, the June record has been simply awful. A Big Hit has occurred 14 times or 40% of the time. Prices fell by less than 5% in nine other years and rose just 12 times (or 34% of the time) resulting in an average loss of -2.60%, equal to 86 points on a FT-SE 100 of 3300.

Here are some other ways to tell if this is a Big Hit year:

Watch May

▶ If a Big Hit is experienced in May, the odds are small that one will also occur in June. Out of 15 May Big Hits, two were followed by a June Big Hit. One was in 1940, during the darkest days of the war when there

Figure 8.1:   **JUNE MONTHLY PRICE TREND: 1919–1993**

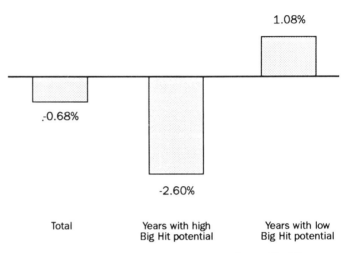

Figure 8.1: It is dangerous to hold shares when a Big Hit warning flashes. But in other years, prices usually rise and profits are likely.

---

was a real risk we might lose. June prices fell -22.10%, one of the biggest monthly falls in history, after a May fall of -11.60%. The other exception was in the worst stretch of the 1973–74 bear market, the spring of 1974, when prices fell -19.55% in March, -8.08% in May and -10.48% in June. So, unless market conditions are catastrophically poor, the odds of back-to-back Big Hits in May and June are quite low.

June's first quarter

▶ Since 1936, when daily indices were first published in the United Kingdom, there have been 11 June Big Hit years. In nine of them, prices fell during the first quarter of June. The two exceptions were in the tumultuous years of 1974 and 1975 when Big Hits occurred despite a first-quarter price rise. As a rough rule of thumb, if the first-quarter price trend is up, it is likely that June will not be subjected to a Big Hit. Prices might fall, but by less than 5%.

May's second
half

▷ The third backup signal to watch is the direction of prices in the second half of May. Nine of the 11 post-1936 Big Hits occurred after a price decline on the FT-Ordinary Share Index (the FT-30). The two exceptions: 1992 when second-half prices rose by just +0.04%, the equivalent of one point on the FT-SE 100 and in the atypical 1975. Implication: If prices rise in the second half of May, a Big Hit is not very likely, even if one of the historical price trends flashed a red flag warning signal.

INCREASE YOUR PROFIT ODDS

Past-12-months
signal

Even if Big Hits are not expected, it is still possible for share prices to fall. Investors must pick their time carefully to avoid a money-losing June. One price trend that does a very good job of tipping when June's prices will fall is the direction of prices in the preceding 12 months (1 June to 31 May). If prices have fallen in the preceding 12 months by any amount, and have fallen between -0.06% to -11.88% in the past six months, June prices will probably fall. Out of 11 years which followed this scenario, June prices fell in 10 of those years. Five of the 10 were Big Hits.

Rose (1)   ▯

Fell (10) ▭

June record after a preceding-12-month fall and a six-month fall of -0.06% to -11.88%.

166

February–May signal

Shares are also likely to fall if they have fallen during the February to May period within a range of -2.67% to -15.90%. Since 1940, prices have fallen within this range on 12 occasions in the four month run-up to June. Shares fell in June in 11 of those years by an average of -5.03%. Seven of the 11 falls were Big Hits. This signal last flashed in 1994 and June prices fell on cue.

Rose (1)

Fell (11)

June record after four-month fall of -2.67% to -15.90% (since 1940)

April–May signal

On the up-side, if shares rise in April by +3.75% to +13.03%, and shift in May by -1.61% to +3.96%, the odds favour a June price rise. Since 1935, there were 14 years with a price shift of this magnitude in the run-up to June Shares rose in 12 of these years. Be warned, though. The two exceptions to the rule were whoppers: -8.25% in 1961 and -7.45% in 1992.

Rose (12)

Fell (2)

June record after an April rise of +3.75% to +13.03%, and a May shift of -1.61% to +3.96% (since 1935)

The message to long-term investors is quite clear. Despite June's poor reputation, it is safe to invest in June if you pick your years carefully.

167

FIRST QUARTER OF JUNE – JUNE 1ST TO 8TH

During the last two decades, first-quarter prices have risen in three out of four years. Profits are especially good on 6 June, one of the best trading days of the entire year.

Small price increases in May are often associated with a first quarter profit.

Recently
profitable

Although June is often terrible for investors, the first quarter has been a consistent money-maker. The last bad stretch ran from 1961 to 1972 when first-quarter prices fell in 10 out of 12 years. But things suddenly changed for the better. From 1973 to the present, prices rose in 17 of 22 years at an average rate of +1.30% per year *(see Table 8.2)*.

Despite the fact that the first quarter tends to be profitable, our analysis of share price trends on a day-by-day basis reveals that the first few trading days tend to be merely average gainers in most years. 6–7 June are quite profitable, especially 6 June which rises 70% of the time. It is the eighth most profitable day of the entire year, quite surprising for so poor a month *(see Figure 8.2)*.

INCREASE YOUR PROFIT ODDS

Looking at the overall first-quarter trend, there are several historical relationships that increase the odds of correctly forecasting which way prices will move.

Big Hit signal
is important

One important signal to watch out for is the possibility of a Big Hit using the signals discussed earlier. If 1996 turns out to be a potential Big Hit month, the odds are high that first-quarter prices will fall, even if no monthly Big Hit occurs. Since 1936, out of 24 years classified as being a possible Big Hit June, first-quarter prices fell 16 times (67%). But if no Big Hit is forecast, there is a 74% probability of turning a first-quarter profit *(see Figure 8.3)*.

UPDATE

Table 8.2

PERCENTAGE PRICE CHANGE: JUNE 1936–1994

	June 1–8	June 9–15	June 16–23	June 24–30
Average annual price change				
1936–39	-0.22%	-1.30%	1.39%	-0.13%
1940–49	-0.49%	-0.09%	-1.71%	-0.18%
1950–59	0.94%	0.00%	0.86%	-0.56%
1960–69	-0.53%	-0.56%	-0.84%	0.81%
1970–79	0.55%	-3.09%	-0.59%	-0.76%
1980–89	1.47%	0.16%	0.17%	-0.09%
1990–94	0.26%	0.65%	-1.40%	-1.57%
Average quarterly price change	0.34%	-0.64%	-0.38%	-0.27%
Number of years in which prices:				
rose	34	25	28	27
fell	24	34	30	31
remained unchanged	1	–	1	1

Source: Datastream

Table 8.2: The first quarter is the month's only profitable segment. The next three tend to be losers, especially the second quarter, which is the year's worst performer.

UPDATE (margin note)

May fourth-quarter signal (margin note)

In months with a low probability of a Big Hit, the odds of a first-quarter profit are especially high if prices rose in May's fourth quarter by +0.27% to +1.51%. Out of 10 years with a May price move in the designated range, first-quarter prices rose each time.

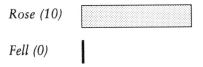

Rose (10)

Fell (0)

First-quarter record after a price rise of +0.27 % to +1.51% in May's fourth quarter (in 'safe' years)

169

Figure 8.2: **PERCENTAGE OF TIME PRICES RISE EACH TRADING DAY IN JUNE'S FIRST QUARTER**

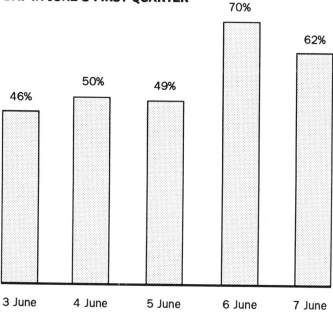

Figure 8.2: The first quarter is profitable in most years. If you do plan to buy or sell shares, be sure to factor the strength of 6 and 7 June into your thinking, especially 6 June.

May signal

Another trend that tips first-quarter prices is the direction of prices during the month of May. This trend is operative in all years, regardless of the Big Hit potential. If May prices rise moderately, first-quarter prices will probably rise too. There have been 10 occasions since 1936 when May prices rose by +2.47% to +3.96%. June's first quarter rose in nine of those years. The single exception was in 1971.

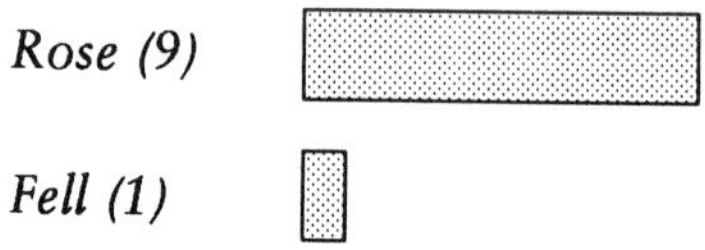

Rose (9) �largebar

Fell (1) ▯

First-quarter record after a price rise of +2.47% to +3.96% in May

Figure 8.3: **STOCK MARKET TREND IN JUNE'S FIRST QUARTER: 1936–1993**

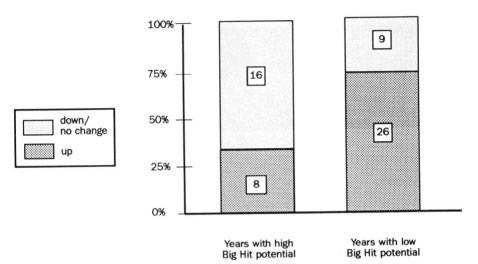

Figure 8.3: In years with a high likelihood of a Big Hit, stand aside. Prices fall 70% of the time. But first-quarter prices rise 74% of the time in safe years.

May second-half signal

By watching the price trend during May's second half, it is possible to pin-point years when prices are especially likely to fall. The losses are often large.

Since 1948, there have been 14 years with a decline in the second half of May of under -5.00% and a fourth-quarter decline of -0.20% to -2.98%. Prices fell in June's first quarter in 12 of those years (86%). The average loss during those 14 years was -1.30%.

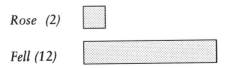

Rose (2)

Fell (12)

First-quarter record after a price fall of up to -5.00% in May's second half and fourth-quarter price fall of -0.20% to -2.98% (since 1948)

Second Quarter of June – June 9th to 15th

> Here comes the year's worst quarter. Even if a Big Hit does not threaten, the odds of a profit are just 50:50.
>
> Fortunately, you can move the odds into your favour by watching price shifts that occur in May's fourth quarter and June's first quarter.

Low profit odds

The average share price in the second quarter of June drops -0.64% each year, the worst quarterly performance of the year. The quarter is third-lowest in terms of the percentage of time in which prices rise (42%). Even during the 1980s' bull market decade, the record was four up, six down and an average increase of +0.16%. Subtract the +6.53% increase of 1980 – the largest increase ever realised in June's second quarter – and this decade also would have been a loser for investors *(see Table 8.3)*.

13 June

Analysis of prices on a day-to-day basis reveals a poor pattern, but no worse than many other segments of the year *(see Figure 8.4)*. Why, then, is this quarter the year's biggest loser? The main reason is the size of the average daily loss, driven higher by the occasional Big Hits that periodically strike June.

Note that shares are often weak on 13–15 June when they land on a Thursday. Since 1936, prices rose just 25% of the time for any of these three days when they landed on Thursday. 13 June lands on a Thursday in 1996.

As with the first quarter, an important signal to watch for is the possibility of a Big Hit. If 1996 turns out to be a potentially dangerous month, there is a 67% chance that second-quarter prices will fall. Unless you feel very positive about market conditions in such a year, it would be a good time to stand aside. But if no Big Hit is forecast, there is roughly a 50:50 chance of turning a second-quarter profit *(see Figure 8.5)*.

Table 8.3

PERCENTAGE PRICE CHANGE: 1985–1994

	June 1–8	June 9–15	June 16–23	June 24–30
Annual quarterly price change				
1985	-0.09%	-2.25%	-1.62%	-2.55%
1986	1.19%	-1.74%	1.86%	2.16%
1987	0.88%	3.44%	-1.96%	1.77%
1988	1.94%	2.09%	0.75%	-0.90%
1989	0.99%	-0.80%	2.21%	-0.73%
1990	2.03%	1.75%	-0.67%	-0.68%
1991	-0.10%	1.08%	-1.47%	-3.56%
1992	-2.69%	-1.50%	-1.47%	-2.72%
1993	0.88%	1.16%	1.13%	-0.22%
1994	1.18%	0.74%	-4.51%	-0.64%
Average quarterly price change				
1985–1994	0.62%	0.40%	-0.57%	-0.81%
Number of years in which prices:				
rose	7	6	4	2
fell	3	4	6	8

UPDATE

Source: Datastream

Table 8.3: First-quarter prices have risen in seven of the past 10 years. The trend for the other three segments grows steadily worse The fourth-quarter trend is especially weak, dropping seven consecutive times since the 1987 crash.

INCREASE YOUR PROFIT ODDS

Clearly, the only way to profit consistently in the second quarter is to invest selectively when market conditions are favourable. To help you improve the odds of a profitable investment, the market sends several useful signals. One of the best is the interaction between May's fourth quarter and June's first quarter. In previous editions, we reported on several correlations involving these two periods. Here is an update.

Figure 8.4:   **PERCENTAGE OF TIME PRICES RISE EACH TRADING DAY IN JUNE'S SECOND QUARTER**

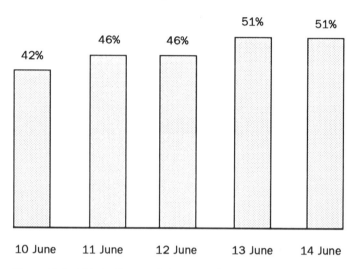

10 June   11 June   12 June   13 June   14 June

Figure 8.4: This is the year's least profitable quarter. The odds favour standing aside during this segment of the month unless a unique situation arises. When 13 June lands on a Thursday, the odds of a price rise are just 25%.

Previous-two-quarter signal No 1

If strong May fourth-quarter prices (+0.64% to +2.90%) are followed with a first-quarter price rise of at least +0.18%, prices will probably continue to rise in the second quarter. Second-quarter prices rose in 11 out of 12 years with the two prior price trends in the appropriate range. The sole exception was in 1953. The average second-quarter increase is +1.07%.

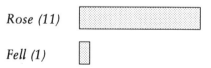

Rose (11)

Fell (1)

Second-quarter record after a price rise in May's fourth quarter of +0.64% to +2.90% and a first-quarter price rise of at least +0.18%

Figure 8.5:   **STOCK MARKET TREND IN JUNE'S SECOND QUARTER: 1936–1993**

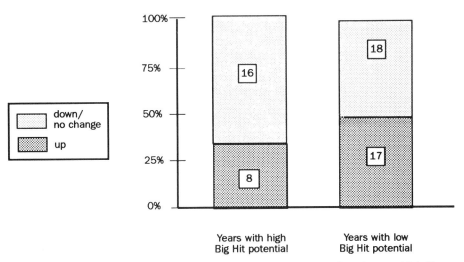

Figure 8.5: The risk of a second-quarter loss is very high if any Big Hit warning signals have flashed at the beginning of the month. But even in the best of times, there is a 50:50 chance of turning a profit.

Previous-two-quarter signal No 2

On the other hand, if weak prices in May's fourth quarter are followed by strong prices in June's first quarter – look out. Second-quarter prices will probably fall once the first quarter up-move is finished. Here is the evidence: there have been 13 years when the price of the average share shifted in May's fourth quarter within a range of -4.13% to +0.27%, and rose in the first quarter by at least +0.20%. Second-quarter prices declined in 11 of these years (85%). The average quarterly decline during those 13 years was -1.39%, equal to 46 points on an FT-SE 100 in the area of 3300.

IMPROVEMENT	*Rose (2)* ▢
	Fell (13) ▭

Second-quarter record after a price shift in May's fourth quarter of -4.13% to +0.27% and a first-quarter price rise of at least +020%

First-quarter
signal

A final signal to watch for is a decline of -0.60% to -2.69% in June's first quarter. If prices fall in this range, the odds are good that they will continue to fall in the second quarter. Out of 13 occasions since 1936 when share prices fell within this range in the first quarter, second-quarter prices declined 11 times (85%). The average decline during those years was -2.16%. That's equal to 71 points on an FT-SE 100 in the area of 3300.

Rose (2) ▢

Fell (11) ▭

Second-quarter record after a price drop in June's first quarter of -0.60% to -2.69%

THIRD QUARTER OF JUNE – JUNE 16TH TO 23RD

> The long-term third-quarter trend is quite poor and things have not improved in the recent past. Prices have fallen in four of the last five years.
>
> If share prices are weak in the beginning of June, the odds are high they will continue to be weak during this segment of the month.

Investors typically lose money by investing during the third quarter. Between 1936 and 1994, the third quarter of June rose 47% of the time and generated an average loss of -0.38% per year. The profit picture may not be as grim as for the second quarter, but it's not good.

Recent trend weak

The price trend has continued to show weakness during the last few decades. Share prices fell in the 1960s and '70s. In the bull market 1980s, the record was five up and five down, and an average yearly share price increase of +0.17%, less than the rate of return at your local building society. The record for the 1990s, so far, is four out of five declines.

19 June

Analysis of share price trends on a daily basis shows weakness throughout the quarter. Be especially cautious on Wednesday, 19 June *(see Figure 8.6)*. There is a long-standing tendency for prices to be weak when 19 or 20 June lands on a Wednesday. Since 1936, these two days have landed on a Wednesday 16 times. Prices rose just once.

INCREASE YOUR PROFIT ODDS

Here again, an important signal is the monthly Big Hit signal. If 1996 turns out to be a 'high potential' Big Hit month, the odds are high (67%) that third-quarter prices will fall. But if no Big Hit is forecast, there is a slightly better than even chance (57%) of turning a third-quarter profit *(see Figure 8.7)*.

Figure 8.6: **PERCENTAGE OF TIME PRICES RISE EACH TRADING DAY IN JUNE'S THIRD QUARTER**

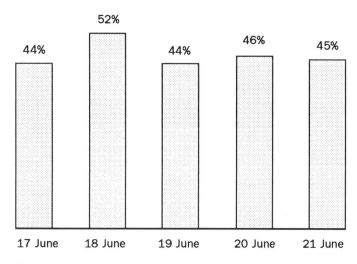

Figure 8.6: Another poor segment of the month. In most years, it makes sense to stand aside. Prices often fall when 19 June lands on a Wednesday.

Second-quarter signal No 1

If you are betting on the down-side, one way to increase your odds of success is to watch second-quarter prices. If they fall by -1.23% or more, the odds of a third-quarter decline increase. Since 1973, second-quarter prices fell within this range 10 times. In nine of them, the fall was immediately followed by a decline in the third quarter. The average loss was -2.29%, equal to 76 points on a 3300 FT-SE 100.

Rose (1)

Fell (9)

Third-quarter record after a price drop in June's second quarter of at least -1.23% (since 1973)

Figure 8.7:   **STOCK MARKET TREND IN JUNE'S THIRD QUARTER: 1936–1993**

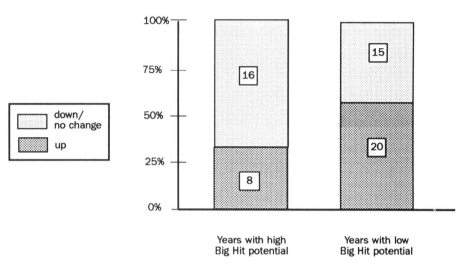

Figure 8.7: There is a big risk of a third-quarter fall if any of the Big Hit warning signals flash at the beginning of the month.

First-half signal

Another trend to watch is the direction of prices in the first half of June. If they fall by -2.79% to -6.83%, the odds are high that prices will also decline in the third quarter. Out of 13 years in which first-half prices fell within the defined range, the third quarter declined 10 times. Two of the exceptions were in 1970 when the Conservatives won a mid-June election (third-quarter prices rose +10.68%) and 1971 when the markets got wind of a July tax cut. These exceptions confirm the point that news-making events can overwhelm even the strongest of trends. If you put these two atypical years aside for the moment, a first-half drop in share prices within a range of -2.79% to -6.83% is associated with a third-quarter drop in 10 out of 11 years.

179

Rose (3)

Fell (10)

Third-quarter record after a price drop in June's first half of
-2.79% to -6.83% (two exceptional years included)

**May second-
half/June first-
half signal**

Large price declines also often occur after prices decline in
the second half of May and first half of June. Out of 16
years in which prices declined in both periods, by at least
-0.33% in May and -0.77% in June, the third quarter
declined 13 times (81%), by an average of -2.34% per year.
In 1937, one of the three exceptions, third-quarter prices
rose by just +0.09%.

Rose (3)

Fell (13)

Third-quarter record after a price drop in May's second half by
at least -0.33% and June's first half by at least -0.77%

**Second-quarter
signal No 2**

There is one ray of sunshine in this cloudy investment
climate. If June's second quarter rises by +1.09% to
+2.50%, third-quarter prices will probably rise. Out of 11
second-quarter shifts within this range, June's third quarter
rose nine times. Unfortunately, the average gain was just
+0.63%.

Rose (9)

Fell (2)

Third-quarter record after a price rise in June's second quarter
of +1.09% to +2.50%

FOURTH QUARTER OF JUNE – JUNE 24TH TO 30TH

> Here comes another quarter with low profit potential. Prices have fallen in each of the last seven years during this segment, the year's worst record.

Poor recent record

In the long-run, investors have lost money by consistently investing during the fourth quarter. The only profitable decade on record was the 1960s. Between 1936 and 1994, the fourth quarter of June rose 46% of the time and generated an average loss of -0.27%. The record since the 1987 crash is seven declines in a row, the worst performance of the year.

28 June

The best day in the quarter is 28 June which rises 55% of the time. The odds of a rise are especially good in 1996. History shows that 28 and 29 June rise 75% of the time when either lands on a Friday, as the 28th will do this year. *(see Figure 8.8)*.

INCREASE YOUR PROFIT ODDS

Third-quarter signal

Big Hits don't seem to affect this quarter as badly as they do other quarters. Prices rise 46% of the time both in 'high potential' and 'low potential' Big Hit years *(see Figure 8.9)*. But the absence of a Big Hit signal does send one useful market-timing signal. In years with a low likelihood of a Big Hit, a third-quarter price rise of +1.13% to +4.18% is associated with a fourth-quarter price drop nine out of 10 times.

Rose (1)

Fell (9)

Fourth-quarter record in low risk years after a third-quarter price rise of +1.13% to +4.18%

Figure 8.8: **PERCENTAGE OF TIME PRICES RISE EACH TRADING DAY IN JUNE'S FOURTH QUARTER**

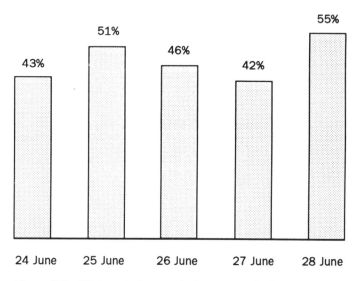

Figure 8.8: 28 June is the quarter's most profitable day. The odds of a rise are especially high when it lands on a Friday, as in 1996.

First-half/third-quarter signal

Despite the difficult general market conditions, we find two good price signals, one tipping up-moves and one tipping down-moves. If prices rise in the first half of June by no more than +2.92%, and shift in the third quarter within a range of -1.24% to +0.53%, fourth-quarter prices will probably rise. There have been 12 years with price shifts within this range. Fourth-quarter prices rose in 11 of those years. The single exception was back in 1950.

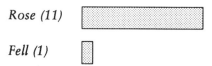

Rose (11)

Fell (1)

Fourth-quarter record after a price rise in June's first half by no more than +2.92% and a shift in the third quarter of -1.24% to +0.53%

182

Figure 8.9:   **STOCK MARKET TREND IN JUNE'S FOURTH QUARTER: 1936–1993**

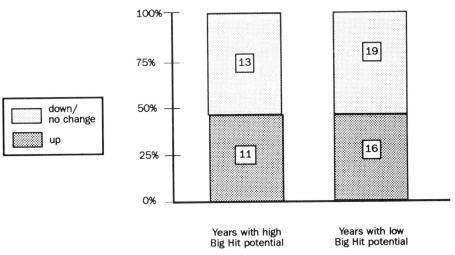

Figure 8.9: It is hard to profit consistently in the fourth quarter. It is a good time to stand on the sidelines unless you have good reason to believe this year will be different.

Last-three-quarters signal

There is also a tendency for prices to fall in the fourth quarter if they rise in June's first, second, and third quarters. It last happened in 1993. Here is the rule that seems to be developing. There have been eight years in which prices rose in the three preceding quarters, with a third-quarter rise of at least +0.50%. Fourth-quarter prices fell in each of those years. The average annual decline was -1.12%.

Fourth-quarter record after a price rise in three consecutive quarters, with a third-quarter rise of at least +0.50%

183

LOOKING AHEAD

Rising prices by
30 June

There is a very pronounced tendency for the June price trend to tip off where prices are heading in the next 12 months, that is, to June 30 of the following year. Since World War I, there were 23 occasions when June prices shifted within a relatively narrow range of -3.14% to + 0.63%. In 20 of those 23 occasions, share prices were sharply higher 12 months later. All but four were in the double digits.

Rose (20)

Fell (3)

Trend to 30 June (next year) after a June shift of -3.14% to +0.63%

There were just three exceptions to the rule: 1937, 1947 and 1973.

After the June 1937 signal flashed, prices remained flat during July and August. But fear of war and of higher taxes to pay for re-armament then hit the stock market hard. In the 10 months that followed, prices dropped by almost 18%.

The cold winter and spring floods of 1947 brought the post-war economy almost to a standstill. Things began to look up in April and May. Sterling was made convertible in June and the June signal flashed. Soon afterwards, the stock market's optimism turned sour. The government was forced to suspend sterling's convertibility in August. Food rations were reduced to well below war-time levels. US aid ran out amidst considerable uncertainty about America's upcoming Marshall Plan aid package. Share prices dropped by over 19% in the year that followed a good June signal.

In 1973, the June signal was followed with a relatively small price drop of around 6% by October. Suddenly, the oil crisis smashed Britain. Crude oil prices rose by 66%. The government was in turmoil. Interest rates rose to 13%. A three-day working week was introduced. A December mini-Budget introduced massive spending cuts, credit controls and tax increases. Labour won a surprise victory in February. By June 1974, prices were down 44% from the previous June, despite a favourable June signal.

Clearly, there are no certainties when it comes to the stock market. Equally clear: throughout all of recorded history, each exception to the June rule was associated with truly extraordinary economic and political events. The June signal flashed most recently (Number 24 in the series) in June 1994 with a drop of -2.6%. Despite the fact that prices barely moved by the end of 1994, we expect a solid price rise by the end of June 1995.

JULY INVESTMENT MONITOR

	LAST MONTH FINAL PRICE	END OF 1ST QUARTER		END OF 2ND QUARTER		END OF 3RD QUARTER		END OF 4TH QUARTER	
		PRICE	PERCENT CHANGE	PRICE	PERCENT CHANGE	PRICE	PERCENT CHANGE	PRICE	PERCENT CHANGE
FT-ORDINARY (FT-30)									
FT-SE 100									
FT-SE 250									
FT-NON-FINANCIAL (FT-500)									
FT-SE-A ALL SHARES									
STANDARD & POORS COMPOSITE									
OTHER INDEX									
ENTER EACH SHARE, UNIT TRUST, ETC, BELOW									

CHAPTER NINE – JULY 1996

It is hard to profit consistently by holding shares during July. Prices rise and fall an equal number of times which makes the profit odds a 50:50 proposition. Over the long-run, the best July investment is a building society savings account.

Be warned: unlike other poor months, for example May, June, and September, prices are weak in the first quarter of July as well as for the rest of the month.

Fortunately, there are a number of price trends that tip which way prices will shift in July. The odds of a price rise are good if there are moderate price moves in the run-up to July. But a large drop in May and June is often associated with further losses in July (see page 188).

Looking ahead, small swings, either up or down, are typically associated with higher prices at year-end. If this signal does flash, don't be too quick to take profits. Past experience suggests the rally will continue throughout the second half of the year (see page 202).

Low profit
potential

July is ranked seventh on monthly profitability. Over the long-run, the July investor has typically made a small profit. Between 1919 and 1994, prices rose at a yearly average of just +0.29%, equal to slightly over 10 points on a 3300 FT-SE 100. A start-up investment of £1,000, placed in shares each July from 1919 to 1994, and in cash for the rest of each year, would have grown to just £1,166. If the same sum were deposited into a risk-free building society savings account each July, earning an average of 4% per year over the past 76 years, it would have grown to £1,288 by 1994.

Recent trend
poor

Worse still, the best decades for the July investor were prior to 1960. Since then, July's performance has weakened. The average return was -2.28% in the 1960s, and -0.22% in the 1970s *(see Table 9.1)*.

In the bull market 1980s, July returned to the profit column. Note though, that the average annual increase of +0.72% merely reached ninth place on the monthly profitability rankings. And most of this profit was due to 1989, when prices rose by +6.10%.

In the last 20 years, the July record was tied with June as the worst of all the 12 months – 10 up and 10 down.

INCREASE YOUR PROFIT ODDS

Despite the poor record, investors can profit if they invest selectively and nimbly. Several historical price trends provide good insight into the expected direction of prices.

January and
April signal

Since 1949, an interesting seasonal pattern has developed which involves January and April, the opening month of each quarter. Moderate rises in both of these months seem to tip rising prices in July.[1] Here is the evidence.

---

[1] Reminder: All monthly calculations are based on the FT-Non-financial Index, formerly the FT-'500'; unless otherwise stated, they are based on data from 1919–1994. All daily, quarterly, and bi-monthly calculations are based on the Ordinary Share Index, also known as the FT-30; unless otherwise stated, they are based on data from 1936–1994.

Table 9.1   **JULY PRICE RISES AND DECLINES: 1919–1994**

	Average July price change	Up	Down/ no change
1920–29	-0.86%	3	7
1930–39	1.51%	6	4
1940–49	2.20%	6	4
1950–59	0.73%	6	4
1960–69	-2.28%	4	6
1970–79	-0.22%	4	6
1980–89	0.72%	6	4
1990–94	1.00%	3	2
Average July price change	0.29%	38	38

UPDATE

Source: BZW and Datastream

Table 9.1: July is a lacklustre month, especially in the recent past. The three most profitable decades were prior to 1960. Even in the Bull Market 1980s, its +0.72% profit was merely eighth-ranked.

There have been 10 occasions with a January price rise of +0.84% to +5.38% and an April rise of +1.14% to +5.77%. July rose in nine of those years at an average annual rate of +1.66%. The single exception was in 1961 when the government sharply increased interest rates to protect sterling against speculative out-flows. Shares fell by 6%.

NEW

Rose (9)

Fell (1)

July's record after a January price rise of + 0.84% to +5.38% and an April rise of +1.14% to +5.77% (since 1949)

First-half signal

Another good signal for which to watch is a small price shift, in either direction, in the first half of the year. If prices fluctuate in January to June by -2.22% to + 9.85%, and in the preceding two months within a range of -1.98% to

+4.25%, July prices will probably rise. Out of 16 years which followed this scenario, July prices rose 15 times.

Rose (15)

Fell (1)

July's record after a previous six-month price shift of -2.22% to +9.85% and a previous two-month shift of -1.98% to +4.25%

May/June signal No 1

Here is a variation of the 'moderation' theme which is based on a moderate price shift in May and June, regardless of how prices shifted during the broader six-month period. Since 1963, there have been 13 years with a May/June price shift of -4.81% to +2.99%. Prices rose in 11 of those years. Both exceptions were whoppers. Prices fell by over 5% in 1973 and 1986, despite a favourable May/June signal.

Rose (11)

NEW

Fell (2)

July's record after a May/June price shift within a range of -4.81% to +2.99% (since 1961)

May/June signal No 2

Since 1961, a price decline of at least -5.10% during May and June signalled that July prices will probably continue to fall. Out of 13 years with a drop of this magnitude, July prices fell 11 times. Be warned: both exceptions were big (almost 6%).

Rose (2)

UPDATE

Fell (11)

July's record after a drop of -5.10% or more during May and June (since 1961)

FIRST QUARTER OF JULY – JULY 1ST TO 8TH

> The recent record is weak. The odds of a price drop are especially high if prices have fallen moderately in June's second half. One window of opportunity on the up-side is signalled by a moderate price rise during June's second half.

Recent record poor

At first glance, the first quarter looks to be a profitable time period in which to invest. Its record since 1935 is 33 up months (55%), 24 down months, three unchanged and an average profit of +0.49% per year. Unfortunately, much of that profit was achieved in 1935–1959. In the more recent decades, a first-quarter investor has been a consistent money-loser *(see Table 9.2)*.

1975 was an exception

In the 1960s, first-quarter prices rose just three times. The profits of the 1970s were entirely due to an +11.86% increase in the abnormal year of 1975, the largest-ever price rise at this point in the year. On 1 July of that year, Denis Healey electrified the markets by warning unions he would introduce wage controls unless they voluntarily reduced their wage demands. Share prices exploded upwards. The record for the rest of the decade was three up and six down, and an average annual loss of -0.57%.

In the bull market 1980s, the first quarter lost, on average, -0.04% per year. The 1990s continues to disappoint investors. The score to date is two up and three down.

Analysis of daily price trends over the long-run reveals a pattern of profitable trading conditions on 1 July and 4 July, both among the best trading days of the entire month *(see Figure 9.1)*.

5 July looks promising

5 July rises 49% of the time over the long-run. But shares traditionally do better than average on first quarter Fridays. Since 1935, 3–5 July has risen 65% of the time when they land on Friday. 5 July lands on Friday in 1996.

Table 9.2   **PERCENTAGE PRICE CHANGE: JULY 1935–1994**

	July 1–8	July 9–15	July 16–23	July 24–31
Average annual price change				
1935–39	0.65%	-0.46%	0.66%	0.80%
1940–49	1.77%	0.34%	0.21%	-1.13%
1950–59	1.07%	0.08%	0.06%	-0.50%
1960–69	-0.52%	-0.91%	-0.52%	-1.27%
1970–79	0.67%	1.00%	-1.28%	-1.16%
1980–89	-0.04%	0.28%	-0.71%	0.80%
1990–94	-0.65%	1.39%	-0.20%	0.16%
Average quarterly price change	0.49%	0.21%	-0.34%	-0.46%
Number of years in which prices:				
rose	33	35	30	29
fell	24	25	30	31
remained unchanged	3	–	–	–

UPDATE

Source: Datastream

Table 9.2: At first glance, the first quarter looks to be the month's most profitable segment, but its performance has been relatively poor in the past few decades. The profit of the 1970s was due to a +11.86% increase in 1975. The second quarter has been the stronger of the two in recent years. The third and fourth quarters are often money-losers.

INCREASE YOUR PROFIT ODDS

Here are several ways to help investors to improve the odds of a profitable first quarter investment. Three involve an upturn in June's second half.

June second-half signal No 1

There have been 14 years when June's second half rose by +0.94% to +3.01%. First quarter prices rose in 12 of those years. The average increase was +0.94%.

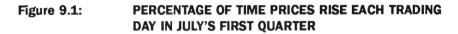
Figure 9.1:   **PERCENTAGE OF TIME PRICES RISE EACH TRADING DAY IN JULY'S FIRST QUARTER**

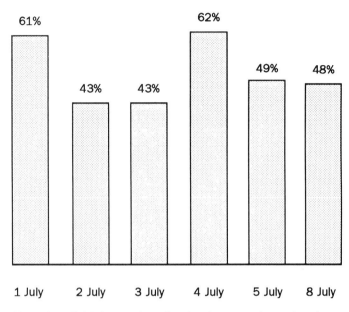

Figure 9.1: 5 July is a weak trading day. One exception to the rule: prices often rise when it lands on a Friday, as it will in 1996.

Rose (12)

Fell (2)

First-quarter record after a rise of +0.94% to +3.01% in June's second half

June second-half signal No 2

Here is a variation of the second-half theme which is based on the direction of prices in June's third and fourth quarters. There is some duplication with the previous signal but it sometimes flashes independently of the second-half signal. Since 1936, an increase in share prices in both quarters has been frequently associated with an increase during July's first quarter. Out of 11 years in which prices rose by at least +0.09% in the third quarter and at least +0.27% in the fourth quarter, first-quarter prices rose 10 times (91%). The average increase was +0.98%.

Rose (10)

Fell (1)

First-quarter record after a rise of at least +0.09% in June's third quarter and at least +0.27% in June's fourth quarter

June second-half signal No 3

Since 1948, there were 11 years in which prices dropped in both June quarters by a small or moderate amount, no more than -2.79% in the third quarter and no more than -2.72% in the fourth quarter. July's first quarter rose twice. One was an increase of just +0.29%. In other words, prices rose by a reasonable margin in just one out of 11 years following a small or moderate decline in the third *and* fourth quarters.

Rose (2)

Fell (8)

No change (1)

First-quarter record after a fall of up to -2.79% in June's third quarter and of up to -2.72% in June's fourth quarter (since 1948)

SECOND QUARTER OF JULY – JULY 9TH TO JULY 15TH

Share prices rise in most second quarters. The trend in the second half of June and the first quarter of July often tip which way second-quarter prices will shift.

Mostly profitable

Although the month as a whole often disappoints investors, the second quarter tends to be profitable. The only full decade on record in which the price of the average share dropped in value each year was back in the 1960s. Since 1970, the second-quarter record is 15 up (60%) and 10 down, and an average increase of +0.79% per year. The recent record remains profitable. Since 1990, prices have risen four out of five times *(see Table 9.3)*.

12 July:
be careful

Analysis of daily price trends finds that the odds of a profit are good on most days in the second quarter. But one word of caution. Since 1984, trading conditions on the 12th have worsened. We noted in last year's edition that its recent record was one up and six down. 1994 followed the norm. The recent record is now one up and seven down. We don't suggest that prices will decline each and every 12 July from now on but the recent weakness is a point to consider for anyone planning to buy or sell around this time in the month *(see Figure 9.2)*.

INCREASE YOUR PROFIT ODDS

The market sends some useful signals to help second-quarter investors improve the odds of profiting – the direction of prices in the last half of June and the first quarter of July. If they both rise or both fall within certain limits, the odds are good that prices will rise in the second quarter.

Table 9.3   **PERCENTAGE PRICE CHANGE: 1985–1994**

	July 1–8	July 9–15	July 16–23	July 24–31
Annual quarterly price change				
1985	1.34%	-1.47%	-1.72%	2.39%
1986	-3.61%	-1.15%	-1.21%	-1.15%
1987	2.50%	4.45%	-3.80%	0.89%
1988	1.59%	-0.62%	-1.21%	0.63%
1989	1.80%	3.84%	0.34%	1.01%
1990	-1.84%	0.81%	-0.69%	-1.21%
1991	0.71%	3.16%	2.82%	-0.11%
1992	-2.64%	0.27%	-4.65%	-0.24%
1993	-1.90%	-0.28%	0.59%	3.71%
1994	2.40%	2.97%	0.93%	-1.37%
Average quarterly price change				
1985–1994	0.04%	1.20%	-0.86%	0.46%
Number of years in which prices:				
rose	6	6	4	5
fell	4	4	6	5

UPDATE

Source: Datastream

Table 9.3: The third and fourth quarters have been weak in recent years. Fourth-quarter prices have risen just once in the 1990s.

June second-half/July first-quarter signal No 1

There have been eight occasions since 1965 when the price of the average share fell in June's second half (by any amount) and July's first quarter (by at least -0.52%). Second-quarter prices rose each time.

Rose (8)

Fell (0) |

Second-quarter record after a fall in June's second half and in July's first quarter by at least -0.52% (since 1965)

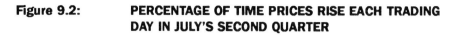

Figure 9.2:   **PERCENTAGE OF TIME PRICES RISE EACH TRADING DAY IN JULY'S SECOND QUARTER**

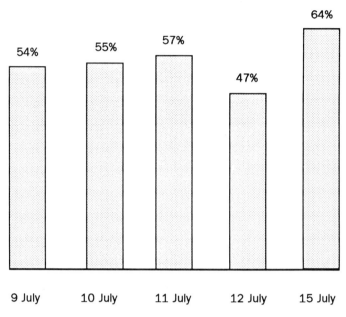

Figure 9.2: 12 July is profitable slightly less than half the time over the long-run. Unfortunately, the recent trend has weakened. Since 1984, prices rose once but fell seven times.

June second-half/July first-quarter signal No 2

There have been 11 other occasions when the price of the average share rose in June's second half by +1.38% to +5.35%, and shifted in July's first quarter within a range of -2.76% to +5.55%. Second-quarter prices rose in 10 of those years. The average increase during this period was +1.80%.

Rose (10)

IMPROVEMENT

Fell (1)

Second-quarter record after a rise in June's second half by +1.38% to +5.35%, and a shift in July's first quarter of -2.76% to +5.55%

THIRD QUARTER OF JULY – JULY 16TH TO JULY 23RD

In the last few decades, third-quarter prices have disappointed investors frequently. But shares often rise following a moderate price increase in the first half of the month.

Investors typically lose -0.34% per year by investing every third quarter. That's equal to a drop of 11 points on a 3300 FT-SE 100.

Recent trend poor

Like the first quarter of July, third-quarter investors made money in the 1930s, '40s, and '50s. The trend has been poor ever since. The average share fell in value during the 1960s, '70s, and '80s. The record during this period was just 13 up months and 17 down.

22 July: be careful

Analysis of price trends on a daily basis finds a tendency for red ink in mid-quarter. The record on the 22nd is worth noting. Prices have risen 44% of the time over the long-run, with no improvement in sight in recent years. Since 1974, shares have risen just five times out of 16 tries *(see Figure 9.3)*.

Another straw to the wind. Prices tend to rise less often on 20–23 July if they land on Monday, compared with other weekdays (24% odds of a rise on Monday versus 51% on Tuesday to Friday). 22 July lands on a Monday in 1996.

INCREASE YOUR PROFIT ODDS

Don't get disheartened. History provides several clues to help investors to spot short-term trading opportunities.

First-half signal

Price increases are often tipped off by the price trend in the first half of July. Prices have risen in the first half of the month by +1.07% to +2.95% on 12 occasions. Third-quarter prices rose in 10 of those years.

Figure 9.3: **PERCENTAGE OF TIME PRICES RISE EACH TRADING DAY IN JULY'S SECOND QUARTER**

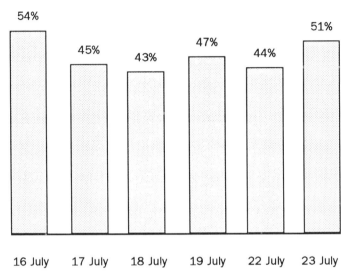

| 16 July | 17 July | 18 July | 19 July | 22 July | 23 July |

Figure 9.3: 22 July has a poor trading record and has weakened in recent years. The odds of a decline are highest when it lands on a Monday, as in 1996.

Rose (10)

Fell (2)

Third-quarter record after a rise in the first half of +1.07% to +2.95%

Second-quarter signal

If second-quarter prices shift slightly, within a range of -0.45% to +0.44%, it is a good sign that third-quarter prices will rise. Out of 12 years with a second-quarter shift within this range, third-quarter prices rose 10 times.

Rose (10)

Fell (2)

Third-quarter record after a shift in the second quarter of
-0.45% to +0.44%

**Previous-three-
quarters signal**

Another signal to look for is the trend over the previous
three quarters: the last quarter in June and the first two in
July. If shares steadily move in the same direction in all three
periods, they are likely to move in the opposite direction in
the third quarter.

▶ Shares fell in three consecutive quarters on seven
occasions since 1936. Third-quarter prices rose all
seven times. The last time this signal flashed was in
1993. After a drop of over 2% in the three preceding
quarters, prices rose in the third quarter.

▶ On six other occasions, prices rose in each of the three
preceding periods, with a second-quarter rise of at
least +0.94%. Third-quarter prices fell each time.

What of the remaining years not preceded by three steady
rises/declines? Here too, the market sends a clear signal.

Since 1969, there were nine years not touched by the
three prior up/three prior down rule in which first-half
prices fell. Each of the nine falls was immediately followed
by a decline in the third quarter. The average loss was a
staggering -2.57%, equal to 85 points on a 3300 FT-SE 100.

Rose (0)

Fell (9)

Third-quarter record after a drop in the first half in years unaf-
fected by the three-prior-up/three-prior-down rule (since 1969)

FOURTH QUARTER OF JULY – JULY 24TH TO 31ST

Here comes another money-loser. We find no pockets of opportunity to help you to profit consistently during this segment of the month.

Poor recent trend

The fourth quarter of July offers poor investment potential. In the long-run, investors have consistently lost money by investing during the fourth quarter. The only full decade on record in which profits were made was during the bull market 1980s. The trend for the 1990s has reverted to form with four out of five declines.

Between 1935 and 1994, the fourth quarter of July rose 48% of the time and generated an average loss of -0.46%, the fifth-worst quarterly performance of the entire year.

29 July

Much of the damage occurs on the 25th which rises just 38% of the time, the worst trading day of the month. On the bright side, the 29th has been especially good to investors since 1984 with a record of seven up and one down *(see Figure 9.4)*.

INCREASE YOUR PROFIT ODDS

Previous-three-quarters signal

Unfortunately, we find no way to increase the odds of spotting an up-move during this quarter of the month. But, if you wish to bet on the down-side, here is a relationship that has been in effect since 1938. If shares shift slightly in the first three quarters of July, no more than +0.28% on the up-side and no more than -1.49% on the down-side, they are likely to fall in the last quarter of July. Out of 13 years with this pattern, fourth-quarter prices fell 11 times.

Figure 9.4:   **PERCENTAGE OF TIME PRICES RISE EACH TRADING DAY IN JULY'S FOURTH QUARTER**

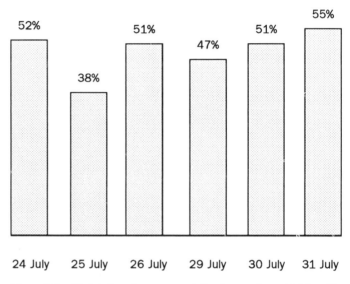

| 24 July | 25 July | 26 July | 29 July | 30 July | 31 July |

Figure 9.4: 29 July has been especially strong since 1984, with a record of seven up and one down.

Rose (2)

Fell (11)

Fourth-quarter record after a shift in the first three quarters of -1.49% to +0.28% (since 1938)

LOOKING AHEAD

Rising prices by next 31 January

July provides a useful insight about the direction of shares in the months ahead. A small shift during July, no more than -1.49% on the down-side and no more than +1.06% on the up-side, is a good sign that prices will rise six months ahead.

Since 1924, there have been 14 years with a small price shift within the defined range. By the end of January of the following year, prices rose each time.

Rose (14)

Fell (0)

Trend to 31 January (next year) after a July price shift of -1.49% to +1.06% (since 1924)

If the July signal does flash, don't be too quick to sell before the end of next January. In 13 of the 14 years when the signal flashed, prices reached their high point in January.

Buried in this statistic is another interesting price signal to help you to maximise next year's January profits. In a roundabout way, the data is telling us that January prices rise 13 out of 14 times following a July shift of -1.49% to +1.06%.

AUGUST INVESTMENT MONITOR

	LAST MONTH FINAL PRICE	END OF 1ST QUARTER		END OF 2ND QUARTER		END OF 3RD QUARTER		END OF 4TH QUARTER	
		PRICE	PERCENT CHANGE	PRICE	PERCENT CHANGE	PRICE	PERCENT CHANGE	PRICE	PERCENT CHANGE
FT-ORDINARY (FT-30)									
FT-SE 100									
FT-SE 250									
FT-NON-FINANCIAL (FT-500)									
FT-SE-A ALL SHARES									
STANDARD & POORS COMPOSITE									
OTHER INDEX									
ENTER EACH SHARE, UNIT TRUST, ETC, BELOW									

CHAPTER TEN – AUGUST 1996

August is the third most profitable month for investors. Share prices rise +1.26% in the average year. It is not surprising that investors are advised: enjoy the August sun and miss the stock market fun.

Prices are especially likely to rise if shares have been rising strongly in the 12-month run-up to August. Prices often fall if the trend is weak during this period.

Another historical trend that does a good job of forecasting which way August prices will shift is the direction of prices on Wall Street in June and July.

The first quarter is the year's third-best and the other three are also good profit-makers. But don't linger – September storm clouds hit hard in some years.

The August price trend often tips where prices are heading in the five months to follow, that is, to the end of next January (see page 223).

The August ditty: 'Shares will climb during August holiday time' is alive and well. Summer slumps often end dramatically with the arrival of August. Just as investors depart to sunnier climes, the market begins to rise.

Price rise likely

Between 1919 and 1994, August prices rose 64% of the time. The average price rise was +1.26%, equal to 42 points on an FT-SE 100 in the area of 3300. Historically, August is the third-best month in which to invest in shares. A hypothetical investor who invested in August only, from 1919 to 1994, would have run up his £1,000 to £2,334.

1947 was an exception

The last losing decade for the August investor was the 1940s when prices dropped at an average annual rate of -0.32%. But under the surface, things looked pretty good even then. Prices rose in seven of the decade's 10 years. A -17.04% drop in 1947, in response to the sudden suspension of sterling's convertibility, caused all of that decade's losses. It was the worst-ever month for August investors and the fourth-worst in history.

Since then, the month has been consistently profitable. In the 1980s, prices rose in seven out of 10 years, with an average price rise of +2.40% per month, the decade's third-best performer *(see Table 10.1)*.

Unfortunately, the window of opportunity that the month provides is small. The month that follows, September, is one of the worst months of the year in which to own shares. So act quickly.

INCREASE YOUR PROFIT ODDS

Despite the good overall record, investors can make even more profit if they invest selectively.[1] There are several

---

[1] Reminder: All monthly calculations are based on the FT-Non-financial Index, formerly the FT-'500'; unless otherwise stated, they are based on data from 1919–1994. All daily, quarterly, and bi-monthly calculations are based on the Ordinary Share Index, also known as the FT-30; unless otherwise stated, they are based on data from 1936–1994.

Table 10.1

AUGUST PRICE RISES AND DECLINES: 1919–1994

	Average August price change	Up	Down/ no change
1920–29	1.59%	6	4
1930–39	-1.07%	4	6
1940–49	-0.32%	7	3
1950–59	3.12%	8	2
1960–69	2.13%	8	2
1970–79	1.46%	5	5
1980–89	2.40%	7	3
1990–94	0.53%	3	2
Average August price change	1.26%	49	27

Source: BZW and Datastream

Table 10.1: August is the year's third-best month. The last losing decade for the August investor was back in the 1940s. Since then it has been a profitable time period for investors. A great deal of volatility has occurred in the 1990s including a price decline of -8.05% in 1990 and increases of +6.28% in 1993 and +5.63% in 1994.

UPDATE

Wall Street signal

historic price trends that provide good insight into the expected direction of August's prices.

One that is sure to intrigue *Schwartz Stock Market Handbook* readers is the relationship between Wall Street and the UK stock market.

If US prices have fallen during June and July by -1.95% to -11.24%, the odds are especially good that UK prices will rise during August. Since 1928, there have been 18 occasions when Wall Street's Standard & Poors 500 Index fell within the defined range. In 16 of those years, UK prices rose.

The two exceptions were whoppers. In 1966, the UK stock market was wrong-footed by a set of July Measures which included increases in the Bank Rate, taxes, a £50 overseas travel allowance and a wage/price freeze. August prices fell -8.22%.

In 1974, prices fell -11.78% in the midst of our worst-ever bear market around the time that Tony Benn's White Paper set out plans to nationalise large segments of British industry.

Rose (16)

Fell (2)

August's record after a US June/July price drop of -1.95% to -11.24% (since 1928)

Previous-12-months signal No 1

As far as UK-only indicators are concerned, one of the best predictors of the August price trend is the direction of prices in the preceding 12 months.

Out of 13 years in which prices rose between +5.47% to +11.86% from 1 August to 30 July, August rose 12 times.

Rose (12)

UPDATE *Fell (0)*

Unchanged (1)

August's record after previous 12-month price rise of +5.47% to +11.86%

This indicator last flashed in 1994 when a +6.86% rise in the 12-month run-up to August was followed with a rise of +5.63% in August.

Previous-12-months signal No 2

Also look for price increases between +28.59% to +49.70% in the preceding 1 August to 30 July. There have been nine years with a price rise of this magnitude. August's prices rose each time.

Rose (9)

Fell (0)

August's record after previous 12-month price rise of +28.59%
to +49.70%

January/March
signal

Here is a new one for *Schwartz Stock Market Handbook*
readers. We can't explain why it works but consistently it
has been flagging August up-moves for most of this century.

If January prices rise by any amount, and March prices
rise by +2.92% or more, the odds of an August price rise are
quite good. January and March prices have shifted within
the appropriate ranges on 20 different occasions. August
prices rose in 18 of those years. In both exceptional years,
prices steadily fell in May, June and July.

Rose (18)

Fell (2)

August's record after a January price rise (any amount) and
March price rise of +2.92% or more

Previous-
12-month signal
No 3

Stock markets don't always rise, even in historically good
months. Here is a useful down-side indicator for August
which utilises the price trend over the past 12 months. Since
1919, there have been seven occasions when prices fell in the
preceding 12 months by -18.21% or more. August prices fell
in six of those years. The single exception was in 1940.

Rose (1)

Fell (6)

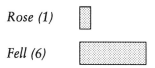

August's record after previous-12-month price drop of -18.21%
or more

209

FIRST QUARTER OF AUGUST – AUGUST 1ST TO 8TH

Here comes the third most profitable quarter of the year. Prices rise in seven out of ten years.

Shares are especially likely to increase in value following a moderate price rise in the second half of July. But a small decline in July's fourth quarter often signals that prices will continue to fall in this quarter.

Although August is a good month in which to invest, there are widely different profit potentials associated with investments made during different segments of the month.

Month's best quarter

The best segment is the first quarter. It has risen 68% of the time (third-best of the entire year) and produced an average annual profit in every single decade on record. Between 1935 and 1994, the average first-quarter profit was +0.96% per year, also the year's third-best *(see Table 10.2)*.

In the 1980s first-quarter profitability lagged behind the second quarter. Some analysts wonder if this was the start of a trend change. We think not. Much of the recent damage is due to 1987 when first-quarter prices fell -6.78% and 1990 with a decline of -5.20%. We shall, of course, continue to watch the situation closely.

Recent volatility

There is one distressing pattern worthy of note that affects all August quarters including this one. When prices do fall, the drop is often a large one. Since 1980, there were 21 quarterly drops in August (out of 60 quarters in total). Eleven were in excess of 2.5%. Unfortunately, we find no forecasting tool which systematically anticipates all or even most of these Big Hits.

1 and 8 August look good

Analysis of daily price swings finds very profitable trading conditions throughout the quarter. Five of the best trading days of the entire month land in this quarter. Recent conditions have been especially favourable on the 1st and

Table 10.2   **PERCENTAGE PRICE CHANGE: AUGUST 1935–1994**

	August 1–8	August 9–15	August 16–23	August 24–31
Average annual price change				
1935–39	0.63%	0.28%	-2.55%	0.37%
1940–49	0.99%	0.05%	-0.11%	0.29%
1950–59	0.74%	1.02%	0.14%	0.57%
1960–69	2.12%	0.82%	0.27%	-0.09%
1970–79	1.61%	0.38%	0.22%	-0.16%
1980–89	0.10%	1.39%	0.48%	0.20%
1990–94	-0.30%	0.17%	-1.14%	1.07%
Average quarterly price change	0.96%	0.65%	-0.14%	0.25%
Number of years in which prices:				
rose	41	37	33	35
fell	18	23	27	23
remained unchanged	1	–	–	2

Source: Datastream

Table 10.2: The first-quarter trend is very strong, the year's third-best. Recent weakness is due to large declines in 1987 and 1990. The third quarter looks to be a long-term loser, but has been steadily profitable in the 1950s to 1980s.

UPDATE

8th of the month. Since 1984, prices have risen seven times and fallen once on each of these days *(see Figure 10.1)*.

July second-half signal

INCREASE YOUR PROFIT ODDS

Happily, it is possible to pin-point years with above-average prospects. Since 1941, there have been 28 years when prices shifted in the second half of July by -0.61% to +5.42%. Prices rose in August's first quarter in 25 of those years.

Figure 10.1: **PERCENTAGE OF TIME PRICES RISE EACH TRADING DAY IN AUGUST'S FIRST QUARTER**

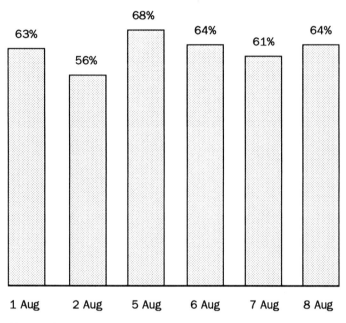

Figure 10.1: Prices often rise during this quarter of the month. The 5th is the best day of the entire month. Share prices have risen in seven of the last eight trading days on 1 and 8 August.

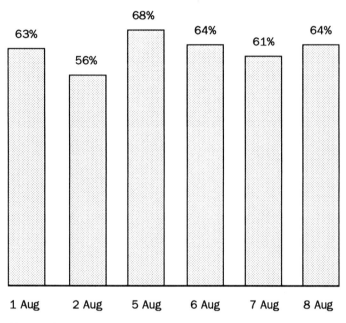

Rose (25)

Fell (3)

UPDATE

First-quarter record after a price shift of -0.61% to +5.42% in July's second half (since 1941)

This signal last flashed in 1994 and first quarter prices rose by +3.64%.

July fourth-
quarter signal
No 1

Another trend worth tracking is July's fourth quarter. There have been 27 years in which fourth-quarter prices shifted -0.18% to +2.64%. Prices rose in August's first quarter in 24 of those years (89%).

Rose (24)

Fell (3)

First-quarter record after a price shift of -0.18% to +2.64% in July's fourth quarter

July fourth-
quarter signal
No 2

A good down-side indicator is a small decline in July's fourth quarter. Prices fell by -0.24% to -1.23% on 10 occasions since 1938. First-quarter prices fell still further in nine of those years.

Rose (1)

Fell (9)

First-quarter record after a price fall of -0.24% to -1.23% in July's fourth quarter (since 1938)

SECOND QUARTER OF AUGUST – AUGUST 9TH TO 15TH

> There has been little down-side risk associated with holding shares during the second quarter in recent years. Although the record since 1985 is five up and five down, four of the five falls were under 1%. Three were less than one-tenth of 1%, equivalent to three points or less on a FT-SE 100 in the area of 3300.

Second-quarter prices rose 62% of the time between 1935 and 1994, slightly less often than the first quarter. Prices rose +0.65% on average, also less than the first quarter but still highly respectable.

Recent
improvement

The trend has improved since 1980. A consistent second-quarter investor received an average annual quarterly profit of +1.39% during that decade *(see Table 10.3)*.

Analysis of price trends on a day-by-day basis reveals that first quarter strength often continues through the first two trading days of the second quarter.

9 and 14 August
look good

The odds of a price rise on 9 August are even better than usual in 1996. History shows that the odds of a price rise are 76% when 5–10 August land on a Friday versus 55% when they land on a Monday to Thursday. 9 August lands on a Friday in 1996.

The recent record for August 14 has improved. Since 1984, prices rose seven times and fell just once *(see Figure 10.2)*.

INCREASE YOUR PROFIT ODDS

July fourth-
quarter/August
first-quarter
signal

As if these results aren't good enough, the market sends several useful signals that help second-quarter investors obtain even better returns.

If July's fourth quarter is weak and August's first quarter strong, second quarter prices will probably rise. Here is the evidence.

214

Table 10.3

PERCENTAGE PRICE CHANGE: 1985–1994

	August 1–8	August 9–15	August 16–23	August 24–31
Annual quarterly price change				
1985	1.58%	1.95%	1.51%	2.27%
1986	-4.29%	4.40%	0.02%	3.20%
1987	-6.78%	3.38%	-3.25%	1.89%
1988	1.75%	-3.24%	0.03%	-3.87%
1989	2.63%	-0.74%	1.44%	0.09%
1990	-5.20%	-0.02%	-8.24%	5.57%
1991	1.00%	0.92%	1.31%	0.48%
1992	-2.80%	0.03%	0.09%	-4.26%
1993	1.87%	-0.01%	0.54%	1.72%
1994	3.64%	-0.09%	0.60%	1.82%
Average quarterly price change				
1985–1994	-0.66%	0.66%	-0.60%	0.89%
Number of years in which prices:				
rose	6	5	8	8
fell	4	5	2	2

Source: Datastream

Table 10.3: The recent second-quarter price trend is looking good. Three of the five recent second-quarter declines fell less than one-tenth of 1%. But when things go wrong in August, they sometimes go wrong in a big way. Nine of the 13 down-quarters since 1985 fell in excess of 2.5% (over 82 points on an FT-SE 100 in the area of 3300).

UPDATE

There have been 16 years when the fourth quarter shifted within a range of -7.45% to +0.17% and the first quarter rose by up to +4.29%. Prices rose in the second quarter in 14 of those years. The two losses were near misses, a decline of -0.22% in 1963 and -0.09% in 1994.

Figure 10.2   **PERCENTAGE OF TIME PRICES RISE EACH TRADING DAY IN AUGUST'S SECOND QUARTER**

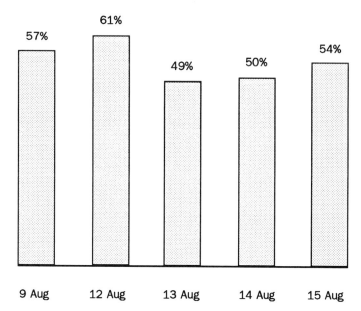

Figure 10.2: First-quarter strength often continues into the second quarter. 9 August frequently rises when it lands on a Friday. 14 August has been especially strong since 1984 with a record of seven up and one down

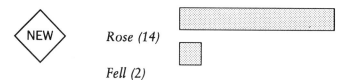

NEW

Rose (14)

Fell (2)

Second-quarter record after a price shift in July's fourth quarter of -7.45% to +0.17% and rise in August's first quarter of up to +4.29%

July second-
half/August first-
quarter signal
No 1

Another useful signal is contained in the price trend during July's second half and August's first quarter. If shares steadily shift in the same direction through both periods, the second quarter will probably rise.

Since 1949, there have been 12 years in which prices rose in July's second half and August's first quarter. The price rise continued through August's second quarter in 10 of those years (83%). One of the two exceptions occurred in 1993 when second-quarter prices fell by a minuscule -0.01% after a steady price rise in the two preceding periods.

Rose (12)

Fell (2)

Second-quarter record after a price rise in July's second half
and August's first quarter (since 1949)

July second-half/
August first-
quarter signal
No 2

There were 11 other years since 1957 in which prices fell in July's second half and August's first quarter. Prices bounced back with an increase in August's second quarter in nine of those years. And one of the exceptions to the rule, in 1990, saw a second-quarter drop of just -0.02%.

Rose (9)

Fell (2)

Second-quarter record after a price fall in July's second half
and August's first quarter (since 1957)

Also since 1957, there were 17 years when prices did not steadily rise or steadily fall in the second half of July and the first quarter of August. The second-quarter record was seven up and 10 down.

Third Quarter of August – August 16th to 23rd

> Here comes another profitable August segment. Prices are especially likely to rise if they fell in the second quarter.

A hidden message

Over the 60 year period studied, the third quarter averaged a -0.14% loss each year.

But a closer look at the raw data tells a different story. There were big losses in the last half of the 1930s when share prices fell five years in a row, and in 1990 when the average share dropped -8.24%. In the intervening period, the results weren't all that bad – price rises in most years and average annual profits during the 1950s, '60s, '70s and '80s. In the most recent 10 years, from 1985 to 1994, prices rose eight times, one of the year's best quarterly records.

Analysis of daily price swings finds that prices are weakest on the first two days of the quarter *(see Figure 10.3)*.

23 August looks good

23 August often rises when it lands on a Friday, a good sign for 1996. Between 1935 to the present day, 22–23 August landed on a Friday 17 times and produced a record of 13 up (76%) and four down. On the remaining days of the week, 22–23 August rise just 47% of the time.

Increase your profit odds

Prior-two-quarter signal

Since 1967, a potentially profit-making statistical relationship has emerged. During this period, there have been 11 years when prices dropped in August's second quarter. They bounced back with a third-quarter increase in ten of these years. The average annual increase was +0.73%. And this average was pulled down quite substantially by the sole exception to the rule, the -8.24% decline of 1990. In the recent past, the second-quarter signal flashed in 1993 and in 1994 and prices rose both times, right on cue.

Figure 10.3

PERCENTAGE OF TIME PRICES RISE EACH TRADING DAY IN AUGUST'S THIRD QUARTER

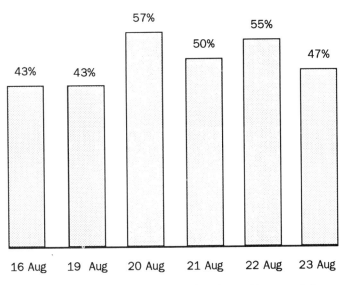

Figure 10.3: The quarter starts and ends weakly, especially 19 August, the worst day of the month. But the trend improves during the middle of the quarter. 23 August lands on a Friday in 1996, increasing the odds of a price rise.

UPDATE

Rose (10)

Fell (1)

Third-quarter record after a price drop in August's second quarter (since 1967)

UPDATE

A new trend is in the process of developing. Since 1980, prices shifted in the first half of August within a range of -2.77% to +1.93%, on eight occasions. Third-quarter prices rose each time. In the remaining seven years, third-quarter prices fell five times.

219

FOURTH QUARTER OF AUGUST – AUGUST 24TH TO 31ST

> The odds of making money in this segment of August are high. But be quick. Money-losing September is right around the corner.
>
> A consistent price move in the run-up to this quarter (up or down), often signals impending price increases.

Recent trend looks good

Prices rise 58% of the time during the fourth quarter of August. The average annual gain is +0.25%. The recent trend remains strong. Between 1985 and 1994, the fourth-quarter record is eight up and two down, like the third quarter, one of the year's best quarterly records.

27 August: be careful

Analysis of daily price shifts shows a generally strong pattern of profitable days. 27 August is a notable exception. Prices rise 44% of the time. Worse still, they have never risen on a Tuesday out of nine tries and 27 August lands on a Tuesday in 1996 *(see Figure 10.4)*.

No long-term investment

If you are contemplating a purchase to take advantage of a good trading environment, be careful. Don't make any long-term investments. The impending arrival of risky September trading conditions means that, in some years, investors should begin closing out their open positions at the end of this quarter or during September's first quarter.

INCREASE YOUR PROFIT ODDS

Prior-three-quarters signal No 1

If you do decide to make a purchase in the fourth quarter, the best time to do it is if prices have risen steadily or fallen steadily in the preceding periods. There have been ten occasions since 1952 when prices rose in the first half of August by up to +3.56% and the third quarter. Fourth-quarter prices rose in eight of them.

Figure 10.4   **PERCENTAGE OF TIME PRICES RISE EACH TRADING DAY IN AUGUST'S FOURTH QUARTER**

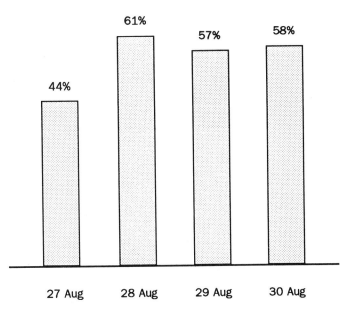

Figure 10.4: Prices rise throughout the quarter, except for 27 August.

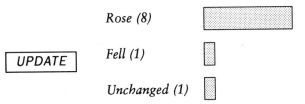

Rose (8)

Fell (1)

Unchanged (1)

Fourth-quarter record after a price rise in August's first half by up to +3.56% and a rise in the third quarter (since 1952)

This signal last flashed in 1994 with a first half rise of +3.55%, just within the range. Fourth-quarter prices followed with a rise of +1.82%.

221

Prior-three-quarters signal No 2

Likewise, if prices fall in the first half and the third quarter, the odds favour a fourth-quarter rise. There have been 11 occasions on record since 1939 where a decline occurred in the first half and third quarter. Fourth-quarter prices rose nine times.

Rose (9)

Fell (1)

Unchanged (1)

Fourth-quarter record after a price decline in August's first half and third quarter (since 1939)

Since 1952, there have been 27 years untouched by a steady up or down move in the first half and third quarter. The fourth quarter record was disappointing, 11 up and 16 down.

Third-quarter signal

Here is one final signal to help you to increase the odds of a fourth quarter profit. If third quarter prices rise by +0.81% to +1.53%, the fourth quarter is likely to rise, regardless of what happened nearer the beginning of the month. Here is the evidence to date. There have been 13 occasions with a third-quarter rise within the designated range. Fourth-quarter prices rose in 11 of those years. The signal last flashed in 1994 and fourth quarter prices rose as expected.

Rose (11)

Fell (2)

Fourth-quarter record after a third-quarter price rise of +0.81% to +1.53%

LOOKING AHEAD

Here are two price signals that do a good job of forecasting where prices are headed in the months ahead.

Rising prices by 31 December

If prices have risen in the first seven months of the year (to 31 July), and rise still further in August by +4.30% or more, there is a very good chance they will continue to rise by year-end.

There have been 15 years on record with price increases within these parameters. Shares rose still higher in 14 of those years. The sole exception was in 1981 when prices suddenly dropped by -16.94% in September in response to a sudden drop on Wall Street. But even here, the loss on 31 December was under 5%, a recovery of 12% during the last three months of the year.

Rose (14)

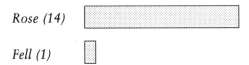

Fell (1)

Trend to 31 December after a January–July price rise and an August price rise of +4.30% or more

Rising prices by next 31 January

An August price rise of +3.57% to +10.44% is a clear signal that prices will rise even higher in the next five months, that is, to the end of January.

Out of 24 times with a price shift within this range, prices rose in the next five months 23 times. The single exception was in 1929.

Rose (23)

Fell (1)

Trend to 31 January (next year) after an August price rise of +3.57% to +10.44%

223

SEPTEMBER INVESTMENT MONITOR

	LAST MONTH FINAL PRICE	END OF 1ST QUARTER		END OF 2ND QUARTER		END OF 3RD QUARTER		END OF 4TH QUARTER	
		PRICE	PERCENT CHANGE	PRICE	PERCENT CHANGE	PRICE	PERCENT CHANGE	PRICE	PERCENT CHANGE
FT-ORDINARY (FT-30)									
FT-SE 100									
FT-SE 250									
FT-NON-FINANCIAL (FT-500)									
FT-SE-A ALL SHARES									
STANDARD & POORS COMPOSITE									
OTHER INDEX									
ENTER EACH SHARE, UNIT TRUST, ETC, BELOW									

CHAPTER ELEVEN – SEPTEMBER 1996

September investments are money-losing propositions. A £1,000 investment in 1919, placed in shares every September and in cash for the rest of each year, would have shrunk to £757 by 1994.

Sad to say, that's the good news. The bad news is we forecast that September's record will get worse.

The source of the problem is Wall Street. September is the worst month of the year on Wall Street and the US stock market is exerting an increasingly large influence over the UK market with each passing year. Since 1985, September prices fell in eight out of 10 years in the US and UK prices fell in unison in seven of those years.

But not all the news is bleak. Profits are good in the first quarter of each month. When troubles do occur, they often cluster in the second-to-fourth segments of the month.

Despite the red ink, you can profit by following key price signals. For example, poor Septembers frequently have been tipped in advance by poor Januarys. Another danger signal to watch for is a small price shift in May–August. There also are some signals associated with rising prices as well. See page 228 for further details.

Looking ahead, the September trend has become an excellent tool with which to forecast the odds of profiting in October–December, and in the 12 months ahead.

Prices rose in July/August, 1994 by 11%, one of the best summer rallies in history, only to sharply fall in September by over 7%. Sadly, it was a typical September performance.

Tenth-ranked

September has not been a good month in which to own shares in the long-run. It is ranked a lowly tenth on monthly investment potential. Only May and June are worse. Between 1919 and 1994, September prices fell at a yearly average of -0.24%, equal to seven points on a 3300 FT-SE 100 *(see Table 11.1)*.

Future looks bleak

Even worse, there is a good chance that the future September record will weaken further. The source of the problem is the close relationship between US and UK stock market price trends.

While all western economies are growing increasingly dependent upon each other, the problem for UK stock market investors is especially significant if it is the US economy that is rocking the boat. Because of its sheer size, when things go well in America, many large UK companies with extensive US holdings do well. (FT-SE 100 companies gain about 25% of their profits from the US.) When US economic conditions are poor, it affects our profits as well.

A second issue: until recently, US investors were very domestically focused. Compared with Europeans, they allocated a very small percentage of their stock market investments to non-US companies. This practice is starting to change which means that US domestic issues, political as well as economic, will have a growing effect on the UK stock market.

London follows Wall Street

As far as September is concerned, an increasingly close relationship is worrisome because September is Wall Street's worst month. Since 1974, Wall Street had four Big Hits in September. UK prices fell by over 5% each time. Since 1985, Wall Street fell eight times in September. UK prices fell in seven of those years.

Big Hits also a problem

Putting aside the influence of Wall Street for the moment, the UK's September price trend shares an important charac-

Table 11.1

SEPTEMBER PRICE RISES AND DECLINES: 1919–1994

	Average September price change	Up	Down/ no change
1920–29	-1.01%	3	7
1930–39	-0.37%	6	4
1940–49	1.26%	8	2
1950–59	-0.08%	5	5
1960–69	0.87%	5	5
1970–79	-0.83%	6	4
1980–89	-1.01%	5	5
1990–94	-1.80%	1	4
Average September price change	-0.24%	40	36

UPDATE

Source: BZW and Datastream

Table 11.1: Each decade from 1930–1989, prices rose at least half the time. September's problem was occasional Big Hits which ruined its record for the entire decade. But in recent years, September has been heavily affected by a poor Wall Street record.

teristic with May and June. In the past, the month was often good to investors. But every so often, it got slammed by the markets. The 'hit' was so severe that it hurt the average performance of the entire decade.

Take the 1930s as an example: the average share price dropped during this decade because of 1939 when prices fell by -12.13%. In that month, the market was buffeted by the declaration of war, news that Germany and Russia invaded Poland, the loss of 20 allied ships to U-boats and a War Budget which raised income tax to its highest-ever figure. The record for the rest of the decade was six up and three down, and an average annual increase of +0.94%.

The 1940s had no out-of-the-ordinary monthly decline. The September record was eight up and two down, and an average increase of +1.26%. The 1950s losing performance of -0.08% per year was caused by 1957's decline of -9.08%. The decline was in response to an increase in base rates to counter inflation. The rest of the decade saw five ups and four downs and an average increase of +0.92%.

The 1960s saw five up months, five down months, no unusual price action, and an average monthly price increase of +0.87%. The poor results of the 1970s were affected by 1972 (down -11.01%) and 1974 (down -12.35%). Inflation dominated September's economic news in both years. Here is one September 1974 headline: 'UK nurses get raises of up to 58%'. The rest of the decade saw six ups and two downs, and an average increase of +1.88%.

And in the last complete decade, the bull market 1980s, poor results were due to a -16.94% decline in 1981. The record for the rest of the decade was five ups, four downs and an average increase of +0.74%.

Poor prospects ahead

Based upon all available facts, our working hypothesis is that the September price trend will get worse. You may profit in any single year but over the long-run, profitable months will be in the small minority. Note, however, that conditions are not uniform throughout the month. The first quarter has been quite profitable in most years. The problems, when they occur, tend to cluster in the second, third, and fourth quarters.

INCREASE YOUR PROFIT ODDS

If you can't predict when a surprise event will occur, or when markets suddenly decide to take fright of events that have been unfolding over a long period of time, be warned that sudden, often unexpected, September price declines can wipe out years' worth of accumulated September profits. But if you can figure out how to avoid the bad years, or at least some of them, there's money to be made in this month. Fortunately, there are a number of ways.

May–August signal

Here is a newly discovered trend that has done a good job of tipping off losing Septembers.[1] Since 1952, there have been nine occasions when prices shifted within a range of -0.86% to +2.89% in the last four months, May to August. September prices fell in each of those years. It flashed in 1994 and September prices fell by -7.38%.

Rose (0)

Fell (9)

September's record after a May–August price shift of -0.86% to +2.89% (since 1952)

January signal

Another winning strategy: hold no shares (or move into Puts) in years when January share prices drop. We have refined the strategy a bit since last year. Here is an up-to-date version of it. Since 1937, there were 14 years when January prices dropped by up to -7.57%. In 12 of those years, September prices also dropped (86%). The average September price decline during these 14 years was -4.69%, equal to 155 points on an FT-SE 100 in the area of 3300. And one of the two exceptions was a mere +0.20% increase in 1978. The last time the January Signal flashed was in 1993. September prices fell -2.59%, right in the middle of a very strong bull market run.

Rose (2)

Fell (12)

September's record after a January fall of up to -7.57% (since 1937)

---

[1]Reminder: All monthly calculations are based on the FT-Non-financial Index, formerly the FT-'500'; unless otherwise stated, they are based on data from 1919–1994. All daily, quarterly, and bi-monthly calculations are based on the Ordinary Share Index, also known as the FT-30; unless otherwise stated, they are based on data from 1936–1994.

Historical trend analysis reveals several other trends that have done a good job of anticipating the direction of September price shifts.

Previous-
12-months
signal

If prices have fallen between -11.79% to -32.01% in the past twelve months, and the preceding three-month trend (June to August) is negative, September prices will probably rise. Out of 11 years which followed this scenario, September prices fell just once. This signal last flashed in 1992. After a -16.19% drop in the three months ending 31 August, September prices shot up by +9.01%, in response to our withdrawal from the ERM.

Rose (10)

Fell (1)

IMPROVEMENT

September's record after previous 12-month fall of -11.79% to -32.01% and a three-month fall

January signal

If the preceding six-month trend has risen within a range of +15.04% to +24.67%, September prices will probably rise. Out of 11 years with a price rise of this magnitude in the run-up to September, September prices rose 10 times. The average increase during these 11 years was +2.42%, equal to 80 points on a 3300 FT-SE 100.

Rose (10)

Fell (1)

September's record after previous six month rise of +15.04% to +24.67%

230

FIRST QUARTER OF SEPTEMBER – SEPTEMBER 1ST TO 8TH

> The first quarter tends to be profitable in most years, despite the poor prospects for the month as a whole.
>
> Small shifts in August's final quarter are often associated with a price rise at the beginning of September.

First quarter profitable

Although the month of September can be painful to investors, its first quarter is a consistent money-maker. Prices have risen in each of the five full decades on record. The average rate of increase is +0.32% per year. Prices rise in 60% of all Septembers *(see Table 11.2)*.

6 September looks good

Analysis of price trends on a day-by-day basis reveals a pattern of strength on most days of the quarter. The odds of a price rise on 6 September are higher than usual in 1996. Since 1935, 6–7 September rose 71% of the time if either date landed on a Friday versus just 48% if either landed on a Monday to Thursday. 6 September lands on a Friday in 1996 *(see Figure 11.1)*.

INCREASE YOUR PROFIT ODDS

August signal

The direction of first-quarter prices is frequently tipped off by the August price trend. Since 1957, a shift of -4.74% to +4.69% in August is often followed by a price increase in September's first quarter. Out of 21 years with an August shift within this range, September's first quarter rose 19 times and generated an average profit of +1.27% per year. This signal last flashed in 1992 when first-quarter prices rose +1.79% after an August drop of -3.77%.

Table 11.2   **PERCENTAGE PRICE CHANGE: SEPTEMBER 1935–1994**

	September 1–8	September 9–15	September 16–23	September 24–30
Average annual price change				
1935–39	-0.16%	-2.63%	-1.54%	0.67%
1940–49	0.11%	0.48%	0.12%	-0.08%
1950–59	0.06%	0.15%	-0.58%	-0.09%
1960–69	1.09%	-0.38%	0.50%	-0.77%
1970–79	0.87%	0.00%	-0.89%	-1.53%
1980–89	0.43%	-0.94%	-0.50%	-0.93%
1990–94	-1.14%	-1.09%	-0.08%	-0.33%
Average quarterly price change	0.32%	-0.42%	-0.36%	-0.54%
Number of years in which prices:				
rose	36	24	29	27
fell	24	36	31	33

Source: Datastream

Table 11.2: The first-quarter investor made money in every full decade since the 1940s. The second- to fourth-quarter investor has been a steady money-loser in recent decades, including the bull market 1980s.

Rose (19)

Fell (2)

First-quarter record after an August shift of -4.74% to +4.81% (since 1957)

Above +4.69% in August and the prospects for September's first quarter decidedly weaken, with the odds of a loss higher than 50:50.

Figure 11.1   **PERCENTAGE OF TIME PRICES RISE EACH TRADING DAY IN SEPTEMBER'S FIRST QUARTER**

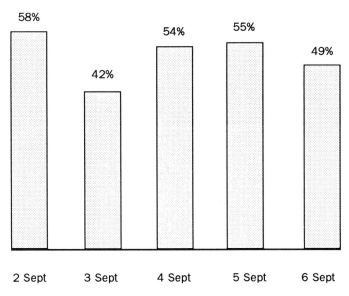

| | 2 Sept | 3 Sept | 4 Sept | 5 Sept | 6 Sept |

Figure 11.2: Prices rise on most days in the first quarter. The odds of a price rise on Friday 6 September is higher than average in 1996.

August fourth-quarter signal

Since 1960, if prices shift in the fourth quarter of August within a range of -0.66% to +1.19%, shares usually rise in value during September's first quarter. Out of 14 years with a shift within the defined range, first-quarter prices rose 12 times.

Rose (12)

Fell (2)

First-quarter record after an August fourth-quarter shift of -0.66% to +1.19% (since 1960)

233

SECOND QUARTER OF SEPTEMBER – SEPTEMBER 9TH TO 15TH

Here comes the start of three consecutive quarters with very high odds of falling prices.

The likelihood of a price drop is especially good if shares have been weak in September's first quarter or August's fourth quarter.

As a general rule, think twice before buying any shares in the second quarter of September. Not only are the odds of making a profit against you, but the third and fourth quarters of the month are also generally money-losers. If you are thinking of selling shares you already own, the odds favour doing it at the beginning of the quarter.

Recent record remains poor

The average share price drops -0.42% each year during this quarter. Prices have risen in just 24 of the last 60 years (40%). Even during the 1980s' bull market decade, the record was four up, six down and an average decrease of -0.94%. Thus far into the 1990s, prices have fallen in four out of five years *(see Table 11.3)*.

6 September look out

Analysis of daily price trends confirms this general pattern of weakness *(see Figure 11.2)*. You should be especially cautious on 9 September because shares often fall when the second Monday of September lands on the 9th–11th. Since 1935, second Monday prices rose just six out of 19 times (32%). In 1996, the 9th lands on a Monday.

INCREASE YOUR PROFIT ODDS

The only way to make money consistently in the second quarter is to bet against the market. To help you improve the odds of identifying periods when prices will decline, the market sends several useful signals.

Table 11.3 **PERCENTAGE PRICE CHANGE: 1985–1994**

	September 1–8	September 9–15	September 16–23	September 24–30
Annual quarterly price change				
1985	0.68%	-0.87%	-1.64%	0.41%
1986	0.90%	-2.58%	-1.37%	-3.53%
1987	0.88%	0.01%	3.82%	0.57%
1988	-0.50%	1.40%	1.74%	2.05%
1989	1.32%	-2.70%	-0.01%	-3.27%
1990	-3.25%	-1.76%	-4.49%	-0.10%
1991	0.69%	-1.23%	-2.48%	0.25%
1992	1.79%	0.88%	10.20%	-2.17%
1993	-1.72%	-2.17%	-0.38%	0.26%
1994	-3.18%	-1.15%	-3.26%	0.12%
Average quarterly price change				
1985–1994	-0.24%	-1.02%	0.21%	-0.54%
Number of years in which prices:				
rose	6	3	3	6
fell	4	7	7	4

Source: Datastream

Table 11.3: In the last 10 years, the second to fourth quarters of September have performed especially poorly. The third-quarter average would have been in negative territory had it not been for 1992's whopping +10.20% rise in prices in response to our withdrawal from the ERM.

January signal

One of them is the January rule which does such a good job of anticipating September's monthly declines. If you are toying with the idea of buying Puts, your short-term profit potential will improve if you buy them in years that January's prices declined by up to -7.57%. Out of 15 years in which January prices declined by up to -7.57%,

Figure 11.2   **PERCENTAGE OF TIME PRICES RISE EACH TRADING DAY IN SEPTEMBER'S SECOND QUARTER**

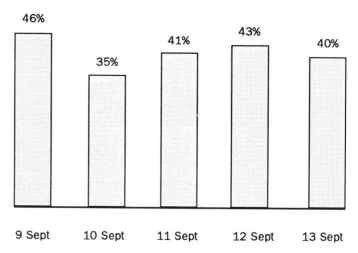

Figure 11.2: Trading conditions are poor throughout the quarter. Prices are especially likely to fall when 9 September lands on a Monday, as will happen in 1996.

September second-quarter prices fell 13 times (87%). The average price loss was -1.25%.

Rose (2)

Fell (13)

Second-quarter record after a January fall of up to -7.57%

This signal last flashed in 1993 and second quarter prices fell by -1.15%, right on cue.

First-quarter signal

In the short-run, if prices fall in the first quarter by -1.35% or more, the chances are good they will continue to fall in the second quarter as well. Out of 11 occasions that prices fell by a large enough amount, second-quarter prices fell 10 times.

NEW

Rose (1)

Fell (10)

Second-quarter record after a first quarter fall of -1.35% or more

The signal last flashed in 1994 when a first quarter decline of -3.18% was followed by a second quarter drop of -1.15%.

August fourth-quarter/ September first-quarter signal

A third signal which improves your odds of profiting on the down-side is the direction of prices in the preceding few quarters. If they shift in the fourth quarter of August by -2.29% to +0.52% and rise in the first quarter of September, the odds are especially good they will fall in the second quarter. Out of 12 occasions since 1957 when the price of the average share shifted in the preceding periods within the appropriate range, second-quarter prices declined 11 times (92%). The average quarterly decline during those 12 years was -1.47%.

Rose (1)

Fell (11)

Second-quarter record after an August fourth-quarter shift of -2.29% to +0.52% and September first-quarter rise (since 1957)

Third Quarter of September – September 16th to 23rd

> You may or may not make money in any single third quarter but over the long-run, you will be a loser by steadily investing at this point in the year.
>
> Watch the price trend during the first half of September. It often tips which way third-quarter prices will shift.

As in the second quarter, investors usually lose money by investing during the third quarter. Between 1935 and 1994, the third quarter of September rose 48% of the time and generated an average loss of -0.36% per year.

Recent trend is poor

A review of recent price trends reveals that the average share price fell in both the 1970s and '80s. So far in the '90s, prices have declined in four out of five years. But the single exception, a +10.20% increase in prices in 1992 in response to Britain's withdrawal from the ERM, will exert a strong influence on this decade's average performance and disguise the period's poor results among lazy investors who merely look at the overall average.

Be cautious on 16 and 23 September

The daily price trend confirms this poor record of overall performance. Prices rise just 34% of the time on 16 September, the 10th-worst day of the year, and 30% of the time on 23 September, the year's fourth-worst day *(see Figure 11.3)*.

Increase your profit odds

January signal

If you wish to bet on the down-side, here are two signals to increase your chance of success. Since 1952, a January decline of up to -7.57% correlates with a poor third-quarter performance. Third-quarter prices declined in nine of 11 years in which January prices fell by this amount. The average decline was -2.24%.

Figure 11.3   **PERCENTAGE OF TIME PRICES RISE EACH TRADING DAY IN SEPTEMBER'S THIRD QUARTER**

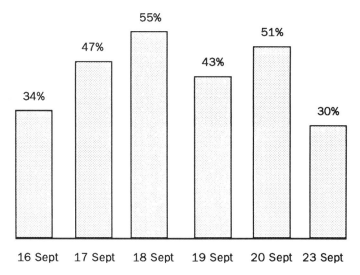

Figure 11.3: Be careful. Two of the year's 10 worst days land in this quarter. The 19th and 20th are among the most volatile days of the month with an above-average likelihood of price shifts (up or down) in excess of 1%.

Rose (2)

Fell (9)

Third-quarter record after a January decline of up to -7.57% (since 1952)

First-half signal No 1

A second useful signal is the direction of prices in the first half of September. If they fall in both the first and second quarter, with a second-quarter decline of no more than -3.08%, the odds of a third-quarter decline increase. Since 1946, there have been 13 occasions when first-half prices fell within the designated range. In 11 of those years, the fall continued into the third-quarter.

239

UPDATE

Rose (2)

Fell (11)

Third-quarter record after a first-quarter fall (any amount) and second-quarter fall of up to -3.08% (since 1942)

This signal last flashed in 1994. Prices fell in both the first and second quarters and, on cue, so did the third quarter by a whopping -3.26%.

First-half signal No 2

On the up-side, if the first-half price trend rises, the odds favour a third-quarter rise as well. Since 1958, share prices rose +0.61% to +3.45% in the first half in 11 different years. Third-quarter prices rose each time.

Rose (11)

Fell (0)

Third-quarter record after a first-half price rise of +0.61% to +3.45% (since 1958)

Second-quarter signal

A related measure pertains to the second quarter alone. If second-quarter prices rise by no more than +1.40%, the odds are good that third-quarter prices will also rise. Since 1942, there have been 14 second-quarter rises within this range. Third-quarter prices rose in 13 of those years. The sole exception was back in 1954.

NEW

Rose (13)

Fell (1)

Third-quarter record after a second-quarter price rise of up to +1.40% (since 1942)

FOURTH QUARTER OF SEPTEMBER – SEPTEMBER 24TH TO 30TH

> The fourth quarter is horrid to investors, third-worst of the year.
> Declining prices in the run-up to this quarter often signal that further declines are on the way.

Year's third-worst

The fourth quarter of September offers very poor investment potential. It is the third-worst quarter of the entire year. Investors lose -0.54%, on average, each year they invest in this quarter.

26 September: watch out

Between 1935 and 1994, prices rose in the fourth quarter only 45% of the time. Investors lost money in every single decade on record. 26 September is the worst trading day of the entire year. Prices rise just 21% of the time on this date *(see Figure 11.4 & Table 11.4)*. The recent trend shows no sign of improvement. Since 1984, 26 September has risen once in eight attempts. 24 September is another day to watch: although prices rise half the time over the long-run, the record since 1984 has slipped badly to one up and seven down.

Table 11.4   **THE TEN WORST DAYS OF THE YEAR**

	Percent of time prices rise
September 26	21%
October 9	26%
February 21	29%
September 23	30%
November 22	30%
February 4	33%
March 11	33%
October 10	33%
February 12	34%
September 16	34%

UPDATE

Table 11.4: September and February each have three entries in the year's 10 worst days

INCREASE YOUR PROFIT ODDS

For down-side investors, we find three correlations that are associated with an increased likelihood of a fourth-quarter fall.

January signal

Once again, January prices strongly correlate with a poor September performance. Prices in the fourth quarter declined in 10 of the 11 years in which January prices fell by -1.23% to -7.57%. The average decline was -1.68%.

Rose (1)

Fell (10)

Fourth-quarter record after a January decline of -1.23% to -7.57%

Third-quarter signal

Since 1941, a small third-quarter price decline has often tipped further declines in the fourth quarter. Out of 13 third-quarter drops no greater than -1.37%, fourth-quarter prices fell 10 times.

Rose (3)

Fell (10)

Fourth-quarter record after a third quarter decline of up to -1.37% (since 1941)

The signal issued a false warning in 1993 when a small third-quarter decline was followed by a small rise in the fourth quarter.

Three-prior quarters signal

If prices fall in September's first, second and third quarters, they are especially likely to fall in the fourth quarter. Since 1935, there have been 12 years in which prices fell in each of the three preceding quarters. They fell in the fourth quarter in nine of those years. The signal failed twice in a row in recent years. 1993 saw a price rise of just

Figure 11.4

PERCENTAGE OF TIME PRICES RISE EACH TRADING DAY IN SEPTEMBER'S FOURTH QUARTER

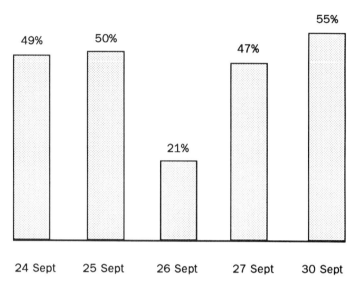

49%	50%	21%	47%	55%
24 Sept	25 Sept	26 Sept	27 Sept	30 Sept

Figure 11.4: The 26th is the worst day of the entire year. The 25th and 27th tend to be very volatile with an above-average likelihood of big (1% or more) price swings. Since 1984, the record for the 24th is one up and seven down.

+0.26% after three consecutive quarterly declines. 1994 saw an even smaller rise of +0.12% after three consecutive falls. Despite the two recent failures, we continue to track this signal. Our reason? Even when it fails, the cost of being wrong is quite small.

UPDATE

Rose (3)

Fell (9)

Fourth-quarter record after prices drop in all three September quarters

Looking ahead

So much for the past. What of the future? One important clue is provided by the August/September price trend. Although it is not widely known, the direction that share prices move in this two-month stretch is an important tool with which to forecast the direction of share prices in the year ahead.

Rising prices by next 30 September

Since 1919, there have been 18 years with price shifts of -14% to +14% in the 12 months ending 31 July and a price rise of +3.86% or more between 1 August to 30 September. In 16 of those years, prices rose still further in the 12 months that followed. The average increase was almost 20%.

One of the two exceptions was the 1965 signal. Prices rose as expected in the next nine months through June 1966. The trend suddenly changed in July in response to Labour's surprise 'July Measures' which increased the Bank Rate to 7%, and added new hire-purchase restrictions, indirect taxes, an overseas travel allowance of £50 and price controls.

Rose (16)

Fell (2)

Trend to 30 September (next year) after a -14% to +14% price shift in the 12 months ending July 31 *and* an August/ September price rise of +3.86% or more

If August/September prices either rise by less than +3.86% or fall, it is strictly a 50:50 gamble that prices will rise in the year ahead, as far as this indicator is concerned.

Rising prices by 31 December

September also serves as an excellent contrarian predictor of fourth-quarter price trends. Since 1959, a price drop in September is usually followed with price increases in the final three months of the year.

Let's start by putting things into perspective. From 1959

to 1994, fourth-quarter prices rose 72% of the time. Share prices increased at an average of +2.73% per year.

During this period, there were 16 years when September prices fell by -0.67% or more. Shares rose in the next three months in 15 of those years (94%) at an average rate of +7.08%. The sole exception occurred in 1974 at the tail end of a vicious two-year-long bear market when prices fell in October to December by -13.07% after a September drop of -12.35%.

Rose (15)

Fell (1)

October to December trend after a September decline of at least -0.67% (since 1959)

The signal last flashed in 1994 when a painful September decline of -7.38% was followed by a small up-move in the year's final three months.

During the other 20 years of this period, when September prices either fell slightly or rose by any amount, the record for the last three months of the year was 11 up and nine down, with an average loss of -0.75%.

OCTOBER INVESTMENT MONITOR

	LAST MONTH	END OF 1ST QUARTER		END OF 2ND QUARTER		END OF 3RD QUARTER		END OF 4TH QUARTER	
	FINAL PRICE	PRICE	PERCENT CHANGE	PRICE	PERCENT CHANGE	PRICE	PERCENT CHANGE	PRICE	PERCENT CHANGE
FT-ORDINARY (FT-30)									
FT-SE 100									
FT-SE 250									
FT-NON-FINANCIAL (FT-500)									
FT-SE-A- ALL SHARES									
STANDARD & POORS COMPOSITE									
OTHER INDEX									
ENTER EACH SHARE, UNIT TRUST, ETC, BELOW									

CHAPTER TWELVE – OCTOBER 1996

Forget the rhyme: 'Bull market bashes end with October crashes.' October is profitable over the long-run.

History provides a number of clues to help investors to anticipate which way prices will shift this October. One interesting signal involves the relationship between July, the start of the third quarter, with October, the start of the fourth quarter. The ebbs and flows of August and September also frequently tip which way October prices will shift.

If you decide to purchase shares in October, history suggests that you act early since profits are often generated in the first quarter of the month. And be very cautious at the end of the month. Prices are especially likely to fall in the fourth quarter. Its record over the past 20 years is six up and 14 down, the year's worst performance.

Looking ahead, a small shift, up or down, in September and October is a good sign that prices will rise by March of next year (see page 269).

Mention October to the average investor and the losses of 1929 and 1987 immediately come to mind.

Profitable despite its reputation

Despite the negative connotation, October investors do pretty well over the long-run. Between 1919, when modern record-keeping first began, and 1994, October prices rose 62% of the time *(see Table 12.1)*.

October investors lost a small amount of money in the 1920s. The source of the problem was not 1929, as many would guess, but 1921 when share prices fell by -9.76%.

Prices rose in six of the other nine years of the 1920s, and produced an average annual profit for the decade, even with 1929's performance included. Incidentally, October fell by just -5.46% in 1929, much less than many modern day investors would guess. 1929 does not even rate a footnote in Table 12.2 which highlights the ten biggest falls in history. It is what happened in the three following years that gives 1929 its notoriety (see pages 250–51).

Despite the Great Depression and the price weakness in the run-up to World War II, October investors made an average annual profit of +3.58% in the 1930s when it was the Number One-ranked month. The month continued to be profitable in the 1940s through to the 1960s.

Recent trend OK

The trend appears to have weakened in the recent past with average annual losses recorded in the 1970s and 1980s. But in each decade, one year accounted for the poor results: 1976 (down -10.12%) and 1987, the worst month since our records began (down -26.32%). The average annual return was positive in the remainder of both decades.

Even with 1921, 1976, and 1987 included in computations, the average October price rise is +0.90%, equal to 30 points on an FT-SE 100 in the area of 3300. Historically, October is the fifth-best month in which to invest in shares. A hypothetical investor who invested only in October, from 1919 to 1994, and switched to cash for the rest of the year, would have run up his £1,000 to £1,724.

Table 12.1

OCTOBER PRICE RISES AND DECLINES: 1919–1994

	Average October price change	Up	Down/ no change
1920–29	-0.11%	6	4
1930–39	3.58%	7	3
1940–49	0.78%	6	4
1950–59	2.87%	7	3
1960–69	1.05%	6	4
1970–79	-0.93%	4	6
1980–89	-0.98%	7	3
1990–94	1.90%	4	1
Average October price change	0.90%	47	29

Source: BZW and Datastream

Table 12.1: October was steadily profitable in the 1930s to '60s. Investors may not have profited every single year but did quite well over the long-run. The apparent losses in the 1970s and '80s were due to a single year in each decade: -10.12% in 1976 and -26.32% in 1987. The average annual return in the rest of each decade was positive.

UPDATE

First quarter is best

If you are planning to purchase shares to catch the October up-turn, be sure to do so at the beginning of the month as the first quarter is the most profitable by far (*see Figure 12.1*). Prices often drop in the rest of the month. The fourth-quarter's performance has been especially poor recently. Prices fell in 14 of the last 20 years, the worst performance of the entire year.

INCREASE YOUR PROFIT ODDS

Investors can increase October profits by identifying specific years when prices are especially likely to rise. Short sellers or Put buyers can also profit by identifying years with a high likelihood of October price drops. There are several historical trends which have done a good job of anticipating the direction of October price shifts.

249

1929: MYTH VERSUS REALITY

For UK investors, there are wide discrepancies between what actually happened in the Crash of '29 and popular myth.

In the US, where many believed the continued, steady growth of the 1920s made economic cycles a thing of the past, share prices were bid up to unsustainable levels until the bubble burst.

Big rises

A leading company like General Motors rose from eight in 1922 to 225 at the end of 1928 after a 50% stock distribution in 1926, a two-for-one split in 1927 and a 2.5 for one split in 1928. The equivalent price, unsplit, would have been almost 1700. An up-start like Radio Corporation of America, riding on the tail of radio's growing popularity, rocketed up from three in 1922 to 574 in September of 1929.

Big falls

When prices eventually started to fall, the drop was equally spectacular. They fell in October and November, 1929 by 20% and 13% respectively, recovered more than half of that loss over the next few months, and then

July signal

Here is a newly discovered trend which underlines the relationship between July, the first month of the third quarter with October, the first month of the fourth quarter.[1]

Since 1922, there have been 16 occasions when July prices shifted by a small amount, no more than -1.49% on the down-side, and no more than +1.06% on the up-side. In each of those years, October prices rose. The average increase was a whopping +4.47%. Part of this spectacular October record is due to 1959 when October rose by +20.41% in the run-up to a Conservative election victory, the third-best monthly

---

[1]Reminder: All monthly calculations are based on the FT-Non-financial Index, formerly the FT-'500'; unless otherwise stated, they are based on data from 1919–1994. All daily, quarterly, and bi-monthly calculations are based on the Ordinary Share Index, also known as the FT-30; unless otherwise stated, they are based on data from 1936–1994.

UK drop milder

dropped for the next few years, ultimately bottoming out in June, 1932, down a mind-numbing 86%.

In contrast, the UK's post World War I economic expansion was less robust than America's and ran out of steam earlier. Consequently, the UK stock market topped out much earlier as well. The April 1928 peak in prices was less extreme than Wall Street's and so was the subsequent fall. October 1929's decline of -5.46% was just one of five months in that year with price declines of this magnitude. When UK prices finally bottomed out in 1932, they had fallen 60%, a softer landing than Wall Street's, but extremely painful nevertheless.

Margin calls make it worse

There is reason to believe that the UK's bear market would have been much milder if not for the practice of many wealthy UK investors of that era to heavily invest on Wall Street, often on margin. When US prices started to fall, they were forced to meet 'margin calls', and sold some of their UK investments to raise cash, intensifying our own bear market.

increase in modern history *(see Table 12.3)*. But even if this atypical monthly increase is removed from the tally, a +3.41% average monthly increase for the remaining 15 Octobers flagged by the July Signal is nothing to sneer at.

Rose (16)

Fell (0) |

October record after a July price shift of -1.49% to +1.06% (since 1922)

Prior-12-months signal

The direction that prices have shifted in the past 12 months is also a good October price signal. There have been 13 years in which prices rose in the past 12 months by

Table 12.2 **THE TEN WORST MONTHS IN HISTORY**

	Percentage decline
October 1987	-26.32%
June 1940	-22.10%
March 1974	-19.55%
August 1947	-17.04%
September 1981	-16.94%
April 1920	-15.75%
November 1974	-15.67%
February 1948	-13.18%
July 1966	-13.00%
November 1973	-12.71%

Table 12.2: The worst month in UK stock market history was October 1987 when shares fell by more than one-quarter. Some commentators call October/November 1987 history's only two-month long Bear Market (prices fell another -10.28% in November). In fact, the market actually peaked in mid-July 1987. Still, the carnage was even worse than in June 1940, when many thought we might lose the war and ran for cover.

Table 12.3 **THE TEN BEST MONTHS IN HISTORY**

	Percentage increase
January 75	51.45%
February 75	23.28%
October 59	20.41%
December 76	17.22%
April 75	16.23%
January 89	14.34%
August 75	14.04%
July 32	13.86%
April 71	13.03%
March 79	12.86%

Table 12.3: Four of the best months in history were in 1975 as the stock market partially recovered from the horror of 1972–74. Putting 1975 aside, October 1959 saw a huge rally as the stock market celebrated the prospects of a Conservative election victory.

Figure 12.1   **PROFITABILITY OF OCTOBER'S FOUR QUARTERS**

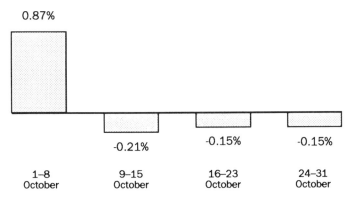

| 1–8 October | 9–15 October | 16–23 October | 24–31 October |

Figure 12.1: Long-term investors make money in the first quarter. The remaining three quarters are steady money-losers.

+13.54% to +20.62%. October share prices rose in 12 of those years. The sole exception was in 1983 when prices fell by -1.79%. The average annual increase during these 13 years is +3.15% which is equal to 104 points on an FT-SE 100 in the area of 3300.

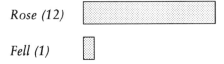

Rose (12)

Fell (1)

October record after a price rise of +13.54% to +20.62% in past 12 months

August/ September signal No 1

In last year's edition, we told investors that if August prices rise by at least 4.00%, and are followed by a September price increase under 5.00%, or by a September fall of any amount, October prices tend to rise. This trend occurred in 1994 and October prices rose as expected. Since 1952, there have been 16 years with August and September price shifts

253

in the correct range, counting 1994. October prices rose each time, at a whopping average annual rate of +4.17%.

| UPDATE |

Rose (16)

Fell (0)

October record after an August price rise of at least +4.00% and a September rise of less than +5.00% or a September fall (since 1952)

August/
September
signal No 2

Here is another variation of the August/September trend to watch: there have been 17 years when prices rose in the preceding two months by +3.19% to +5.88%. October prices rose in 15 of those years.

Rose (15)

Fell (2)

October record after an August/September price rise of +3.19% to +5.88%

August/
September
signal No 3

The August/September trend also tips months when the odds favour a decline. Since 1956, there were 10 years when shares moved up or down by less than 4.00% in August and by +1.22% to -9.08% in September. October prices fell in all 10 years.

Rose (0)

Fell (10)

October record after an August price shift of less than 4.00% (up or down) and a September price shift of +1.22% to -9.08% (since 1956)

FIRST QUARTER OF OCTOBER – OCTOBER 1ST TO 8TH

If you plan to buy shares during October, the odds suggest the best time to do so is near the beginning of the month

Prices are especially likely to rise in years that have witnessed a moderate price rise in September.

As in other months, there are widely different profit potentials associated with investments made during different segments of October.

Here comes October's best quarter

The best segment of the month, by far, is the first quarter. It has risen 63% of the time and produced an average annual profit in every single decade on record. Between 1935 and 1994, the average first-quarter profit was +0.87% per year, fourth-best quarter for the entire year *(see Table 12.4)*.

If you are planning to buy shares during October, past performance suggests that the best time to do it is at the very beginning of the month to take advantage of the anticipated price rise. You will not profit every single year, but in the long-run, the odds favour this investment strategy. Thinking of selling? The odds suggest you will benefit by waiting a few more days.

2 October

Analysis of price trends on a day-by-day basis finds that prices often rise. The most profitable point of the quarter is near the very beginning. Prices rise 62% of the time on 2 October *(see Figure 12.2)*.

3 October

Be cautious on 3 October. Although prices have risen in most years, two negative trends are converging:

▶ The recent record is weak. From 1984 to the present, prices have only risen twice.

▶ 3 October traditionally has disappointed investors when it lands on a Thursday as in 1996.

255

Table 12.4 **PERCENTAGE PRICE CHANGE: OCTOBER 1935–1994**

	October 1–8	October 9–15	October 16–23	October 24–31
Average annual price change				
1935–39	0.46%	0.24%	1.56%	0.47%
1940–49	0.70%	-0.74%	0.42%	0.76%
1950–59	0.31%	1.10%	0.65%	-0.42%
1960–69	0.86%	-0.31%	-1.45%	1.26%
1970–79	1.25%	-0.72%	0.08%	-2.27%
1980–89	0.83%	-0.36%	-2.20%	-0.02%
1990–94	2.04%	-0.66%	1.67%	-0.91%
Average quarterly price change	0.87%	-0.21%	-1.15%	-0.15%
Number of years in which prices:				
rose	38	28	31	27
fell	22	32	27	32
remained unchanged	–	–	2	1

UPDATE

Source: Datastream

Table 12.4: The poor record of the second and fourth quarters is more than a short-term run of poor luck. For both quarters, prices fall in most years. In contrast, the third quarter has been performing better than the averages suggest. Without 1987's decline of -22.95%, the 1980–89 third-quarter average would be +0.10%, and the overall third-quarter average would be +0.24%.

INCREASE YOUR PROFIT ODDS

Although a +0.87% average quarterly profit is nothing to complain about, it is possible to do better than average by investing selectively

Here is a new trend for *Schwartz Stock Market Handbook* readers. A moderate September up-move is often followed by a further rally in the first quarter of October.

Figure 12.2   **PERCENTAGE OF TIME PRICES RISE EACH TRADING DAY IN OCTOBER'S FIRST QUARTER**

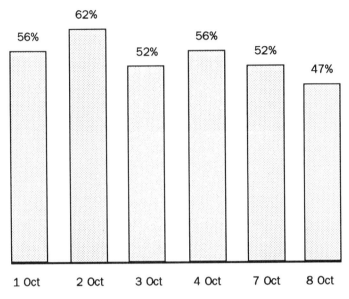

Figure 12.2: The best day of the quarter is 2 October. Be careful on 3 October: the odds are against a rise in 1996.

September signal

There have been 11 occasions when September prices rose +1.58% to +2.93%. October's first quarter rose in 10 of those years. Seven of the up-moves were in excess of 1%. The sole failure of the September Signal occurred in 1945.

Rose (10)

Fell (1)

First-quarter record after a September price rise of +1.58% to +2.93%.

September second-half signal

Prices also tend to rise in years with a neutral or positive trend in September's second-half. Since 1947, there have been 17 years in which September's third-quarter prices either fell by no more than -1.64% or rose, and fourth-quarter prices rose by any amount. Prices continued to rise in October's first quarter in 15 of those years (88%). The average price rise was +1.64% in those 17 years. The two exceptions to the rule occurred in 1964 and 1965.

Rose (15)

Fell (2)

First-quarter record after a September third-quarter price decline of -1.64% or less, or a rise, and a fourth-quarter rise (since 1947)

September fourth-quarter signal

You can also out-perform the averages by watching the direction of prices in September's fourth quarter. Since 1949, if fourth-quarter prices fell by between -1.50% and -5.66%, the odds of a rise in October's first quarter was quite high. Out of 16 years with a fourth-quarter fall of this magnitude, first-quarter prices rose 14 times (88%). The average price rise was +1.46% in those 16 years.

Rose (14)

Fell (2)

First-quarter record after a September fourth-quarter price decline of -1.50% to -5.66% (since 1949)

SECOND QUARTER OF OCTOBER – OCTOBER 9TH TO 15TH

> No one knows what will happen this year but over the long-run, prices fall more often than they rise.
>
> A small change in the preceding quarter often signals that second quarter prices will fall.

Worst quarter of the month

Second-quarter prices rose just 47% of the time between 1935 and 1994, much less than the first quarter. Prices fell -0.21% on average, making the second quarter of October the worst performer of the month over the long-run.

The last profitable decade for the second quarter was in the 1950s. The second-quarter investor lost money in the 1940s, '60s, '70s, and '80s. The second-quarter finally rose in 1994 after five consecutive declines *(see Table 12.5).*

9 & 10 October poor

Analysis of price trends on a day-by-day basis reveals lots of red ink at the beginning. 9 October is the worst day of the month and second-worst of the entire year. Prices rise just 26% of the time. 10 October is not much better with price increases in just 33% of all years, second-worst day of the month and sixth-worst in the year *(see Figure 12.3).*

And if prices fall during the preceding five days, 9 and 10 October are extremely likely to fall. Out of 37 times with a price decline in the previous five trading days, 9 and 10 October rose three times between them.

Rose (3)

Fell (32)

No change (2)

Trend on 9–10 October if prices fell in preceding five trading days

259

Table 12.5   **PERCENTAGE PRICE CHANGE: 1985–1994**

	October 1–8	October 9–15	October 16–23	October 24–31
Annual quarterly price change				
1985	0.78%	1.66%	2.68%	1.69%
1986	1.72%	2.27%	-2.08%	2.84%
1987	0.71%	-2.89%	-22.95%	-2.57%
1988	0.94%	0.24%	1.02%	-0.50%
1989	-1.48%	-2.30%	-2.34%	-2.89%
1990	11.07%	-4.60%	1.69%	-3.73%
1991	-1.48%	-0.91%	-0.37%	-0.19%
1992	0.53%	-1.08%	7.11%	-0.90%
1993	1.76%	-0.20%	2.34%	-0.48%
1994	-1.69%	3.50%	-2.40%	0.78%
Average quarterly price change				
1985–1994	1.29%	-0.43%	-1.53%	-0.60%
Number of years in which prices:				
rose	7	4	5	3
fell	3	6	5	7

UPDATE

Source: Datastream

Table 12.5: The relative strength of the first quarter continued into the 1980s and '90s. The fourth quarter has been quite weak since 1987.

14–15 October good

On the positive side, 14 and 15 October are strong performers. 14 October is especially likely to rise when it lands on a Monday as it will do in 1996 *(see Table 12.6)*.

INCREASE YOUR PROFIT ODDS

In the long-run, it often pays to stand aside or bet against the market during this stretch of the month. We find no signal that tips off a consistent and reasonably-sized profit opportunity on the up-side.

Figure 12.3   **PERCENTAGE OF TIME PRICES RISE EACH TRADING DAY IN OCTOBER'S SECOND QUARTER**

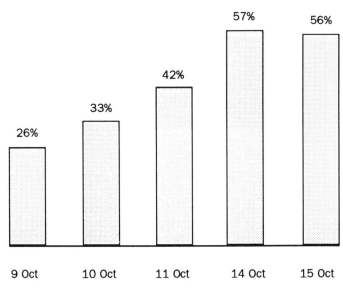

9 Oct	10 Oct	11 Oct	14 Oct	15 Oct
26%	33%	42%	57%	56%

Figure 12.3: 9 October is the second-worst day of the entire year. 10 and 11 October are not very good either. 9 and 10 October comprise the worst two-day stretch of the year.

Prior-five-quarters signal

For readers interested in a short-term bet against the market, watch the trend in preceding five quarters. If prices decline in September's first half, second half, and October's first quarter, they are likely to decline in the second quarter. Since 1935, there have been eight years in which prices fell in all three periods. The price fall continued through October's second quarter in seven of those years.

Rose (1)

UPDATE

Fell (7)

Second-quarter record after a decline in September's first half, second half, and October's first quarter

261

Table 12.6

PERCENTAGE OF TIME PRICES RISE ON 13–14 OCTOBER: 1935–1994

	Prices rise
Total	53%
Monday	82%
Rest of week	46%

Table 12.6: The odds of a price rise on 13 and 14 October are high on Monday. 14 October lands on a Monday in 1996.

This signal's single failure occurred in 1994 when steady declines in the previous three periods were followed by a very strong second-quarter rally.

First-quarter signal

If first-quarter prices shift within a tiny range of -0.18% to +0.71%, second-quarter prices are likely to fall. Out of 10 shifts within this range, second-quarter prices fell nine times.

Rose (1)

Fell (9)

Second-quarter record after a first-quarter shift of -0.18% to +0.71%

September second-half signal

If prices fall in the second half of September within a range of -2.18% to -3.90%, the odds are high that October's second quarter will fall, regardless of what happens in the first quarter. Since 1946, prices fell to the required degree in September's second half on 11 occasions. They continued to fall in October's second quarter in nine of those years.

⟨NEW⟩

Rose (2)

Fell (9)

Second-quarter record after a drop in September's second half of -2.18% to -3.90% (since 1946)

THIRD QUARTER OF OCTOBER – OCTOBER 16TH TO 23RD

> Be careful. Although prices often rise in the middle of this quarter, the quarter to follow is one of the worst of the entire year.

The hidden trend is good

At first glance, the third quarter is not a particularly good time to be in the stock market for long-term investors. Since 1935, it has been averaging an annual loss of -0.15%.

But a closer look reveals some good news. Prices rose 31 times (52%), fell 27 times and were unchanged in two years. The average annual loss is caused by the 1987 crash, which occurred in this quarter, when prices dropped -22.95%. If 1987 were eliminated, a small profit was produced in the remaining 59 years, of +0.24% per year.

Analysis of price trends on a day-by-day basis finds the greatest strength in mid-quarter, the best days of the entire month *(see Figure 12.4)*. But unless you are a very short-term trader, don't be too quick to buy shares. The quarter to follow is one of the year's worst. For this reason, the best advice for long-term investors contemplating a purchase of shares is to wait for the next few weeks to pass.

18 October

Short-term traders will have an interesting trading opportunity this year. Mid-month Fridays rise in three out of four years and 18 October lands on a Friday in 1996 *(see Table 12.7)*.

INCREASE YOUR PROFIT ODDS

It is possible to improve the odds of profit in this quarter by watching the price trend in the first half of October.

First-half signal No 1

Since 1964, there were 10 years when prices dropped in October's first half by no more than -2.49%. They continued to decline in the third quarter in nine of those years.

Figure 12.4   **PERCENTAGE OF TIME PRICES RISE EACH TRADING DAY IN OCTOBER'S THIRD QUARTER**

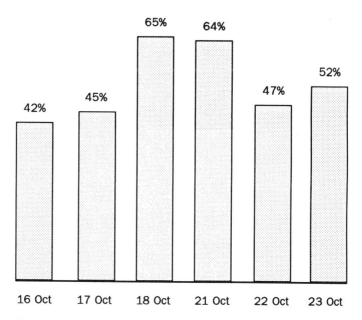

Figure 12.4: The odds of making a profit are above-average once the first two days of the quarter have passed. 18 October is the best day of the month.

Rose (1)

Fell (9)

Third-quarter record after a first-half price decline of up to -2.49% (since 1964)

First-half signal No 2

There were another 15 years when prices rose in October's first half between +1.55% to +4.02%. They continued to rise in the third quarter in 12 of those years (86%).

Table 12.7

PERCENTAGE OF TIME PRICES RISE ON 18–20 OCTOBER: 1935–1994

	Prices rise
Total	57%
Friday	76%
Rest of week	54%

Table 12.7: The odds of a price rise on 18–20 October are high if they land on a Friday. 18 October lands on a Friday in 1996.

UPDATE

Rose (12)

Fell (3)

Third-quarter record after a first-half price rise of +1.55% to +4.02%

This signal failed in 1994. A first half price rise of suitable size was followed by a third quarter fall of -2.40%.

First-half signal
No 3

If prices rise in both the first and second quarters of the month, third-quarter prices are also likely to rise. Since 1942, there have been 14 years in which prices rose in the first quarter by up to +4.96% and in the second quarter by any amount. Third-quarter prices also increased in 12 of those years (86%), at an average annual rate of +1.10%.

Rose (12)

Fell (2)

Third-quarter record after a first-quarter price rise of up to +4.96% and a second-quarter rise of any amount (since 1942)

Prior-three-
quarters signal

And if prices rise three quarters in a row – the last quarter of September, first and second quarters of October – third-quarter prices are especially likely to rise. Since 1942, there have been eight years with price rises in three consecutive quarters. Third-quarter prices rose in seven of those years, at an average annual rate of +1.63%.

Rose (7)

Fell (1)

Third-quarter record after a first-, second-, and third-quarter price rise (since 1942)

FOURTH QUARTER OF OCTOBER – OCTOBER 24TH TO 31ST

No one knows if prices will rise or fall this year. But before you part with any money, consider this: the price rise in 1994 occurred after seven falls in a row.

Long-term trend
poor

The fourth quarter of October is a poor time to be holding shares. Prices decline at an average annual rate of -0.15%. Between 1935–1994, the record was 27 up (45%), 32 down and one no change.

Recent trend
worse

In the last 20 years, from 1975 to 1994, the fourth-quarter record has been atrocious. Prices have fallen 14 times, the worst record of the entire year (see Table 12.8). From 1987 to 1993, fourth-quarter prices fell seven times in a row. The losing streak ended with a small rise in 1994.

Despite the price rise of 1994, the odds favour a price decline in this quarter. So don't be too quick to move into the market.

Table 12.8   **YEAR'S SIX BEST AND SIX WORST QUARTERS IN LAST 20 YEARS: 1974–1993**

Best	Number of increases	Worst	Number of increases
January 4th quarter	18	October 4th quarter	6
January 3rd quarter	16	March 3rd quarter	7
April 2nd quarter	16	May 3rd quarter	7
April 4th quarter	16	June 3rd quarter	7
March 1st quarter	15	June 4th quarter	7
June 1st quarter	15	Several at this level	8

Table 12.8: October's fourth quarter has become the year's worst performer, falling in 14 of the last 20 years.

24–25 October

Analysis of prices on a day-by-day basis reveals a weak trend throughout the quarter. The recent record for 24–25 October is even worse than the long-term average suggests. Since 1974, prices rose about 30% of the time on these two days *(see Figure 12.5)*.

INCREASE YOUR PROFIT ODDS

Prior-three-quarters signal

If you do bet on a price drop, the chance of a successful bet improves if prices have risen weakly or fallen in the preceding weeks. Since 1964, there have been 14 occasions where prices rose by no more than +1.19% in the first half or fell, and rose no more than +1.44% or fell in the third quarter. Fourth-quarter prices continued to drop in 12 of them (86%). The average yearly decline was -1.43%.

Rose (2)

Fell (12)

Fourth-quarter record after a first-half price rise of no more than +1.19 or a fall, and a third-quarter rise of no more than +1.44% or a fall (since 1964)

267

Figure 12.5

PERCENTAGE OF TIME PRICES RISE EACH TRADING DAY IN OCTOBER'S FOURTH QUARTER

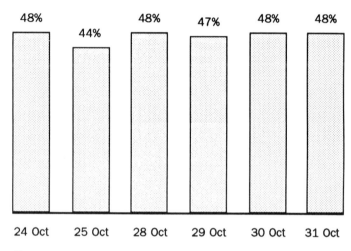

Figure 12.5: Prices rise less than half the time throughout this quarter. Since 1974, the record of 24 and 25 October has weakened.

Third-quarter signal

Another signal to watch is the direction of prices in the third quarter by itself. Since 1970, third-quarter prices have shifted within a range of -0.79% to +2.63% in 13 years. Fourth-quarter prices fell in 12 of those years (92%). This signal last flashed in 1993 and fourth quarter prices fell as expected.

IMPROVEMENT

Rose (1)

Fell (12)

Fourth-quarter record after a third-quarter price shift of -0.79% to +2.63% (since 1970)

LOOKING AHEAD

There are two useful signals that can help to forecast where shares are heading in the months ahead.

Rising prices by next 31 March

If prices shifted during September and October within a range of -3.03% to +3.47%, the odds are very high they will rise in the five months to follow, that is, to the end of next March.

Since 1939, September/October prices shifted within this range 21 times. Prices rose in the five months that followed in 20 of those years.

Rose (20)

Fell (1)

Trend to 31 March (next year) after a September/October shift of -3.03% to +3.47% (since 1939)

Rising prices by next 31 August

And if prices rise strongly during August to October by +4.03% to +15.84%, there is a good chance they will rise still higher 10 months later. Since 1952, out of 16 occasions with a price rise within this range, prices rose still higher by the following 31 August in 15 of those years.

The single exception occurred in 1965. Once the signal flashed, prices rose steadily as expected until July 1966. But a series of July Measures which included higher Base Rates, taxes, price and income freezes, and an overseas travel allowance caught the markets by surprise. Shares fell sharply.

Rose (15)

Fell (1)

Trend to 31 August (next year) after a August–October rise of +4.03% to +15.84% (since 1952)

NOVEMBER INVESTMENT MONITOR

	LAST MONTH	END OF 1ST QUARTER		END OF 2ND QUARTER		END OF 3RD QUARTER		END OF 4TH QUARTER	
	FINAL PRICE	PRICE	PERCENT CHANGE	PRICE	PERCENT CHANGE	PRICE	PERCENT CHANGE	PRICE	PERCENT CHANGE
FT-ORDINARY (FT-30)									
FT-SE 100									
FT-SE 250									
FT-NON-FINANCIAL (FT-500)									
FT-SE-A ALL SHARES									
STANDARD & POORS COMPOSITE									
OTHER INDEX									

ENTER EACH SHARE, UNIT TRUST, ETC, BELOW

Chapter Thirteen – November 1996

Historically, November has been a poor month. Over the long-run, it is ranked ninth in terms of monthly profitability.

Fortunately, there are several windows of opportunity that help investors to shift the odds of a profitable investment a bit more into their favour. For example, the odds of a November price rise are especially high if prices have risen during the first 10 months of the year. On the other hand, a sharp rise in September and October is often associated with a November decline (see page 272).

The November trend will probably change for the better now that Budget Day has been shifted to November, just as March and April benefited when Budgets were a spring-time event. But even if the odds improve for the month as a whole, be careful during the week that precedes Budget Day. Prices fall in seven out of 10 years as nervous investors respond to scare newspaper headlines.

A good preview of what to expect in the first half of 1997 is provided by the November price trend. A small or medium rise is a very powerful sign that good times lie ahead (see page 286).

Historical trend is weak

Between 1919 and 1994, November prices rose 58% of the time, fifth-best of all 12 months on this dimension. Unfortunately, in profitable years, the average price increase was smaller than normal, and in money-losing years, the average decline was larger than normal. As a result, the average price rise over the 76 years studied was just +0.06% per year, a lowly ninth-ranked, and much less than the risk-free return provided by a neighbourhood building society (see Table 13.1).

A hypothetical £1,000 November investment, started in 1919 and moved into cash for the other 11 months each year, would be worth just £963 in 1994. The first and second quarters produced most of the month's profits. The second half lost money in most years (see Figure 13.1).

Budget Day shift will help the trend

We forecast that this pattern of profit will now change because of the 1993 shift to a new, late-autumn unified Budget Day. The effect of Budget Day on share prices is often quite significant, both in the run-up as well as the weeks that follow. When spring Budgets were advanced to mid-April in the 1940s, April's profits sky-rocketed into the Number One-ranked position. When Budget Day was advanced still further into mid-March, March profits similarly rose.

With this latest Budget Day shift, we suspect that the long-term November trend will change. The change will probably affect share prices on Budget Day itself, as well as in the several weeks on either side of it. For this reason, we urge readers to review the contents of Chapter Two before executing any trades during this segment of the year.

INCREASE YOUR PROFIT ODDS

There are a number of trends that once helped investors to improve significantly upon the odds of making a profitable November investment. We don't know the degree to which Budget Day will affect these trends, so use them with caution.

Table 13.1

NOVEMBER PRICE RISES AND DECLINES: 1919–1994

	Average November price change	Up	Down/ no change
1920–29	-0.87%	4	6
1930–39	-0.98%	5	5
1940–49	2.90%	8	2
1950–59	-1.38%	5	5
1960–69	1.35%	7	3
1970–79	-2.39%	5	5
1980–89	1.85%	8	2
1990–94	0.32%	2	3
Average November price change	0.06%	44	32

UPDATE

Source: BZW and Datastream

Table 13.1: November is the fifth-best month in terms of the number of times prices have risen, but only ninth-best in terms of the size of the increase. Over time, investors would have made more profit with their money in a risk-free building society savings account.

October fourth-quarter signal

One formerly useful trend correlates November price shifts with the direction of prices in the last quarter of October.[1] Between 1956 and 1993, there were 14 years when October fourth-quarter prices rose. November prices rose in 13 of those years (93%). Prices increased at a superb average rate of +3.18% per year, equal to 105 points on a 3300 FT-SE 100. The single exception was back in 1965 when Wilson warned the country of yet another economic crisis and imposed an import tax on 26 October, and a 6%

[1] Reminder: All monthly calculations are based on the FT-Non-financial Index, formerly the FT-'500'; unless otherwise stated, they are based on data from 1919–1994. All daily, quarterly, and bi-monthly calculations are based on the Ordinary Share Index, also known as the FT-30; unless otherwise stated, they are based on data from 1936–1994.

Figure 13.1 **PROFITABILITY OF NOVEMBER'S FOUR QUARTERS**

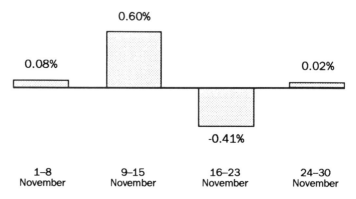

| 1–8 November | 9–15 November | 16–23 November | 24–30 November |

Figure 13.1: Over time, most November profits occur in the first half of the month, especially the second quarter.

income tax increase on 11 November. Even in that year, November prices fell by just -1.09%.

Unfortunately, the signal failed in 1994. We don't know if the failure was an occasional exception to every stock market signal, or a clear warning that the signal is no longer effective because of Budget-related influences. We will watch the situation carefully.

UPDATE

Rose (13)

Fell (2)

November trend after price rise in October's fourth quarter (since 1956)

January–October signal

Another trend which, historically, has done a good job of anticipating the direction of November price shifts is the direction of prices in the preceding 10 months. Since 1958, there have been 14 years in which share prices rose between

2 January to 31 October within a range of +12.46% to +42.89%. November prices rose in 13 of those years.

NEW

Rose (13)

Fell (1)

November trend after price rise in preceding 10 months of +12.46% to +42.89% (since 1958)

May–October signal

There have been 13 years in which prices shifted slightly in the last six months, within a range of -3.91% to +1.53%. November share prices rose in 11 of those years.

UPDATE

Rose (11)

Fell (2)

November trend after price shift in preceding six months of -3.91% to +1.53%

Unfortunately, this signal also failed in 1994, after the Budget Day shift. We will watch the situation carefully.

September/ October signal

The direction of prices over the past two months has flagged some big November falls in the past. There have been nine years with September/October share price increases of +4.93% to +6.96%. November prices fell each time. The average November decrease during these nine years was -1.83%.

Rose (0)

Fell (9)

November trend after price rise in preceding two months of +4.93% to +6.96%

275

FIRST QUARTER OF NOVEMBER – NOVEMBER 1ST TO 8TH

There is only a 50:50 chance of making a profit in the first quarter. But the odds of a price drop are quite high following a decline in the second half of October.

The first quarter is just barely profitable over the long-run. Between 1935 and 1994, the record is 30 up and 30 down and an average profit of +0.08% per year *(see Table 13.2)*. An analysis of daily price trends during this quarter of the month finds that the middle of the quarter is most profitable *(see Figure 13.2)*.

5 November looks good

The odds of a price rise on 5 November are better than average in 1996. The first Tuesday is often profitable and 5 November will land on a Tuesday in 1996 *(see Table 13.3)*.

INCREASE YOUR PROFIT ODDS

October second-half signal

We don't yet know the effect of Budget Day on first-quarter prices. Prior to the Budget Day switch, it was possible to increase the odds of making a profit on the down-side in some years by watching the direction of prices in the second half of October. Since 1935, there have been 16 years in which prices fell in October's second half by -1.16% to -4.03%. In 15 of those years, prices continued to fall in the first quarter of November. The average price drop was -1.31%, equal to 43 points on a 3300 FT-SE 100.

Rose (1)

IMPROVEMENT

Fell (15)

First-quarter trend after price drop in October's second half of -1.16% to -4.03%

276

Table 13.2

PERCENTAGE PRICE CHANGE: NOVEMBER 1935–1994

	November 1–8	November 9–15	November 16–23	November 24–30
Average annual price change				
1935–39	0.70%	0.22%	-2.02%	0.27%
1940–49	0.70%	0.83%	0.74%	-0.05%
1950–59	-0.10%	0.16%	-0.43%	-0.20%
1960–69	-0.53%	2.10%	-1.44%	-0.07%
1970–79	-0.68%	-1.00%	-1.02%	-0.23%
1980–89	0.90%	1.40%	0.49%	-0.15%
1990–94	-0.30%	0.07%	0.39%	1.40%
Average quarterly price change	0.08%	0.60%	-0.41%	0.02%
Number of years in which price				
rose	30	37	27	31
fell	30	20	33	27
remained unchanged	–	3	–	2

Source: Datastream

Table 13.2: The first-quarter investor lost money in the 1950s–'70s, but things improved in the 1980s. The second quarter has been profitable in most decades. In contrast, the fourth quarter of November has been a steady money-loser.

Table 13.3

PERCENTAGE OF TIME PRICES RISE ON 3–5 NOVEMBER: 1935–1994

	Prices rise
Total	52%
Tuesday	73%
Rest of week	47%

Table 13.3: The odds of a price rise on 3–5 November are high if they land on a Tuesday. 5 November lands on a Tuesday in 1996.

UPDATE

Figure 13.2   **PERCENTAGE OF TIME PRICES RISE EACH TRADING DAY IN NOVEMBER'S FIRST QUARTER**

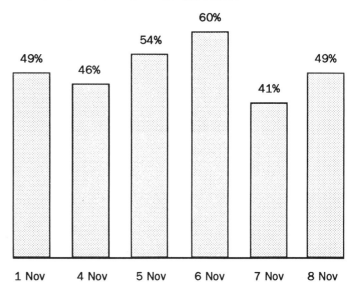

Figure 13.2: The best two days of the quarter are 5 and 6 November.

October signal

Another trend worth watching is the direction of prices in the month of October. There have been nine occasions since 1935 when October prices fell -1.96% to -5.97%. Prices continued to fall in the first quarter of November on all nine occasions. The average first-quarter price decline was -2.05%.

Rose (0)

Fell (9)

First-quarter trend after price drop in October by -1.96% to -5.97%

SECOND QUARTER OF NOVEMBER – NOVEMBER 9TH TO 15TH

Here comes the best quarter of the month. Prices rise in two out of three years.

For some unknown reason, a price rise in October's final quarter is a clear signal that shares will rise in this quarter, regardless of what happened in the first quarter. But if prices fall in October's fourth quarter, the odds of a profit in this quarter are just 50:50

Month's best quarter

Second-quarter prices rose 62% of the time between 1935 and 1994, the best performance of the entire month. They rose at an average annual rate of +0.60%.

The second-quarter investor made money in every complete decade on record except for the 1970s. It was November's Number One-ranked quarter in the 1940s, '50s, '60s, and '80s. Analysis of price shifts on a day-by-day basis shows generally good trading conditions *(see Figure 13.3)*.

INCREASE YOUR PROFIT ODDS

Here is a price trend that has done a good job of tipping second quarter price increases. Once again, we don't know the effect of Budget Day on this trend

October fourth-quarter signal

If prices rise in October's final quarter by +0.59% or more, they are very likely to rise in the second quarter, no matter what happens in the first quarter. Since 1935, there have been 24 years in which prices rose by the appropriate amount. Shares continued to rise in November's second quarter in 22 of those years (92%). The average price rise was +1.54%.

Table 13.4   **PERCENTAGE PRICE CHANGE: 1985–1994**

	November 1–8	November 9–15	November 16–23	November 24–30
Annual quarterly price change				
1985	1.25%	0.33%	4.54%	0.66%
1986	2.47%	-1.82%	-1.47%	1.41%
1987	-6.39%	3.38%	-0.58%	-4.47%
1988	-0.71%	-2.02%	2.50%	-2.63%
1989	3.07%	-0.83%	-0.30%	2.94%
1990	-1.13%	1.57%	7.04%	-1.72%
1991	0.67%	-5.50%	-1.43%	0.00%
1992	2.12%	0.81%	0.63%	3.03%
1993	-3.03%	0.91%	-0.78%	3.89%
1994	-0.14%	2.55%	-3.51%	1.79%
Average quarterly price change				
1985–1994	-0.18%	-0.06%	0.66%	0.49%
Number of years in which prices:				
rose	5	6	4	6
fell	5	4	6	3
remained unchanged	–	–	–	1

Source: Datastream

Table 13.4: Sometimes you have to look beneath the surface to see the real story. The strong second-quarter trend continued into the 1990s with prices up in four out of five years. The average annual loss during this period was due to just one poor year, 1991.

UPDATE

NEW

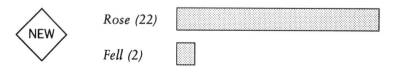

Rose (22)

Fell (2)

Second-quarter trend after price rise in October's fourth quarter of +0.59% or more

Figure 13.3

PERCENTAGE OF TIME PRICES RISE EACH TRADING DAY IN NOVEMBER'S SECOND QUARTER

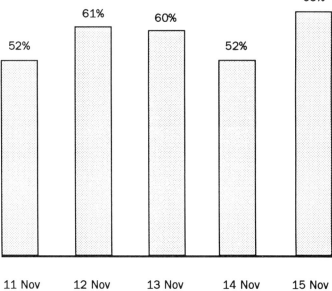

Figure 13.3: It is the best quarter of the month. There is a good chance of rising prices throughout the quarter.

This signal flashed most recently in the fourth quarter of 1994. November's second quarter rose by over 2%, right on cue. No one knows why the fourth quarter of October affects the second quarter of November, regardless of what happens in the first quarter which sits between the two. Whatever the reason, it is a strong signal. And in the 36 years that it did not flash, the second quarter (November's best segment) rose just 18 times and fell 18 times.

One word of caution. Even in years with high odds of a second-quarter profit, remember that prices often fall in the run-up to Budget Day so the odds of an up-move continuing steadily for the rest of November are low.

THIRD QUARTER OF NOVEMBER – NOVEMBER 16TH TO 23RD

> The third quarter has been a poor time to hold shares even before Budget Day was shifted to late November.
>
> The exact date of the 1996 Budget is unknown at press time. Remember: the odds of a price decline in the week preceding Budget Day is high, as frightened investors run for cover due to fear and gloom generated by the media's pre-Budget news coverage.

Month's worst
quarter

Historically, the third quarter is the month's worst performer, averaging an annual loss of -0.41%. Prices rose 27 times (45%) and fell 33 times since our records began.

The third-quarter investor lost money in the 1950s, '60s, and '70s. In the bull market 1980s, the quarter's performance improved with an average profit of +0.49%. But a look under the surface shows that nothing had really changed with a record of three up and seven down.

22 November:
look out

The daily price trend is strongest during the first two days of the quarter, a continuation of good second-quarter trading conditions. Unfortunately, the odds of encountering a profitable trading day then slip dramatically. The 22 November record (prices up just 30% of the time) is the worst trading day of the entire month and fourth-worst of the year *(see Figure 13.4)*.

INCREASE YOUR PROFIT ODDS

First-half signal

Assuming the Government continues to schedule Budget Day in late November, we hypothesise that the third quarter will continue to be painful for investors. Prior to Budget Day being shifted to this part of the year, there was a good short-term down-side signal operating in this quarter. Out of 11 years when prices dropped in November's first half by

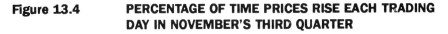

Figure 13.4   **PERCENTAGE OF TIME PRICES RISE EACH TRADING DAY IN NOVEMBER'S THIRD QUARTER**

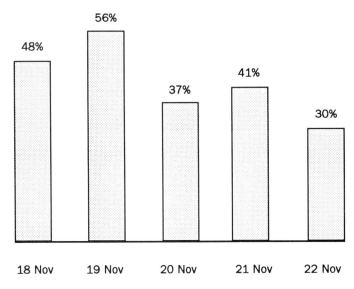

Figure 13.4: Second-quarter strength carries over to the first two days of this quarter. The trend then weakens significantly, especially on 22 November, the month's worst day.

-2.79% or worse, they continued to decline in the third quarter nine times (82%). The average annual decrease was -2.56%. We shall watch with interest to see if this signal remains viable.

Rose (2)

Fell (9)

Third-quarter trend after price drop of -2.79% or more in November's first half

FOURTH QUARTER OF NOVEMBER – NOVEMBER 24TH TO 30TH

> Prior to Budget Day, the final quarter of November wasn't a very good time to be in the stock market. But the recent Budget Day shift changes everything. If Budget Day continues to be scheduled for this part of the month, remember that prices usually fall in the run-up to Budget Day and rise on the day itself, as well as in its aftermath.

Poor trend

The profit trend in the fourth quarter of November used to be disappointing. Prices rose at an average annual rate of +0.02%. Between 1935–1994, the record was 31 up (52%), 27 down and two no change.

Late-quarter
weakness

Fourth-quarter investors lost money in every complete decade for which we have records, from the 1940s to the 1980s. Judging by the daily price records, most of the damage occurs at the very beginning and the very end of the quarter.

Budget Day
trend change

Budget Day will probably change things. Keep on the look out for the actual date that the Budget will be presented. If Budget Day does land in this quarter, be warned: prices fall 71% of the time in the five days before Budget Day, but they usually rise on Budget Day itself and in its aftermath.

INCREASE YOUR PROFIT ODDS

Prior-three-
quarters signal

Here is one historical correlation that has helped investors in the past to make money during this quarter. It involves the direction of prices in the first three quarters of November. There have been eight occasions on record where prices rose in the first three quarters of November. Fourth-quarter prices continued to rise in seven of them (88%). The average yearly increase was +0.91%.

Figure 13.5   **PERCENTAGE OF TIME PRICES RISE EACH TRADING DAY IN NOVEMBER'S FOURTH QUARTER**

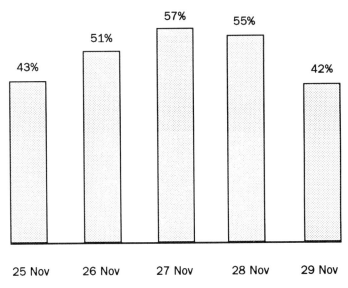

Figure 13.5: Historically, the very end of November has been a money-loser.

Rose (7)

Fell (1)

Fourth-quarter trend after prices rose in the first three quarters of November

Third-quarter signal

Since 1952, there have been 12 years when third-quarter prices shifted very slightly, from -0.40% to +0.57%. Fourth-quarter prices rose in 10 of those years.

Rose (10)

Fell (2)

Fourth-quarter trend after third-quarter prices shifted by -0.40% to +0.57% (since 1952)

We will keep a careful watch on these trends to ensure they are still operative in the new November investing environment.

Looking ahead

For a glimpse of what the year ahead has to offer, November offers two price signals worthy of note.

Rising prices by next 31 July

November shares rose from +0.48% to +4.84% in 31 different years. Prices continued to rise in the next eight months, to 31 July of the following year, in 28 of those years.

Rose (28)

Fell (3)

Trend to 31 July (next year) after a November rise of +0.48% to +4.84%

Rising prices by next 31 July

Here is a second signal that has a good track record tipping where prices will stand by next 31 July. Since 1922, the first 11 months of the year have risen by +15.54% or more in 22 different years. Prices continued to rise in the eight months that follow in 21 of those years.

NEW

Rose (21)

Fell (1)

Trend to 31 July (next year) after a January–November rise of ÷15.54% or more (since 1922)

Since 1922, there have been 37 occasions when one or both of these prices signals flashed. The record on 31 July of the following year was 33 up and four down. In the remaining 35 years untouched by either signal, the record for the next eight months was a disappointing 16 up and 19 down.

DECEMBER INVESTMENT MONITOR

	LAST MONTH FINAL PRICE	END OF 1ST QUARTER		END OF 2ND QUARTER		END OF 3RD QUARTER		END OF 4TH QUARTER	
		PRICE	PERCENT CHANGE	PRICE	PERCENT CHANGE	PRICE	PERCENT CHANGE	PRICE	PERCENT CHANGE
FT-ORDINARY (FT-30)									
FT-SE 100									
FT-SE 250									
FT-NON-FINANCIAL (FT-500)									
FT-SE-A- ALL SHARES									
STANDARD & POORS COMPOSITE									
OTHER INDEX									

ENTER EACH SHARE, UNIT
TRUST, ETC, BELOW

CHAPTER FOURTEEN – DECEMBER 1996

December is a steady money-maker and is growing more profitable with each passing decade.

The first half is often disappointing but things soon hot up. The third quarter is the year's fourth-best. The fourth quarter is the year's best quarter. Five of the year's 10 best days land in this month. Better still, the month to follow is the year's best month over the long-run, making December the start of the best two-month period of the year.

If you are thinking of buying shares, this is the month in which to do it.

Even though the odds of a profit are good, it is possible to improve upon them. A rising price trend over the past few months often signals that shares will continue to rise in December. But if prices have fallen between May and November, look out. They will probably also fall in December.

The trend over the past year gives strong clues about where prices are heading in the year ahead; see page 308 for details.

Fourth-best
month

Investors usually make money in December. Between 1919 and 1994, December prices rose 57% of the time. The average price rise was +1.06%, equal to 35 points on an FT-SE 100 in the area of 3300.[1] The constant December investor made an average annual profit in every decade on record, with the exception of the 1930s *(see Table 14.1)*. A £1,000 December investment in 1919 would have grown to £2,117 by 1994.

Over the 76 years for which we have data, December is fourth-best in terms of monthly profitability, surpassed only by January, April, and August.

Steady
improvement

The December record is getting better. Table 14.2 shows its performance over four successive periods. The size of the average annual profit and the likelihood of a price rise have steadily improved. The improvement continues right up to the present. Since 1980, prices rose in 10 out of 15 years, with an average monthly price rise of +2.08%.

First half
often poor

The month often starts off slowly with losses at the beginning of the month. But things soon start to sizzle. The third and fourth quarters are usually profitable and are ranked, respectively, in fourth and first place for the entire year *(see Figure 14.1)*.

Investors should also recall that Number One-ranked January is just around the corner. The December to January period is the most profitable two-month stretch of the entire year.

Budget Day
should not
affect December

The one fly in the ointment is the recent switch to a late-autumn Unified Budget. We don't know for certain how the Budget will affect December prices. Available evidence suggests there is nothing to fear.

---

[1]Reminder: All monthly calculations are based on the FT-Non-financial Index, formerly the FT-'500'; unless otherwise stated, they are based on data from 1919–1994. All daily, quarterly, and bi-monthly calculations are based on the Ordinary Share Index, also known as the FT-30; unless otherwise stated, they are based on data from 1936–1994.

Table 14.1

DECEMBER PRICE RISES AND DECLINES: 1919–1994

	Average December price change	Up	Down/ no change
1920–29	0.57%	7	3
1930–39	-0.85%	5	5
1940–49	0.66%	4	6
1950–59	1.60%	7	3
1960–69	0.84%	5	5
1970–79	2.13%	5	5
1980–89	1.83%	6	4
1990–94	2.57%	4	1
Average December price change	1.06%	43	33

UPDATE

Source: BZW and Datastream

Table 14.1: The only loss-making decade was back in the 1930s. Since then, December has been consistently profitable.

Table 14.2

DECEMBER HAS BEEN IMPROVING

	Average annual price change	Rank
1920–1939	-0.14%	7
1940–1959	1.13%	6
1960–1979	1.49%	4
1980–1994	2.08%	3

Table 14.2: December's profitability has been steadily improving. In four successive periods, the month's average annual profit and its ranking on monthly profitability have risen.

Figure 14.1   **PROFITABILITY OF DECEMBER'S FOUR QUARTERS**

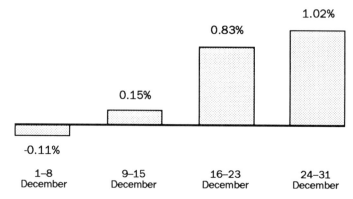

	9–15 December	16–23 December	24–31 December

Figure 14.1: The month often starts off poorly for investors, But profits soon begin to appear in most years. The third and fourth quarters are among the most profitable segments of the year.

▶ The period around Budget Day is usually good for investors.

▶ If a Budget-related problem does occur, its main effect is often felt close to Budget Day, with the worst 'hits' occurring in the quarter or two adjacent to the Budget's presentation.

▶ The strong performance of December's second half is probably influenced by end-of-year money flows and expectations about the year ahead, a pattern we expect to continue.

Our working hypothesis is that even in the aftermath of a poorly received Budget, the second half of December should be distant enough to continue to enjoy favourable trading conditions. All of this is theory, of course. We will watch the situation carefully.

INCREASE YOUR PROFIT ODDS

Prior-12-months
signal

Although the overall December 'story' is a good one, there are several historical price trends that help investors to improve significantly the odds of making a profitable December investment. Here is one of the best. There have been 20 years in which share prices rose in the previous 12 months by at least +8.74% and in the previous two months by +0.96% to +7.94%. December prices rose in 19 of those years. The average profit was +2.37%. The single losing month was December 1941 when prices fell in the aftermath of Japan's 7 December sneak attacks and Britain's Declaration of War on 8 December.

Rose (19)

Fell (1)

December's record after previous 12 month price rise of at least +8.74% and previous two-month rise of +0.96% to +7.94%

September–
November signal

The price trend in the three months that precede December often provides good clues for the December investor. There have been 14 years when prices shifted between -1.74% to +5.96% in the preceding three months and rose by +0.61% to +5.58% in November. December share prices rose in every one of those years.

Rose (14)

Fell (0)

December's record after previous three-month shift of -1.74% to +5.96% and a November rise of +0.61% to +5.58%

If we eliminate duplication within these trends, there are 27 years that are flagged by at least one of them. The December

293

record is 26 up and one down. In years untouched by either one of these two up-trend signals, December's record has been simply terrible: 19 up and 28 down, and two no change. The most recent year to be untouched by either of the two December signals was 1994 and prices dropped.

October/ November signal

Here are two trends to help improve the odds of identifying a declining December. In years untouched by either of the two up-trend forecasts, an October/November price rise within a range of +0.90% to +14.51% is an important red flag danger signal. Out of 22 months with price rises within this range, December prices fell 18 times. This signal preceded the decline of December 1994

UPDATE

Rose (4)

Fell (18)

December's record after an October/November price rise of +0.90% to +14.51% (in years untouched by either up-trend forecast)

May–November signal

If prices are weak in the seven months preceding December, the odds are high that shares will also fall in December. Since our records began, prices have declined 1 May to 30 November within a range of -0.79% to -6.77% on 13 occasions. Shares fell further in December in 11 of these years. The most recent May to November decline occurred in 1994.

NEW

Rose (2)

Fell (11)

December's record after a May–November price drop of -0.79% to -6.77%

294

FIRST QUARTER OF DECEMBER – DECEMBER 1ST TO 8TH

> Before the Budget Day shift, the first quarter was not profitable in most years.
> Given the historical record, the present uncertainty, and the fact that December's second quarter is often weak, the best strategy to follow is to invest cautiously during this part of the month.

Poor trend

December may be a good month in which to invest – but not its first quarter. A decade-by-decade analysis reveals that the first quarter of the month is its least profitable segment. Prices rose in just 43% of all first quarters on record and produced an average loss of -0.11% per year *(see Table 14.3)*.

1990s: still weak

The 1980s were especially weak with a record of four up, six down and an average annual loss of -0.59%. The 1990s have brought more of the same, two up and three down.

4 December

Analysis of daily price trends reveals significant weaknesses on 4 December. Prices rise just 36% of the time. This pattern continues right up to the present. Since 1984, the 4 December record is one up and seven down *(see Figure 14.2)*.

INCREASE YOUR PROFIT ODDS

If you are thinking about betting on a first-quarter price drop, one word of caution. When market conditions suggest a drop is especially likely, be prepared to move fast. Even if the second quarter continues to be weak, a trend that has been apparent in recent years, the year-end rally is likely to begin soon.

November second-half signal

Here is a trend which used to be associated with price drops in the first quarter. Due to the Budget Day switch, we caution investors that historic trend forecasts may be less reliable than usual. Since 1942, there were 10 years with a small price shift in November's second half, no more than

Table 14.3   **PERCENTAGE PRICE CHANGE: DECEMBER 1935–1994**

	December 1–8	December 9–15	December 16–23	December 24–31
Average annual price change				
1935–39	-0.63%	0.12%	0.40%	0.73%
1940–49	0.05%	0.29%	0.54%	0.67%
1950–59	0.18%	1.20%	0.36%	1.11%
1960–69	-0.63%	0.69%	-0.06%	0.88%
1970–79	0.54%	-1.24%	1.93%	1.49%
1980–89	-0.59%	-0.08%	1.33%	1.01%
1990–94	0.17%	0.02%	1.34%	1.18%
Average quarterly price change	-0.11%	0.15%	0.83%	1.02%
Number of years in which prices:				
rose	26	34	43	48
fell	34	24	15	11
remained unchanged	–	2	2	1

Source: Datastream

Table 14.3: The first quarter is December's weak link. Prices rise less than half the time. Fortunately, the third and fourth quarters make up for the poor start. Their strong performance is a long-term phenomenon. On a decade-by-decade basis, they are virtually always the best two quarters of the month.

-0.48% on the down-side and no more than +0.58% on the up-side. First-quarter prices fell in nine of those years at an average of -1.19% per year. The single exception occurred in 1944.

Rose (1)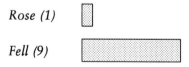

Fell (9)

First-quarter record after a price shift of -0.48% to +0.58% in November's second half (since 1942)

Figure 14.2   **PERCENTAGE OF TIME PRiCES RISE EACH TRADING DAY IN DECEMBER'S FIRST QUARTER**

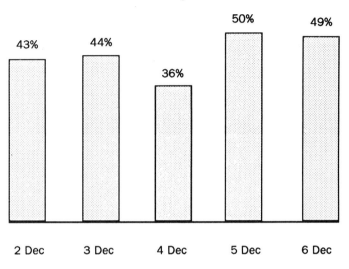

Figure 14.2: Prices often fall on 4 December. Since 1984, the record is one up and seven down.

Second Quarter of December – December 9th to 15th

Be careful. In the last 20 years, prices fell more than half the time.

The odds of a profit improve if prices shift by a small amount in the previous two quarters. On the other hand, even in poor second quarters, the best investment period of the entire year is about to begin, so don't back away from shares too far. A strategy that has worked well in recent years is to buy on second-quarter weakness.

Soon time to buy

Our historical review of all second-quarter closing prices sends an exceedingly clear message. If you were thinking about buying shares in the near future, the time to do it is fast approaching.

Since 1935, second-quarter closing prices rose 57% of the time and produced an average annual profit of +0.15%.

But don't be too quick to jump into the market at the very beginning of this quarter. The long-term trend is changing, unfortunately for the worse. In the last 20 years, from 1975–1994, the second-quarter record has been quite poor – eight up and 12 down. Things have not changed much since 1987. The recent record is two up and five down *(see Table 14.4)*.

11 December

Analysis of daily price trends reveals that the beginning of the quarter is relatively weak. Be especially watchful on 11 December. Since 1984, prices rose once and fell seven times *(see Figure 14.3)*.

Buy on weakness

The implication for investors? Be cautious. But don't back away from shares too far. Keep in mind that the trend for the following seven quarters is quite good. A strategy that worked well recently was to buy on second-quarter weakness.

298

Table 14.4   **PERCENTAGE PRICE CHANGE: 1985–1994**

	December 1–8	December 9–15	December 16–23	December 24–31
Annual quarterly price change				
1985	-2.21%	-1.05%	0.69%	1.61%
1986	-1.29%	0.38%	1.12%	-0.86%
1987	3.52%	2.87%	6.56%	-3.25%
1988	-1.43%	-0.68%	0.62%	1.33%
1989	3.12%	-0.55%	0.89%	2.59%
1990	2.44%	-1.31%	-0.75%	-0.87%
1991	-2.03%	3.39%	-4.43%	6.19%
1992	-0.22%	-1.14%	4.62%	1.04%
1993	2.45%	0.59%	3.26%	0.40%
1994	-1.78%	-1.44%	3.99%	-0.84%
Average quarterly price change				
1985–1994	-0.26%	0.11%	1.66%	0.73%
Number of years in which prices:				
rose	4	4	8	6
fell	6	6	2	4

UPDATE

Source: Datastream

Table 14.4: The recent trend for each quarter mirrors the patterns of the past. First- and second-quarter prices are relatively weak, third- and fourth-quarter prices relatively strong.

INCREASE YOUR PROFIT ODDS

November fourth-quarter/ December first-quarter signal

Here is one trend that has done a good job of forecasting rising second-quarter prices. If shares shift within a narrow range of -1.00% to +2.96% in November's fourth quarter, and -1.54% to +0.39% in December's first quarter, they will probably rise in the second quarter. There have been 20

Figure 14.3 **PERCENTAGE OF TIME PRICES RISE EACH TRADING DAY IN DECEMBER'S SECOND QUARTER**

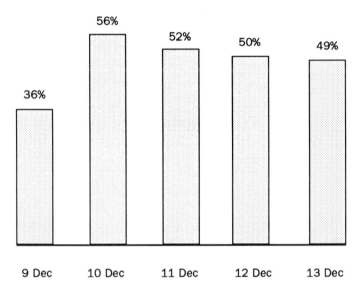

Figure 14.4: 11 December rises 52% of the time. Unfortunately, since 1984, its record has been poor – one up and seven down.

years with price shifts within these ranges. Second-quarter prices rose in 18 of them. The average increase was +1.01%.

IMPROVEMENT

Rose (18)

Fell (2)

Second-quarter record after a price shift of -1.00% to +2.96% in November's fourth quarter, and -1.54% to +0.39% in December's first quarter

Keep in mind that Budget Day may have affected this trend. We shall watch the situation carefully.

300

THIRD QUARTER OF DECEMBER – DECEMBER 16TH TO 23RD

> Here comes the start of a profitable stretch that runs to the first quarter of February.
>
> Prices rise in three out of four years during this quarter. A small price shift in the second quarter usually signals a price rise in this quarter.
>
> This segment is becoming quite volatile. Prices have shifted by over 3% in each of the last four years.

Very profitable

December's third quarter has been a nice little money-earner during the past 60 years. Even more important, it marks the beginning of a profitable stretch that runs through to early February. While you would not have profited in every single quarter nor in every single year, the record shows that between 1935 to 1994, the average share price rose sharply during this seven-quarter stretch.

A hypothetical start-up investment of £1,000 in 1974, placed in shares during these seven quarters, and in cash for the rest of the year, would have grown to over £6,000 by the beginning of 1995. If you consider that the investment was at risk for just over 700 trading days in total (roughly three years of normal trading) the size of this profit is easier to grasp.

Rises in three out of four years

Focusing on December's third quarter reveals that prices have risen in 72% of all years on record. The only segment of the year which rose more often was December's fourth quarter which rose 80% of the time. Third-quarter share prices have increased by an average annual rate of +0.83%.

The worst-ever decade for the third quarter was in the 1960s when investors lost at an average rate of -0.06% per year. But even then, the record was six up and four down. Many of the price moves of that decade were small. As a result, the biggest decline of the decade, a relatively small -3.84% in 1967 had a much larger effect on the decade's average than similar sized declines usually have.

Recent trend strong

The 1980s continued the good profits trend with a record of nine up and one down, and an average annual profit of +1.33%.

We shall have to wait and see whether the pattern continues through the 1990s. The record since 1990 is three up and two down and an average annual profit of +1.34%.

20 and 23 December

Analysis of share price trends on a day-by-day basis reveals that prices often fall near the beginning of the quarter. But things soon improve. Prices rise 71% of the time on 23 December, one of the year's Top 10 days *(see Table 14.5 and Figure 14.4)*.

The odds of a price rise are also quite high when 20 December lands on a Friday which it does in 1996 *(see Table 14.6)*.

In the 1995 edition of the *Schwartz Stock Market Handbook*, we noted that the third quarter has been quite volatile in the past three years. The drop of -4.43% in 1991, the biggest ever, was followed by increases of +4.62% in 1992 and +3.26% in 1993. The pattern continued into 1994 with a third quarter rise of +3.99%. We shall watch these new developments with great interest.

UPDATE

INCREASE YOUR PROFIT ODDS

There are a number of ways to improve the odds of making a third-quarter profit. One trick is to watch the price trend in the first two quarters of the month. If prices rise in both periods, or if they fall in both periods, the chance of a third-quarter profit improves significantly.

December first-half signal No 1

Since 1943, there have been 13 occasions when the price of an average share rose in each of the first two quarters of the month. The third-quarter record in those 13 years was 11 increases (85%), two losing quarters and an average annual third-quarter profit of +1.25%. This signal last flashed in 1993 and prices rose +3.26% in the third quarter.

Table 14.5

THE BEST DAYS OF THE YEAR

	Percentage of time prices rise
December 24	80%
December 27	79%
April 27	74%
December 22	74%
August 3	72%
December 23	71%
December 29	71%
April 15	70%
June 6	70%
April 3 & August 5	68%

| UPDATE |

Table 14.5: It's simply unbelievable. Five of the year's best days arrive in December. All occur after 21 December.

Table 14.6

PERCENTAGE OF TIME PRICES RISE ON 17–21 DECEMBER: 1935–1994

	Prices rise
Total	46%
Friday	70%
Rest of week	41%

Table 14.6: The odds of a price rise on 17–21 December are high if they land on a Friday. 20 December lands on a Friday in 1996.

Rose (11)

Fell (2)

Third-quarter record after a price rise in the first and second quarter of December (since 1943)

December first-half signal No 2

There were 12 additional years when the price of the average share fell in both preceding quarters. Prices rose in

303

Figure 14.4　　**PERCENTAGE OF TIME PRICES RISE EACH TRADING DAY IN DECEMBER'S THIRD QUARTER**

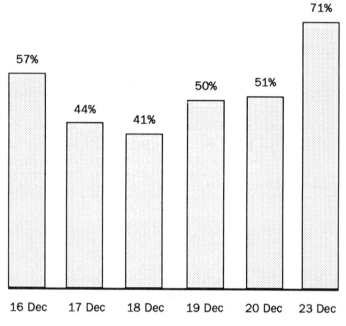

Figure 14.4: The week before Christmas has a secret weapon, 23 December, where prices rise 71% of the time, one of the year's best performances. The odds of a price rise on the Friday before Christmas is also quite good – this year 20 December.

nine of those years, remained unchanged in two and fell just once. This signal last flashed in 1994 and was followed by a third quarter rally which drove up prices by +3.99%.

| UPDATE |

Rose (9)

Fell (1)

No change (2)

Third-quarter record after a price drop in the first and second quarters of December

Second-quarter signal

The second-quarter trend, by itself, also does a fine job of forecasting third-quarter increases in share price. There have been 24 years with a very small second-quarter price shift in the range of -1.14% to +0.61%. Third-quarter prices rose in 23 of those years. The single exception was back in 1957.

Rose (23)

Fell (1)

Third-quarter record after a price shift in the second quarter of -1.14% to +0.61%

FOURTH QUARTER OF DECEMBER – DECEMBER 24TH TO 31ST

Historically, this is the best quarter of the year. Prices rise four out of five times. Three of the year's best days land in this segment of the month.

Despite the good record, it is possible to increase the odds of a profit by watching price shifts in the preceding weeks. Shares are likely to rise if a small price advance occurred in the third quarter.

Year's best quarter

Investors frequently profit during the fourth quarter of December. It is the very best quarter of the entire year. Three of the 10 best days of the entire year are in this segment of December.

Prices rise four out of five years

Between 1936–1994, prices rose, unbelievably, 80% of the time. The average annual gain was +1.02%. Both figures are the best of all 48 quarters of the year. There are no guarantees for any single year of course. By definition, an 80% likelihood of profit means that shares will fall in one out of five years as well. Still, an 80% likelihood of profit is an impressive record.

The fourth segment of the month has produced an average annual profit in every decade on record. The 'worst' decade was the 1940s when the average annual profit was just +0.67%, equivalent to 22 points on an FT-SE 100 in the area of 3300.

1980s profitable

The recent trend remains strong. The record for the bull market 1980s was eight up, two down, and an average annual profit of +1.01%. Since 1990, the fourth quarter has risen in three of the past five years.

Christmas present

In the period covering the final two trading days before Christmas and the three (or so) trading days between Christmas and New Year's Day, share prices fell just nine times in the 60 years between 1935 and 1994 (15%). It is the closest thing to a guaranteed profit that the stock market will ever offer.

24 and 27 December

Analysis of share price trends on a daily basis shows above-average strength throughout this quarter *(see Figure 14.5)*. The recent record for 24 and 27 December shows no sign of weakness.

INCREASE YOUR PROFIT ODDS

Third-quarter signal

The third quarter does a fine job of helping investors to increase the odds of catching a profitable fourth quarter. There have been 29 third quarters with small price shifts within a range of -0.19% to +0.89%. Fourth-quarter prices fell in just one of those years, a -0.09% fall (equal to three points on a 3300 FT-SE 100) back in 1950. The average annual increase was +1.33%.

Rose (28)

Fell (1)

Fourth-quarter record after a price shift in the third quarter of -0.19% to +0.89%

Figure 14.5   **PERCENTAGE OF TIME PRICES RISE EACH TRADING DAY IN DECEMBER'S FOURTH QUARTER**

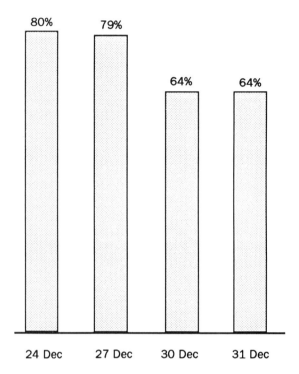

Figure 14.5: The fourth quarter may be holiday-shortened, but prices tend to rise on the few days that trading does occur. 24 December is the year's best day and 27 December is the year's second-best day.

Prior-three-quarters signal

Although the odds of losing money are low, most fourth-quarter declines occur when prices in the first three quarters of the month shift by a small amount. Since 1946, there have been 11 occasions when prices shifted by -0.45% to +1.30% in the first three quarters. Fourth-quarter prices fell in eight of those years. In two of the exceptional years, the fourth-quarter profit was tiny, +0.35% in 1977 and +0.26% in 1963.

Rose (3)

Fell (8)

Fourth-quarter record after a price shift of -0.45% to +1.30% in the first three quarters of December

In the remaining 38 years since 1946, the fourth-quarter record was 36 up and two down.

LOOKING AHEAD

For a preview of what the first three months of 1997 has in store for you, the price trend over the past 12 months provides a useful clue.

Rising prices by next 31 March

Since 1956, there have been 16 years when prices shifted within a range of -13.19% to +7.88% in the year ending 31 December. On each occasion, prices rose in the next three months (to 31 March of the year ahead).

Rose (15)

Fell (0)

Trend to 31 March (next year) after a January–December price shift of -13.19% to +7.88% (since 1956)

In the remaining 24 years of this period, the first-quarter record was little better than 50:50, 13 up and 11 down.

Extremely large price shifts in the November/December time period often tip price declines in the first six months of the year ahead.

Falling prices by next 30 June

There have been 14 years on record with a November/December price decline of -3.34% or worse. Prices fell still further by 30 June of the following year in 10 of those years. There were six other years with a

November/December price rise of +8.82% to +10.63%. Prices fell by 30 June of the following year in five of those years.

Rose (5)

Fell (15)

Trend to 30 June (next year) after a November/December price drop of -3.34% or worse, or a price rise of +8.82% to +10.63%

CHAPTER FIFTEEN –
WALL STREET JANUARY 1996

Great speech. Too bad '96
was an even-numbered year

January is often money-making time on Wall Street as well as in the UK. Prices rise in two out of three years.

The recent trend continues to be strong. There is no sign of a trend change. You will not make money in every single year with a January investment, but the odds favour a January profit over the long-run.

The likelihood of a January profit is especially high if December prices rose strongly. But if a strong November rally peters out in December, history suggests January will be a loser.

The so-called January Rule which describes the relationship between January price shifts and the stock market's trend during the rest of the year continues to operate, but only in odd-numbered years, due to the US political cycle. So don't try to use the rule for forecasting purposes in even-numbered years like 1996. However, a strong December/January up-move increases the odds of a profit in the next six months in all years, odd and even.

Steady profits

January is Wall Street's second-best month, a steady money-maker since our records began. From 1930 to the present, prices have risen 65% of the time, at an average rate of +1.47% per year. A hypothetical investor, who held shares each January, from 1930 to the present, and converted to cash for the rest of the year would have run a $1,000 investment up to $2,393. This is not a bad return considering that the money was placed in shares for just 65 months.[1]

While you would not have profited in every single year, your investment would have grown in every completed decade since the 1930s *(see Table 15.1)*. It is the only month of the year on Wall Street that can make this claim.

Recent record good

There is no sign of recent weakness. Prices have risen in eight of the last 10 years. It is Wall Street's Number Two-ranked month during this period.

INCREASE YOUR PROFIT ODDS

Although the chance of profiting in January is quite good, it is possible to improve the odds of making money in this month by monitoring several historical trends.

December signal

One of the best is the price trend during the previous month. There have been 15 occasions since 1926 when December prices rose strongly, within a range of +3.89% to +8.62%. January prices continued to rise in 14 of those years. The only exception was in 1977 when January fell by -5.05% despite a favourable December signal. Even with 1977 included, prices rose by an average of +2.32% each time the December signal flashed.

Rose (14)　▭

Fell (1)　▯

January record after a December price rise of +3.89% to +8.62%

---

[1] All Wall Street data based on the S & P composite (500).

Table 15.1   **JANUARY PRICE RISES AND DECLINES: 1930–1994**

	Average January price change	Up	Down/ no change
1930–39	2.02%	7	3
1940–49	0.86%	7	3
1950–59	1.24%	7	3
1960–69	0.89%	6	4
1970–79	1.24%	5	5
1980–89	3.38%	7	3
1990–94	-0.15%	3	2
Average January price change	1.47%	42	23

Source: Datastream

Table 15.1: January is the only month that was steadily profitable in every decade since the 1930s.

July to
December signal

Another trend that does a good job of anticipating January profits is a large decline in the preceding six months. Since 1926, there have been 11 years when prices fell by -7.42% to -31.49% in the second half of the year. Prices rose each time in the January that followed. The average increase was a whopping +4.70%.

Rose (11) ▭

Fell (0) ▌

January record after a July to December price drop of -7.42% to -31.49% (since 1926)

November/
December signal

On the down-side, when a strong November up-move peters out in December, the odds are high that January prices will also fall. Since 1934, there have been seven occasions when shares rose in November by at least +2.70% and either fell in December or rose by no more than +0.32%. January prices fell each time, by an average of -3.57%.

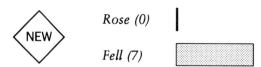

Rose (0)

Fell (7)

January record after a price rise in November of at least +2.70% and either a decline in December or a rise by no more than +0.32% (since 1934)

LOOKING AHEAD

Predictive in odd-numbered years

As in the UK, there is a relationship between January price shifts and the direction of prices in the next 11 months. But the nature of that relationship is very different on Wall Street from that in the UK. In America, the ability of January to forecast the direction of prices in the next 11 months is quite impressive in odd-numbered years, less so in even-numbered years. To understand why this is so, a brief description of the American political system is in order.

The US Congress is divided into two branches, the Senate whose members serve a six year term (one-third come up for re-election every two years) and the House of Representatives whose members serve a two year term. The president is on a four-year cycle. National elections are held near the beginning of November in even numbered years, and the newly elected officials take office two months later in January of the following year.

Because of this schedule, price trends in odd-numbered Januarys are incredibly useful to investors, serving as an important bell-wether for the year ahead. In this month, campaign posturing and promises are either side-lined or put to the test. The President gives his annual State of the Union address which lays out his budget and goals for the year ahead. New congressional leaders are elected by their fellow members of the Senate or House of Representatives, and present their own political and economic agendas. And most important of all, the degree to which the newly-elected members of Congress will support the President and/or their congressional leaders is revealed for the first time.

Odd-year signal No 1

Not surprisingly, the stock market pays a great deal of attention to politics in odd-numbered Januarys. And Wall Street's initial reaction of how politics will affect the economy is usually quite accurate. Since 1949, odd-year January prices fell six times. By 31 December, prices fell even lower all six occasions.

Rose (0)

Fell (6)

Trend to 31 December after a January price drop (since 1949)

Odd-year signal No 2

During this period, January rose by up to 12.28% in 16 years. Prices continued to rise in every one of those years.

Rose (16)

Fell (0)

Trend to 31 December after a January price rise of up to 12.28% (since 1949)

The sole exception was in 1987. A January price rise of over 13% proved to be not sustainable. Although prices continue to rise until mid-year, the October crash caused 1987 to be a money-loser despite a January up-move.

Odds of profit in even-numbered years is 50:50

During even-numbered years, when members of Congress are better known, and fewer brand new legislative programmes are initiated, there is less opportunity for a January-related event to affect the stock market and the January Rule does not work as well.

▶ In even-numbered years since 1950, January prices rose 12 times. By 31 December, prices rose still higher 10 times and fell twice.

▶ Also in even-numbered years, January prices fell 11 times. By 31 December, prices rose nine times and fell even lower twice.

Although the point of this analysis is to show that the January Rule is useless as a forecasting tool in even-numbered years, the alert reader has probably spotted one other useful investment insight: the odds of a January price rise in even-numbered years, like 1996, is poor: roughly 50:50.

Rising prices by 31 July

Another tool with which to forecast the months ahead is the size of the combined December and January up-move. Since 1936, December/January prices rose by +4.75% or more in 30 different years. Prices rose still higher in the six months to follow (31 July) in 28 of those years. One of the two exceptions occurred in 1971 when February to July prices fell by a mere one-third of a percent.

Rose (28)

Fell (2)

Trend to 31 July after a December/January price rise of +4.75% or more (since 1936)

As you use this information, keep in mind that 31 January is not necessarily the low point of the period nor is 31 July necessarily the high point. Prices could spurt in February, hypothetically, drift down over the next few months, yet qualify as a February–July up-move. By the same token, shares could fall in February or March, allowing investors to buy at an even lower price in some years.

CHAPTER SIXTEEN –
WALL STREET FEBRUARY 1996

February has been a dead loss for US investors during most of the twentieth century. Although prices have risen slightly more than half the time, the size of the typical February advance is often quite weak.

Despite the disappointing long-term trend, it is possible to profit handsomely by investing sporadically and avoiding the stock market in years with a high likelihood of a February decline. One signal for which to look is a sluggish price trend in the run-up to February, either a small gain or a small loss. Small pre-February moves often signal that shares will fall in February.

Some more good news: there has been a noticeable improvement during the last 10 years. February prices have risen eight times.

Small average annual loss

As in the UK stock market, February is frequently a disappointment to American investors. It is Wall Street's tenth-best month. From 1930 to the present, a steady February investor lost money at a small average rate of -0.02% per year. A hypothetical investor, who held shares each February, from 1930 to the present, and converted to cash for the rest of the year would have run down his $1,000 start-up investment to $927, before factoring in inflation.

The February investor lost money in the 1940s, '50s and '60s. Two big profit years, 1970 and 1975, were responsible for the profits of the 1970s. The record for the remaining eight years was two up and six down. Things seem to have improved in the bull market 1980s, as did other months. Thus, its average annual profit of +0.58% during this period was merely ninth-ranked *(see Table 16.1)*.

Weakness

Despite the poor record, you may be surprised to learn that prices rise in most years. The problem with February is that prices tend to rise weakly in the years that they do rise.

Table 16.1   **FEBRUARY PRICE RISES AND DECLINES: 1930–1994**

	Average February price change	Up	Down/ no change
1930–39	0.51%	7	3
1940–49	-0.94%	3	7
1950–59	-0.51%	5	5
1960–69	-0.57%	5	5
1970–79	0.11%	4	6
1980–89	0.58%	6	4
1990–94	1.32%	4	1
Average February price change	-0.02%	34	31

Source: Datastream

Table 16.1: February investors lost money in the 1940s–1960s and squeaked out a small profit in the 1970s. But in recent years, the trend has improved markedly.

Recent improvement

But in the recent past, from 1985 to 1994, there has been a noticeable improvement. Prices have risen eight times. It is the first time since records began that February prices have risen in eight out of 10 consecutive years.

INCREASE YOUR PROFIT ODDS

Despite the weak profit prospects over the long run, it is possible to profit in February by investing selectively. Here are three trends that have been associated with February price declines. Avoiding the stock market in years that any of these three trends issued a warning signal will ensure good odds of a profit in years when you do invest.

December/ January signal

Since 1942, a price shift in December and January within a range of -3.19% to +4.29% has occurred in 15 different years. Shares fell in February in 14 of those years. The sole failure of this rule occurred in 1993 when a small rise in December/January was followed by a further rise in

February. But things quickly got back on track in 1994 when February prices fell after a small December/January price change, right on cue.

Rose (1)

Fell (14)

February record after a December/January price shift of -3.19% to +4.29% (since 1942)

January signal

Another signal to watch for is a small January price shift within a range of -1.75% to +0.73%. There have been 14 shifts of this small magnitude since our records began in 1926. February prices fell in 12 of those years. The two exceptions occurred in 1986 and 1993, both late in the day in multi-year bull markets.

Rose (2)

Fell (12)

February record after a January price shift of -1.75% to +0.73% (since 1926)

September–
January signal

The third warning signal is a moderately weak price trend in the five month run-up to February. There have been 13 years with a price shift of -5.95% to +0.72% in the 1 September–31 January period. February's prices fell each time, at an average annual rate of -3.20%.

Rose (0)

Fell (13)

February record after a September to January price shift of -5.95% to +0.72%

319

Since 1942, there have been 22 years flagged by one or more of these three warning trends. February's record in these years was 2 up and 20 down. In the remaining 31 years, the February record was a very respectable 24 up and 7 down. While you would not have made money every single year, a 77% success rate is nothing to be ashamed of either.

LOOKING AHEAD

The February price swing often provides a good clue about the direction of prices 12 months ahead.

Rising prices by next 28 February

Since 1944, there have been 15 years with a small February price shift, no more than -0.25% on the down-side and no more than +1.05% on the up-side. Prices rose in the 12 months that followed in each of those 15 years.

Rose (15)

Fell (0)

Trend to 28 February (next year) after a February price shift of -0.25% to +1.05% (since 1944)

Falling prices by next 28 February

On the down-side, since 1939, there have been 10 years with a small three-month December to February price shift of -2.23% to +0.52%. The record for the year ahead was just two rises and eight declines.

Rose (2)

Fell (8)

Trend to 28 February (next year) after a December–February price shift of -2.23% to +0.52% (since 1939)

CHAPTER SEVENTEEN –
WALL STREET MARCH 1996

> Since World War II, March prices have risen in two out of three years. In years where there has been a moderate price rise in the run-up to March, prices are especially likely to rise.
>
> Looking ahead, a good sign to watch for is a price rise in the first quarter of the year. It almost always means that prices will rise still further by year-end.

1930s were horrid

At first glance, February and March seem to share similar trading patterns. Both frequently disappoint American investors. Over the long run, March is Wall Street's ninth best month *(see Table 17.1)*.

Investors lost heavily in the 1930s, an average annual loss of -4.76%, the second-worst ever performance on record for any month. Only September did worse, also in the 1930s. There is no getting away from it. The '30s was a horrid period for March investors. Three years did most of the damage: 1932, -11.82%; 1938, -25.04%; 1939, -13.54%. The 1938 decline was the second worst monthly 'hit' ever experienced on Wall Street since our records began. The only month to cost investors more dearly was September 1931 when prices fell by almost 30% during the height of the 1929–32 stock market collapse *(see Table 17.2)*.

Trend positive since 1940

But a peek beneath the surface finds the prospects for a March investor to be much better than they appear to be at first glance. Even with the 1930s included, March prices have risen 60% of the time, and made money for investors at a small average rate of +0.09% per year. A hypothetical investor, who held shares each March, from 1930 to the present, and converted to cash for the rest of the year would have run down his $1,000 start-up investment to $966.

Table 17.1

MARCH PRICE RISES AND DECLINES: 1930–1994

	Average March price change	Up	Down/ no change
1930–39	-4.76%	3	7
1940–49	1.07%	7	3
1950–59	1.55%	7	3
1960–69	1.03%	6	4
1970–79	1.38%	7	3
1980–89	0.35%	6	4
1990–94	-0.05%	3	2
Average March price change	0.09%	39	26

Source: Datastream

Table 17.1: The 1930s pull the long-term March average down. The record from 1940–1994 is 36 up and 19 down. The trend in the last 10 years is positive with a record of six up and four down.

Table 17.2

TOP 10 MONTHLY DECLINES: 1926-1994

	Percent decrease
September 1931	-29.94%
March 1938	-25.04%
May 1940	-23.95%
May 1932	-23.33%
October 1987	-21.76%
April 1932	-20.25%
October 1929	-19.93%
February 1933	-18.44%
June 1930	-16.46%
December 1931	-14.53%

Table 17.2: When things go wrong on Wall Street, they can go wrong in a *big* way. Both May and October have two entries on this Top 10 list. Seven out of 10 occurred between 1929–32, American's worst-ever bear market.

Excluding the 1930s from the long-term computations and his average annual profit would be close to one percent. A $1,000 March investment starting in 1940 instead of 1930, would now be worth $1,655. During this period, prices rose 36 times (65%) and fell 19 times.

INCREASE YOUR PROFIT ODDS

It is possible to improve your profit prospects in March over the long-run by investing selectively. Here are two trends that have been consistently associated with March price increases.

February signal From 1956 to 1994, February prices have risen by at least +1.90% on 10 occasions. Shares rose in March in nine of those years. The average annual increase was +1.83%. The sole failure of this signal occurred in 1988.

Rose (9)

Fell (1)

March record after a February price rise of at least +1.90% (since 1956)

September– February signal Since 1959, prices rose in the six-month run-up to March by at least +7.09% in 17 different years. March prices rose in 16 of those years. The average annual increase during these 17 years was +2.46%. The single failure occurred in 1985 when March prices fell by a tiny -0.29%.

Rose (16)

Fell (1)

March record after a September–February rise of at least +7.09% (since 1959)

Since 1959, there were 17 years when neither signal flashed. The March record was a money-losing six up and 11 down.

LOOKING AHEAD

Rising prices by
31 August

A small-to-medium March price rise is often associated with further price rises in the five months ahead. Here is the evidence. Since 1941, there have been 21 years when March prices rose +0.40% to +3.31%. By 31 August, prices stood still higher in 20 of those years. In the recent past, this signal flashed in 1991 and 1993 and prices rose in the months ahead both times.

Rose (20)

Fell (1)

Trend to 31 August after a March price rise of +0.40% to +3.36% (since 1941)

Rising prices by
31 December

The price trend for the first three months of the year provides a good clue about where prices will stand at the year-end. Since 1950, there have been 26 occasions when prices rose by at least +0.42% in the first three months of the year, up through March 31st. They rose still further by the year-end in 24 of those years. The two exceptions were in 1957 when shares were down by just -3.73% at year-end, and in 1987 when the up-trend was badly fractured by the October crash.

Rose (24)

Fell (2)

Trend to 31 December after a January–March price rise of at least +0.42% (since 1950)

CHAPTER EIGHTEEN – WALL STREET APRIL 1996

Not a great month but things could be worse . . .

Despite a poor record in the 1930s and '40s, April is the year's fourth-best month.

The trend was helped by a series of good years in the 1950s and 1960s when prices rose 15 out of 20 times. Since then, prices have risen less frequently and the month has become just mildly profitable. By way of example, in the last 10 years, prices rose five times and fell five times.

The price trend between December and March often tips off which way April prices will move. A small shift, up or down, frequently signals an April price drop. A healthy four-month long advance is usually followed by an April price rise.

Historically profitable

April is Wall Street's fourth-best month. Prices rise 57% of the time at an average rate of +1.03%. You will not have made money every year but over the long-run, an April investment has been solidly profitable. Between 1930 and 1994, a hypothetical April investor who placed his money in cash for the rest of the year, would have run-up his $1,000 to $1,664 *(see Table 18.1)*.

Table 18.1   **APRIL PRICE RISES AND DECLINES: 1930–1994**

	Average April price change	Up	Down/ no change
1930–39	1.58%	3	7
1940–49	-0.33%	4	6
1950–59	2.16%	7	3
1960–69	1.80%	8	2
1970–79	-0.06%	6	4
1980–89	1.70%	6	4
1990–94	-0.25%	3	2
Average April price change	1.03%	37	28

Source: Datastream

Table 18.1: The Golden Years for April investors were in the 1950s and '60s when prices rose 15 times out of 20 years. But since then, April's performance has been only modestly profitable.

But beneath the surface, the April trend is more erratic than it appears to be at first glance.

Losses in the 1930s and '40s

During the 1930s and 1940s, April was not very profitable. The combined record during this period was seven up and 13 down. The 1930s poor performance was disguised by an enormous rally in 1933 when April prices soared 42%. A wave of bank closures and bank holidays severely frightened the stock market in the late winter and early spring of 1932–33. Newly elected president Roosevelt took office on 3 March. He shortly removed the country from the Gold Standard and took steps to stimulated the economy. The stock market responded with an enormous rally, the largest monthly increase on record.

Recent record poor

Things improved in the 1950s and 1960s, the best-ever period for April investors. Prices rose 15 times in 20 years. Since then, the trend has been mildly profitable, but nowhere near the level of profits obtained by UK investors.

The recent record continues to be unimpressive. Prices have risen five times and declined five times in the past 10 years, and returned a small average annual profit of +0.17%.

INCREASE YOUR PROFIT ODDS

Although the recent odds of profiting in April are nothing to brag about, it is possible to improve upon them by monitoring several historical trends which do a good job of tipping price increases.

February/March signal

One of the best is the direction of price shifts in the previous two months. Since 1951, there have been 13 occasions when shares drifted slightly in the previous two months, no more than -2.59% on the down-side and no more than +0.56% on the up-side. April prices rose in 12 of those years.

Rose (12)

Fell (1)

April record after a February/March price shift of -2.59% to +0.56% (since 1951)

December–March signal No 1

The preceding four months often tip off where shares are heading in April, down as well as up. There have been 12 occasions on record when prices shifted within a tight range of -2.06% to +4.71% from 1 December to 31 March. April prices fell in nine of those years.

Rose (3)

Fell (9)

April record after a December–March price shift of -2.06% to +4.71%

December–
March signal
No 2

Above this level and the odds favour a price rise. There have been 15 other occasions when prices rose by +4.97% to +8.80% in the four month run-up to April. Shares rose in 13 of those years. Both exceptions to the rule occurred in the 1950s.

Rose (13)

Fell (2)

April record after a December–March price rise of +4.97% to +8.80%

January signal

January does a superb job of forecasting where April's prices are heading. No one knows for certain why January is such a good April forecaster although the fact that both are opening months of adjacent quarters is an obvious connection. Since 1954, January prices rose within a range of +1.81% to +7.22% 17 times. April prices rose each time.

Rose (17)

Fell (0)

April record after a January price rise of +1.81% to +7.22% (since 1954)

LOOKING AHEAD

Rising prices by
31 July

April price shifts provide several good clues about where prices are heading in the months ahead. A small price swing is often associated with further price rises in the next three months. Since 1943, there have been 15 years when April prices shifted within a range of -2.12% to +0.61%. By 31 July, prices stood still higher in 14 of those years. The sole exception was in 1972 when a small April shift was followed by a decline in share prices in the next three months. But even then, the three-month decline was a tiny -0.26%.

NEW

Rose (14)

Fell (1)

Trend to 31 July after an April price shift of -2.12% to +0.61% (since 1943)

Rising prices by 31 August

A small price rise in the three months ending 30 April is a good sign that prices will rise further in the next four months. There have been 15 years when prices rose by +3.14% to +8.36% during this three-month stretch. They rose still further in the four months that followed each rise.

NEW

Rose (15)

Fell (0)

Trend to 31 August after February–April price rise of +3.14% to +8.36%

Rising prices by 30 September

Here is a third useful signal, this one based on a longer time frame. Since 1939, there have been 21 years when prices rose in the 11 month period between 1 June to 30 April by +5.98% to +20.16%. They continued to rise still higher in the next five months in 20 of those years. The sole exception to the rule occurred in 1981.

NEW

Rose (20)

Fell (1)

Trend to 30 September after a June–April price rise of +5.98% to +20.16% (since 1939)

Falling prices by
30 November
No 1

The price trend at this point of the year also provides two useful down-side indicators. If either one flashes, history suggests the need for extreme caution in the months ahead. Prices fell in the five months between 1 December and 30 April by -4.35% to -12.25% on 11 different occasions. They fell still further over the next seven months in nine of those years.

Rose (2)

Fell (9)

Trend to 30 November after a December–April price drop of
-4.35% to -12.25%

Falling prices by
30 November
No 2

There have been 11 occasions when shares rose by just +0.28% to +5.09% in the 11-month period between 1 June and 30 April. They fell over the next seven months in nine of those years. One of the two exceptions was a rise of under 1% in 1953.

Rose (2)

Fell (9)

Trend to 30 November after a June–April price rise of +0.28% to +5.09%

330

CHAPTER NINETEEN – WALL STREET MAY 1996

May is Wall Street's eleventh-best month and has been a sub-standard performer for most of the century.

But the recent trend change has caught most investors by surprise. From 1985 to 1994, prices have advanced 10 years in a row, a rare event for any month.

Even when times are poor, it is possible to increase the odds of a May profit by picking your investment opportunities carefully. Moderate price increases in the months that precede May often signal that May prices will also rise.

There are also several useful signals to help forecast where prices will be in the months ahead. A strong price rise in the first five months of the year usually signals that prices will rise even further by year-end.

Constant losses

Historically, May has been a frequent disappointment for American investors, just as it has been for UK investors. It is Wall Street's eleventh-best month. Only September is worse. From 1930 to the present, the May investor lost money at an average of -0.34% per year. A hypothetical investor who held shares each May from 1930 to the present, and converted to cash for the rest of the year would have run down his $1,000 start-up investment to $698, before factoring in the effects of inflation.

Its performance in the 1930s was simply awful with an average loss of -2.24% per year. The record would have been even worse had it not been for 1933 when President Roosevelt's actions during his first 100 days in office caused the stock market to rocket upwards. May prices rose by almost 16% in that year, seventh-best in history.

May's performance improved in the 1940s and '50s. The

Table 19.1   **MAY PRICE RISES AND DECLINES: 1930–1994**

	Average May price change	Up	Down/ no change
1930–39	-2.24%	4	6
1940–49	-0.20%	7	3
1950–59	0.55%	6	4
1960–69	-1.20%	5	5
1970–79	-1.62%	3	7
1980–89	0.80%	6	4
1990–94	3.33%	5	0
Average May price change	-0.34%	36	29

Source: Datastream

Table 19.1: The May trend has been chronically sub-standard for half a century. But prices have risen steadily since 1985, 10 times in a row.

1940s record was pulled down by a 24% drop in 1940 as Wall Street reacted to Germany's blitzkrieg and the Allies being swept from Europe. The record for the rest of the decade was seven up and two down, one of the better monthly performances of that decade.

Unfortunately, this period was May's high water mark. In the 1960s and '70s, May was 11th and 12th ranked. Investors did especially poorly in the 20 years from 1965 to 1984 when shares fell 15 times and rose just five times.

Trend change   But since 1985, May's performance has been nothing short of miraculous. Prices increased in each of the past 10 years, a very rare event for any month and something that has never happened in May before. The average price has risen by over 3% per annum during this stretch. This positive trend, coupled with the effect of Wall Street on London, helps to explain why May shares have performed so well in the UK in recent years.

INCREASE YOUR PROFIT ODDS

Even in bad stretches, it is possible to profit in May by investing selectively. Here are three trends that have been associated with May price rises.

February–April signal

If prices rise moderately in the three month run-up to May, the odds are good they will continue to rise during May. There have been 11 occasions when prices rose by +3.92% to +8.36% between February 1 to April 30. Shares rose in May each time.

Rose (11)

Fell (0)

May record after a February–April price rise of +3.92% to +8.36%

November–April signal

Over the longer run, a moderate price rise in the six-month run-up to May is also a good omen. There have been 13 occasions when prices rose by +5.14% to +12.67% between 1 November and 30 April. Shares rose in May in 12 of those years.

Rose (12)

Fell (1)

May record after a November–April price rise of +5.14% to +12.67%

September–April signal

The third trend to look for is a strong price rise in the eight-month run-up to May. There have been 10 occasions when prices rose by +16.37% to +21.64% between 1 September and 30 April. Shares rose in May each time.

Rose (10)

Fell (0)

May record after a September–April price rise of +16.37% to +21.64%

There is some overlap among these three trends. Since 1927, there have been 22 years touched by one or more of them. The May record is 21 up and one down. In the remaining 46 years, the May record is 17 up and 29 down (63%). You might make money in some of these years but over the long-run, a May investment is a money-losing proposition if none of the three signals is flashing.

Looking ahead

The extent to which May prices shift often provides a good clue about the months ahead. Here are three good signals to help you to forecast where prices are heading in the months ahead.

Rising prices by 30 September

Since our records began, there have been 15 Mays when prices shifted by a small amount, no more than -0.13% on the down-side and no more than +1.73% on the up-side. By 30 September, four months later, prices had risen further each time.

Rose (15)

Fell (0)

Trend to 30 September after a May price shift of -0.13% to +1.73%

Rising prices by 31 December

Since 1950, there were 21 years when prices rose in the first five months of the year within a range of +6.10% to

+15.47%. By the year-end, they rose still further each and every time.

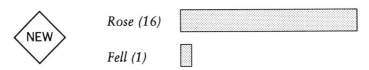

Rose (14)

Fell (0)

Trend to 31 December after a January–May price rise of +6.10% to +15.47%

Rising prices by next 31 May

If prices have fallen in the last 12 months, it is also a good sign for the year ahead. Since 1932, there have been 17 occasions in which prices fell in the 12 months preceding 31 May by at least -2.60%. In all but one of those occasions, the stock market rose in the 12 months ahead. The single exception occurred in the 1973 bear market.

Rose (16)

Fell (1)

Trend to 31 May (next year) after a 12-month (1 June–31 May) price drop of at least -0.31%.

335

Chapter Twenty –
Wall Street June 1996

Until recently, June has been steadily profitable over the long-run.

Unfortunately, the recently improved May trend has been affecting June for the worse. Since 1989, prices have fallen in five of the past six years. The single exception was a very tiny rise in 1993. June seems to be developing the habit of giving back some of May's profits.

Given the possibility of a major June trend change, it is wise to invest during this month with caution. History provides some useful clues. In the past, a moderate price rise in the few months preceding June often tipped off that June prices would fall.

Looking ahead, a moderate June price rise often signals that prices will continue to rise in the year ahead.

June is Wall Street's sixth-best month. Prices rise 54% of the time at an average rate of +0.93%. The only losing decade for the June investor was in the 1960s. You would not have made money every year, but over the long-run, this month has been solidly profitable. Between 1930 and 1994, a June investor who placed his money in cash for the rest of the year, would have run-up his $1,000 to $1,656.

Possible trend change

There is one fly in the ointment. Recent Junes have been weak. Prices fell four times in a row between 1989 and 1992, the first time ever they fell in four consecutive years, and in five of the last six years. The single increase between 1989 and 1994 was a minuscule +0.08% in 1993. We also note that recent Mays on Wall Street have, uncharacteristically, become quite profitable, suggesting the June drop may be nothing more than a normal reaction that usually follows a good rally.

How long will these poor trading conditions continue?

Table 20.1   **JUNE PRICE RISES AND DECLINES: 1930–1994**

	Average June price change	Up	Down/ no change
1930–39	3.47%	6	4
1940–49	2.30%	7	3
1950–59	0.89%	5	5
1960–69	-1.89%	4	6
1970–79	0.68%	5	5
1980–89	1.59%	7	3
1990–94	-2.00%	1	4
Average June price change	0.93%	35	30

Source: Datastream

Table 20.1: June has tended to be profitable throughout most of the 20th century but the trend has weakened noticeably since 1989. It may be nothing more than a short spell of turbulence or the first sign of a major trend change. We will watch the situation carefully.

No one knows. We note though that the last very bad stretch for June investors was in 1961 to 1974 when prices fell in 10 out of 14 years. Two of the four increases during this period were under 1%.

There is no question that the four recent falls in a row could be 'just one of those things' that occurs occasionally, but we are concerned about returning to a 1960s-type era of sub-standard performance. One straw to the wind: even in those sorry old days, three downs in a row was the worst that occurred before prices finally rose. This time around, we have seen four declines in a row. We shall watch future June developments with great interest.

Increase your profit odds

As in other months, it is possible to profit in June by investing selectively. This is especially useful if we are going through another 1960s-type bad patch. Here are three trends that have been associated with June price declines in the past.

March–May signal

A moderate price rise in the three months preceding June is often associated with a price decline during June. Since our records began, there have been 10 occasions when prices rose between +4.92% to +9.06% in March to May. The stock market declined in June in nine of those years.

Rose (1)

Fell (9)

June record after a March–May price rise of +4.92% to +9.06%

February–May signal

There have been 11 years when prices rose in the four month run-up to June by +5.88% to +11.43%. June prices fell in 10 of those years. There is some over lap with the previous three-month indicator, but this signal also flags some falls that were not spotlighted by the March to May signal.

Rose (1)

Fell (10)

June record after a February–May price rise of +5.88% to +11.43%

September–May signal

The third warning signal for which to watch is a large increase in the nine months preceding June. Since 1945, there have been 10 years with a price increase in the range of +16.83% to +23.66% between September to May. Shares fell in June in nine of those years. The sole exception was a +0.07% increase in 1971.

Rose (1)

Fell (9)

June record after a September–May price rise of +16.83% to +23.66% (since 1945)

If none of these three signals flashes, things are looking good for June. Since 1945, there were 34 years untouched by any of these three signals. The June record was 21 up and 13 down. You would have lost money in some years but the profits would have far out-weighed the losses.

LOOKING AHEAD

Rising prices next 30 June

June price shifts often provide clear signals about where prices are heading in the next few months. A small price rise is frequently associated with further price rises in the next 12 months. There have been 18 years when June prices rose within a range of +1.21% to +4.43%. One year later, prices stood still higher 17 times. The sole exception was in 1983, when a small June shift was followed by a decline in share prices in the next 12 months.

Rose (17)

Fell (1)

Trend to 30 June (next year) after a June price rise of +1.21% to +4.43%

Rising prices by 31 December No 1

Another good signal for which to look is a small price swing, up or down, in the period between 1 April and 30 June. Shifts like this are often associated with further price rises in the next six months. Since our records began, there have been 18 years when prices shifted within a range of -2.44% to +1.47%. By 31 December, shares stood still higher in 17 of those years. The sole exception was in 1941 when a small June shift was affected by falling prices in the run-up to America's entry into World War II.

Rose (17)

Fell (1)

Trend to 31 December after an April–June price shift of -2.44% to +1.47%

Rising prices by 31 December No 2

Here is another indicator that often signals further price rises in the second half of the year. Since 1935, there have been 18 years when prices rose in the first half of the year between +7.08% to +14.72%. By 31 December, prices stood still higher in 17 of those years. The sole exception was back in 1948.

Rose (17)

Fell (1)

Trend to 31 December after a January–June price rise of +7.08% to +14.72% (since 1935)

If nether of the two December signals flashes, the odds are just 50:50 that prices will rise in the second half of the year. Since 1935, there were 31 years when neither signal flashed. Prices rose from 1 July to 31 December in 15 years and fell 16 times.

CHAPTER TWENTY-ONE – WALL STREET JULY 1996

July was once a great month on Wall Street. Sadly, things change. Since the 1960s, it has risen about half the time. No improvement has been detected in recent years.

Fortunately, the price trend in the run-up to July sends some good clues about the direction of prices. A June price decline often precedes a July advance. A mild June advance is often followed by a decline in July.

Looking ahead, a small price shift in June/July is usually associated with rising prices over the next seven months.

Historically, July is Wall Street's best month. Between 1930 and 1994, a July investor who held shares during this month and converted his capital to cash for the rest of the year, would have run-up his $1,000 nest egg to $2,897. Prices have risen by 5% or more on 18 occasions since our records began, double the average for the other 11 months.

Large 1932 rise

The long-term average was helped by the profits of the 1930s when July prices rose by an average of +5.71% per year. It was the best performance ever, for any decade. A large part of this amazingly high average annual increase

Table 21.1   **TOP 10 MONTHLY INCREASES: 1926–1994**

	Percent increase
April 1933	42.22%
July 1932	37.70%
August 1932	37.54%
June 1938	24.70%
September 1939	16.46%
October 1974	16.30%
May 1933	15.87%
April 1938	14.12%
June 1931	13.90%
January 1987	13.18%

Table 21.1: Five of the top ten monthly increases were associated with the 1929–32 bear market or its immediate aftermath. It was the most volatile period on record.

---

was due to 1932 when prices rose by +37.70% *(see Table 21.1)*, marking the end of the worst bear market in Wall Street's history. It was the second-best month since our records began, followed one month later with an almost identical 37.54% rise in August 1932.

But even without 1932, July's prices rose by an average of +2.16% during the rest of this profitable decade. The 1950s produced an even more noteworthy trend. Prices rose in each of the decade's 10 years, the only time this has ever occurred on Wall Street in any month, since our records began *(see Table 21.2)*.

Average since the 1960s

Unfortunately, July's Golden Years have past. Since the 1960s, the July record has been decidedly average, with prices rising about half the time and producing a small average annual profit. It was ranked in eighth place on monthly profitability in the 1960s, and ninth and seventh place in the two decades that followed. During the 1980s, prices fell steadily from 1982 to 1986, the heart of one of the best bull markets of the century.

Table 21.2

JULY PRICE RISES AND DECLINES: 1930–1994

	Average July price change	Up	Down/ no change
1930–39	5.72%	7	3
1940–49	0.42%	5	5
1950–59	3.79%	10	0
1960–69	0.52%	5	5
1970–79	-0.31%	5	5
1980–89	0.82%	3	7
1990–94	2.10%	3	2
Average July price change	1.85%	38	27

Source: Datastream

Table 21.2: The Golden Years for the July investor ran from the 1930s to the 1950s. Prices rose in almost three out of four years. The '50s were the best decade ever, the only month for which prices rose in all 10 years. Since then, prices have risen about half the time and produced a small average annual profit.

INCREASE YOUR PROFIT ODDS

Even though the bloom is off the rose as far as July is concerned, it is still possible to profit in most years by investing carefully. Here are four trends that have been associated with fairly distinctive July trading patterns.

June signal No 1   If stock market prices fall by a sizeable amount in June, the odds favour a price rebound in July. There have been 15 years with a June price drop of -2.18% or more. July prices rose in 13 of those years.

Rose (13)

Fell (2)

July record after a June price drop of -2.18% or more

December–June
signal

If prices rise moderately in the seven month run-up to July, the odds are good they will continue to rise during July. There have been 11 occasions when prices rose by +7.23% to +11.41% between 1 December and 30 June. Shares rose in July each time.

Rose (11)

Fell (0)

July record after a December–June price rise of +7.23% to +11.41%

February–June
signal

On the down-side, here are two signals for which to watch. The first occurs very infrequently, but when it does – look out. There have been six years on record when prices rose by +13.96% or more in the five months preceding July. July's prices fell each time. Five were in excess of -5%.

Rose (0)

Fell (6)

July record after a February–June price rise of +13.96% or more

June signal No 2

Also keep an eye peeled for a small price rise in June. Since 1943, there have been 11 years with a June rise in the range of +0.07% to +2.08%. July prices fell in nine of those years.

Rose (2)

Fell (9)

July record after a June price rise of +0.07% to +2.08% (since 1943)

LOOKING AHEAD

Rising prices by next February

The extent to which the stock market shifts in June and July often provides a good clue about the trend for the months ahead. Since records began, there have been 23 years when prices were weak during June and July, shifting within a range of -5.01% on the down-side to +0.86% on the up-side. By 28 February of the following year, seven months later, prices had risen further in 22 of those years. The sole exception occurred in 1981.

Rose (22)

Fell (1)

Trend to 28 February (next year) after a June–July price shift of -5.01% to +0.86%

Falling prices by November

One note of caution: if prices rise strongly in July, within a range of +3.49% to +5.48%, look out for a down-turn. Since 1929, prices rose within this range on 13 occasions. By 30 November, four months later, shares were lower in 11 of those years. Five of the 11 falls were in double digits.

Rose (2)

Fell (11)

Trend to 30 November after a July price rise of +3.49% to +5.48% (since 1929)

CHAPTER TWENTY-TWO – WALL STREET AUGUST 1996

> The typical August profit is small, and half of it is attributable to a massive 38% increase in 1933.
>
> Fortunately, the stock market provides some useful clues which often tip off the direction of prices in August and the months that follow. Sharp declines in the run-up to August are frequently associated with August price rises. Small August price shifts, up or down, are usually associated with rising prices for the rest of the year.
>
> But if prices shift by a large amount during this sleepy summer month, the odds of making a profit in the final four months of the year are just 50:50.

Back around the turn of the century, when agriculture was largely a domestic affair, good crop years meant high traffic for the nation's railroads and lower costs for processors and manufacturers. August often gave investors their first clear view of what the summer growing season would deliver and the stock market moved accordingly.

Generally profitable

But in the more recent times covered by this survey, August has become a sleepy, largely uneventful month. Between 1930–1994, it was Wall Street's fifth best month. Prices rose 58% of the time at an average rate of +0.96%. During this period, an August investor who placed his money in cash for the rest of the year, would have run-up his $1,000 to $1,656.

1950s was a loser

The only losing decade for the August investor was in the 1950s when August prices fell in seven out of 10 years (see Table 22.1). Many of those falls followed strong July advances (which have been occurring less often in recent years).

Table 22.1   **AUGUST PRICE RISES AND DECLINES: 1930–1994**

	Average August price change	Up	Down/ no change
1930–39	4.37%	7	3
1940–49	0.20%	7	3
1950–59	-1.40%	3	7
1960–69	0.80%	7	3
1970–79	0.30%	5	5
1980–89	2.24%	6	4
1990–94	-0.53%	3	2
Average August price change	0.96%	38	27

Source: Datastream

Table 22.1: Prices rise in most decades. The two most profitable decades were helped by atypical years: a +37.54% increase in 1933, marking the end of the 1929–32 bear market, and two double-digit increases in 1982 (+11.60%) and 1984 (+10.63%).

In most decades, August prices move by a small amount. When big moves do occur, as in the 1930s or 1980s, it is usually due to an atypical price shift in one or two years.

1933 big rise ▶ Prices rose by an average of +4.37% per year in the 1930s, the second-best decade in any month of the year. The advance was helped by a +37.54% increase in 1933, marking the end of the 1929-1932 bear market. This single year accounts for one-half of all August profits during the 65 years surveyed. The record for the rest of the decade was six up, three down and a smaller +0.69% average annual increase.

1982 and 1984 ▶ The 1980s average annual profit of +2.24% was helped by two double digit increases, in 1982 (+11.60%), and 1984 (+10.63%). The record for the rest of the decade was four up, four down and a tiny +0.02% average annual profit.

On balance, you will not make money every year but can expect to make a small average annual profit over the long-run. Up-moves large enough to affect the August averages do occur from time to time but, unfortunately, not very often.

INCREASE YOUR PROFIT ODDS

History reveals several price signals which can help investors to improve the odds of making an investment profit in August.

July signal No 1 Since our records began, there have been 10 occasions when prices fell by a small amount in July, within a range of -0.25% to -1.30%. August prices fell in eight of those years.

Rose (2)

Fell (8)

August record after a July price drop of -0.25% to -1.30%

July signal No 2 On the up-side, here are two trends which frequently tip that an August price rise is likely. There have been 12 occasions when shares fell in July by a relatively large amount, -1.65% to -6.02%. August prices rose in 11 of those years.

Rose (11)

Fell (1)

August record after a July price drop of -1.65% to -6.02%

348

December–July
signal

There have been 10 occasions when prices were down sharply in the eight months preceding August, December to July, by -9.46% or worse. Shares rose in August in nine of those years.

Rose (9)

Fell (1)

August record after a December–July price drop of -9.46% or worse

LOOKING AHEAD

Rising prices by
December No 1

The extent to which the stock market shifts in August is often a good clue about the price trend for the months ahead. Since 1949, there have been 24 years when August prices shifted by no more than -2.40% on the down-side and no more than +3.45% on the up-side. By the year-end, four months later, prices had risen in 23 of those years. The sole exception occurred in 1978.

Rose (23)

Fell (1)

Trend to 31 December after an August price shift of -2.40% to +3.45% (since 1949)

In the remaining 22 years of this period, the record for the last four months of the year is 11 up and 11 down.

Rising prices by
December No 2

A price rise in the last four months of the year is often tipped off by sharply rising prices in the nine months from 1 December through 31 August. Since our records began, there have been 26 years with a price rise of +9.40% to +23.81% during this period. The stock market continued to rise in the last four months of the year in 25 of those years.

Rose (25)

Fell (1)

Trend to 31 December after a December–August price rise of
+9.40% to +23.81%

Falling prices by November

On the down-side, here are two indicators that suggest prices will probably decline in the months ahead. Since records began, there have been 10 years with a price shift of +0.99% to -7.91% between 1 April and 31 August. In nine of those years, prices fell in the next three months.

Rose (1)

Fell (9)

Trend to 30 November after an April–August price shift of
+0.99% to -7.91%

Falling prices by next June

There have been 11 years with a price drop of -5.16% to -13.86% between 1 February and 31 August. Prices fell in the 10 months ahead in 10 of those years. The single exception to the rule occurred back in 1953.

Rose (1)

Fell (11)

Trend to 30 June (next year) after a February–August price drop
of -5.16% to -13.86%

CHAPTER TWENTY-THREE –
WALL STREET SEPTEMBER 1996

September is *by far* the year's worst month. Prices fall in most years. Sadly, the recent trend shows no sign of improvement.

Prices are especially likely to fall if they have been rising in recent weeks and months.

About the only silver lining in the September cloud is that the third-quarter price trend gives investors a pretty clear picture of where fourth-quarter prices are heading.

Did you hear the story about the investor who was depressed because his portfolio had fallen by 15% since the start of the year? 'Cheer up,' said his broker. 'Things could be worse.' He decided his broker was right, so he cheered up. And sure enough, things got worse.

Big money-loser

That joke springs to mind when we examine Wall Street's sorry September record. September is a frequent disappointment to American investors, as it is to UK investors. It is Wall Street's worst month. From 1930 to the present, the September investor lost money at the incredibly high average rate of -1.36% per year *(see Table 23.1)*. A hypo-

Table 23.1   **SEPTEMBER PRICE RISES AND DECLINES: 1930–1994**

	Average September price change	Up	Down/ no change
1930–39	-5.23%	4	6
1940–49	-0.33%	5	5
1950–59	0.27%	5	5
1960–69	-0.38%	4	6
1970–79	-0.93%	3	7
1980–89	-1.26%	4	6
1990–94	-1.96%	1	4
Average September price change	-1.36%	26	39

Source: Datastream

Table 23.1: September has been a steady loser for American investors. Even the 1950s would have lost money in the average year had it not been for 1954 when prices rose by +8.31%.

thetical investor who held shares each September from 1930 to the present, and converted to cash for the rest of the year would have run down his $1,000 start-up investment to $359, before factoring in the effects of inflation.

Nothing good to say

It is hard to find something nice to say about September. It has the lowest number of up years, the largest number of Big Hits, and the only month to have produced an average annual loss in five of the last six decades.

1954 was an exception

September's best (and only profitable) decade was in the 1950s when it turned an average annual profit of +0.27%. But even then, it was merely the ninth-ranked month in a mainly profitable decade. And without a +8.31% increase in 1954, this decade would also have been a loser for September investors.

No trend change in sight

In case you are hoping for a trend change, forget it. There is no sign of one. September investors continue to have done badly in recent years. From 1984 to 1994, shares

352

fell in nine of 11 years. This horrid trend, coupled with the effect of Wall Street on London prices, helps to explain why the September trend has been so poor in the UK in recent years.

INCREASE YOUR PROFIT ODDS

Despite the poor profit prospects for this lack-lustre month, it is possible to profit in September by investing selectively and avoiding years in which a loss is especially likely. Here are several trends to help you avoid a September decline.

August signal

Since 1951, there have been 19 occasions when August prices rose within a range of +1.53% to +10.63%. Shares fell in September in 16 of those years. In one of the three exceptions, 1979, prices were unchanged.

Rose (2)

Unchanged (1)

Fell (16)

September record after an August price rise of +1.53% to +10.63% (since 1951)

May–August signal

Since 1959, there have been 11 occasions when prices rose in the four month period from 1 May to 31 August, within a range of +3.49% to +7.39%. Shares fell in September in each of those years.

Rose (0)

Fell (11)

September record after a May–August price rise of +3.49% to +7.39% (since 1959)

July signal

Price declines of at least -2.48% in July seem to tip September declines regardless of which direction the stock market moves in August. Since our records began, there have been 12 years with a July decline of sufficient size. September prices fell in 11 of those years. The single exception occurred in 1943.

Rose (1)

Fell (11)

September record after a July price drop of at least -2.48%

Since 1959, one or more of these three signals flashed in 22 years. The September record was two up, 19 down and one no change. In the remaining 14 years of this period untouched by any of these signals, the September record was 10 up and four down.

Looking ahead

Rising prices by next January

The extent to which the stock market rises in August and September often provides a good clue about the likelihood of further rises in the months ahead. Since 1945, there have been 17 years when prices rose within a range of +2.41% to +12.44% during these two months. By 31 January of the following year, four months later, prices had risen further each time.

Rose (17)

Fell (0)

Trend to 31 January (next year) after an August/September price rise of +2.41% to +12.44% (since 1945)

354

Rising prices by December

The price trend during the third quarter of the year often tips off which way shares will move during the year's final quarter. Since 1959, third quarter prices either fell (by any amount) or rose by up to +3.36% in 23 separate years. The record for the fourth quarter that followed was 20 up and three down. Each of the declines was relatively modest: -1.22% in 1969, -1.48% in 1977, and -0.69% in 1983. In other words, even if the signal is wrong, the odds of shares dropping by a large amount is low, based upon past experiences.

Rose (20)

Fell (3)

Trend to 31 December after a July–September price fall (by any amount) or rise by up to +3.36% (since 1959)

Rising prices by next August

To forecast further into the future, watch the price trend over the last six months. Since our records began, there have been 21 years when prices rose moderately between 1 April and 30 September, within a range of +3.37% to +12.49%. They rose still higher in the 11 months that followed (to 31 August of the following year) in 19 of those years. One of the two failures was due to the October, 1987 crash which proved to be too deep a hole out of which shares could climb by August 1988.

Rose (19)

Fell (2)

Trend to 31 August (next year) after a April–September price rise of +3.37% to +12.49%

Rising prices by next December

For a preview of how Wall Street will move in 1997, watch the direction of September price shifts. A drop in excess of 1% is a good sign for 1997. Here is the evidence accumulated to date.

Since 1962, Wall Street has fallen in September by over 1% in 11 different years. Shares rose in the following year each time. The September 1994 decline was Number 12 in the series and we assume that 1995 will follow with a rise.

Rose (11)

Fell (0)

Trend to 31 December (next year) after a September price fall by over 1% (since 1962)

During this same period, there were 21 other years in which September prices either rose or fell by up to 1%. The record for the following calendar year was 13 up and eight down.

356

CHAPTER TWENTY-FOUR –
WALL STREET OCTOBER 1996

October's reputation is worse than its actual performance. The typical year turns a small profit despite the horror of 1987 which pulled the average down.

A moderate price rise in the eight previous months is a good sign that prices will rise further in October. But a very small September price decline is often a prelude to further declines in October.

Looking ahead, a price drop in September/October is a good sign that prices will advance through to the middle of the following year.

October has a bad 'rep'. The mere mention of it conjures up images of 1929, 1987, and investors jumping out of windows from high floors of New York high-rise buildings.

Steady profits

The truth about October is different. Despite the horror of 1929 and 1987, it is Wall Street's seventh-best month. Prices rise 55% of the time at an average rate of +0.34% *(see Table 24.1)*. History suggests you will not make money every year but, over the long-run, this month has a small yet steady record of profitability. Between 1930 and 1994, a hypothetical October investor who placed his money in cash for the rest of the year, would have run-up his $1,000 to $1,113, even with 1987 included.

Recent trend up

The recent record has been good. Since 1985, prices rose seven times and fell three times.

Poor 1930s

Unfortunately, when things go bad in October, they go very bad. Worse still, the bad news seems to come in batches. One of two horrible decades for October investors was the 1930s which was slammed four times by price declines in excess of 8%. And, of course, the -19.93% decline of 1929 was adjacent to the 1930s.

Table 24.1   **OCTOBER PRICE RISES AND DECLINES: 1930–1994**

	Average October price change	Up	Down/ no change
1930–39	-1.54%	4	6
1940–49	1.63%	6	4
1950–59	0.00%	5	5
1960–69	1.66%	8	2
1970–79	-0.46%	3	7
1980–89	0.44%	6	4
1990–94	0.95%	4	1
Average October price change	0.34%	36	29

Source: Datastream

Table 24.1: If you can ignore the shadow of 1929 and 1987, October is a better investment month than its reputation suggests. Trouble seems to come in batches as it did in the 1930s and 1970s.

Worse 1970s

An even worse performer was the 1970s with a record of three up and seven down. The poor record was disguised by the 1974 up-move which marked the end of the 1973–74 bear market on Wall Street. October prices rose +16.30%. If not for 1974, the decade's average annual loss would have been a much larger -2.33% per year.

1929 and 1987 in context

One of our goals for this discussion about October is to help investors understand the pros and cons of an October investment. But we recognise that no matter how much assurance is provided, the mere mention of this month causes alarm bells to go off for many investors. We have no wish to dismiss the pain associated with both major October crashes. October 1987 was a disaster for US stock market investors. But 1987 was Wall Street's fifth-worst fall of modern times. 1929 was the seventh worst fall. March 1938 and September 1931 each experienced bigger falls. May had

Not too disaster-
prone in last 50
years

two bigger falls, in 1932 and 1940. Yet those months don't stimulate the same emotions as October, on either side of the Atlantic. The reason? Probably the shock of each October crash. In both cases, most investors had no inkling of what was about to happen.

Another way to put October's 'disaster potential' into perspective is to tally the number of Big Hits, declines of -5% or more, that occurred in each month of the year. As Table 24.2 shows, October has had 10 Big Hits since 1926, not so different from May, July, August, September, and November. And seven of them occurred before 1944. In the last 50 years, October has experienced just three Big Hits of 5% or more. When you examine the evidence objectively, October's record is not as bad as its reputation.

Table 24.2   **MONTHLY BIG HITS: 1926–1994**

	Total Big Hits	Very Big Hits (-10% or more)	Big Hits (-5.00% to -9.99%)
January	6	—	6
February	3	1	2
March	7	4	3
April	7	1	6
May	10	3	7
June	7	1	6
July	9	1	8
August	9	—	9
September	11	6	5
October	**10**	**4**	**6**
November	9	4	5
December	3	1	2

Table 24.2: October may generate the most fear, but the reality is different. There are many other months that suffer from a similar number of Big Hits and Very Big Hits. There were only three Big Hits in October in the past 50 years.

INCREASE YOUR PROFIT ODDS

Although October's prices rise in most years, it is possible to improve the odds of making a profit in this month. Here are several signals which have tipped past October declines and advances.

September signal No 1

In years when the previous four months either have risen by less than 10% (in other words, when there is no sign of a bull market 'blow off') or have fallen, a September decline of -1.10% to -4.82% is a good sign for October investors. Since our records began, there have been 13 years which have fulfilled these two conditions. The stock market rose in October in 12 of those years. The single exception, in 1952, saw a tiny October decline of just -0.08%.

Rose (12)

Fell (1)

October record after a September drop of -1.10% to -4.82% and a previous four month rise by less than 10%, or a fall

February–
September
signal

A rise in the eight months from February to September usually signals that prices will continue to rise in October. Since 1961, there have been 11 years with an eight-month price rise within the range of +4.59% to +11.39%. October's prices rose in 10 of those years.

Rose (10)

Fell (1)

October record after a February–September price rise of +4.59% to +11.39% (since 1961)

September
signal No 2

On the down-side, there are two leading indicators that are often associated with an October price decline. If September

360

prices drift down by a small margin, no more than -0.97%, the odds of an October fall are high. There have been 12 Septembers with a price decline within this range. The October record following this trend is two rises, one no change and nine declines.

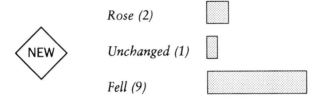

Rose (2)

Unchanged (1)

Fell (9)

NEW

October record after a September price drop of less than -0.97%

December– September signal

A very big rise in the 10 months preceding October is often a signal that prices will soon fall. There have been nine years with a price rise of +24.22% or more in the 10 months leading up to October, that is, from December of the preceding year through to September. October prices fell in eight of those years. The single exception to the rule occurred in 1945, as America began its successful switch-over to a peace-time economy.

NEW

Rose (8)

Fell (1)

October record after a December–September price rise of +24.22% or more

LOOKING AHEAD

Rising prices by next July

A price decline in September and October is often associated with price rises in the next nine months. Since 1946, there have been 18 years when prices fell in September/October by -0.75% or more. In 17 of those years, the stock market rose in the next nine months.

Rose (17)

Fell (1)

Trend to 31 July (next year) after a September/October price drop of -0.75% or more (since 1946)

Falling prices by next September

On the down-side, there have been 14 years when prices rose by +3.90% to +8.58% over the three months ending 31 October. They fell in 11 of those years, in the 11 months that followed.

Rose (3)

Fell (11)

Trend to 30 September (next year) after a August–October price rise of +3.90% to +8.58%

CHAPTER TWENTY-FIVE –
WALL STREET NOVEMBER 1996

> The November price trend has been quite good to investors in recent years. Unfortunately, presidential election years are the exception to the rule. The odds of a price rise are merely 50:50.
>
> But if prices have risen strongly during the last seven months, the odds of a November price rise are quite high.

Looks are deceptive

Be careful when analysing November's 'typical' performance. The long-term averages can deceive. It is easy to reach completely different conclusions about this month's investment potential by adjusting the starting point of your analysis.

On an overall basis, November is Wall Street's eighth best month. Prices rise 54% of the time at an average rate of +0.30%. Between 1930 and 1994, a November investor who placed his money in cash for the rest of the year, would have run-up his $1,000 to $1,124.

1930s and 1940s were poor

But under the surface, some major trend changes are worth noting. November was a significant money-loser in the 1930s and '40s. Shares fell at an average annual rate of -2.09% during this 20-year period. Only September did worse. Between 1937 and 1951, November prices fell 12 times and rose just three times. Two of the gains were less than one-half of one percent *(see Table 25.1)*.

Improvement since 1952

From 1952 to the present, the investment climate radically improved. Prices rose 28 times (65%) and fell 15 times, a remarkable reversal. During this stretch, November investors turned an average annual profit of +1.44%. A $1,000 November investment, starting in 1952, would now be worth $1,775, quite good considering the investment was at risk just 43 months.

Table 25.1   **NOVEMBER PRICE RISES AND DECLINES: 1930–1994**

	Average November price change	Up	Down/ no change
1930–39	-1.33%	4	6
1940–49	-2.84%	3	7
1950–59	2.48%	7	3
1960–69	1.73%	6	4
1970–79	0.27%	6	4
1980–89	1.72%	7	3
1990–94	-0.12%	2	3
Average November price change	0.30%	35	30

Source: Datastream

Table 25.1: The November trend has been strong since the 1950s.

INCREASE YOUR PROFIT ODDS

50:50 in US election years

Even though the odds of a November profit have been good in recent years, it is possible to improve the odds by picking your opportunities with care. This is especially true in presidential election years, like 1996, when the odds of a November profit are not much better than 50:50 (nine up and eight down). However, an interesting trend seems to be developing that might interest investors who think the Republicans will win in 1996. Although the number of observations is very low, the evidence suggests Wall Street reacts positively to first-term Republicans.

Good odds if Republicans win

Since 1926, there have been five different Republicans who won a first term in office. Four of them offered voters a fresh economic programme and the stock market rose each time. The single exception, George Bush, won for the Republicans in 1988 by running on fellow-Republican Ronald Reagan's coat-tails. His slogan: 'Four more years' promised voters a continuation of Reagan's economic programme and the stock market fell in November.

As Table 25.2 shows, second-term Republican presidents are not associated with such favourable stock market trends, probably because their economic programmes are already in place on election day and there are no changing circumstances to which the stock market can react. Democrats, with their traditional emphasis on more taxes and social spending, are not generally greeted with glee by Wall Street, first- or second-term.

The number of observations tallied in Table 25.2 is small. From a statistical point of view, the data is quite 'skimpy'. Still, the data suggests that November 1996 will be a money-maker if the Republicans win the Presidency given that the current occupant is Democrat Bill Clinton.

Table 25.2	**NOVEMBER PROFIT AND LOSS RECORD IN ELECTION YEARS**		
		November prices rose	November prices fell
Republican victories			
	First term	4	–
	Second term	1	3
Democratic victories			
	First term	2	4
	Second term	2	1

Table 25.2: November prices rose each time a Republican presented a new economic programme and won a first term. The trend was less positive for second-term Republican victors, probably because their programmes were no longer new and were already factored into the price. For purposes of this analysis, George Bush's 1988 win was treated as a second term victory. His slogan 'Four more years' explains why. Democrats don't provide much help to November prices, first- or second-term.

August–October signal

Putting the election issue aside, a small decline in the three months from August to October usually signals that prices will rise in November. Since 1952, there have been 14 years with a three month-long price decline within the range of -0.58% to -4.94%. October's prices rose in 13 of those years.

Rose (13)

Fell (1)

November record after an August–October price drop of -0.58% to -4.94% (since 1952)

April–October record

If there is a sizeable run-up in prices in the seven months preceding November, that is from 1 April to 31 October within a range of +13.26% to +53.16%, the odds of a November profit are high. There have been 16 years on record with a seven-month price rise within the designated range. November prices rose in 14 of those years.

Rose (14)

Fell (2)

November record after an April–October price rise of +13.26% to +53.16%

LOOKING AHEAD

December signal

Prices usually rise in election year Decembers, regardless of who wins in November. Either the November rally continues or the stock market's jitters are overcome in the few weeks following the election, leaving the door open to a December up-move. The single exception for which to watch is a price rise in the six-month period between 1 June and 30 November of +9.83% or more. Such a rise frequently indicates that the rally will soon end, at least in the short run.

Here is the evidence accumulated to date. Since 1928, there have been 17 US presidential election years. In six of them, prices rose by at least +9.83% in the six months ending 30 November. The December record in those years was two up and four down. In the remaining 11 years with smaller price rises or a price decline in the six month run-up, December's prices rose each time.

Rose (11)

Fell (0)

Trend to 31 December after a June–November price drop or rise up to +9.82% (since 1928)

Falling prices by next November

The extent to which prices rise in election year Octobers and Novembers often provides a good clue about the likelihood of a further price rise in the year ahead. Since the 1928 presidential election, there have been six election years when prices rose by +4.56% or more during these two months. One year later? Prices had dropped each time, regardless of which party won the election.

Rose (0)

Fell (6)

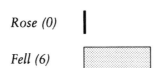

Trend to 30 November (next year) after an October/November price rise of +4.56% or more (since 1928)

367

Chapter Twenty-six –
Wall Street December 1996

The long-term December trend looks good. And under the surface, the trend is even better for investors than the averages suggest.

The recent trend is better yet – eight ups in a row.

Prices are especially likely to rise in December if they have risen moderately in the preceding months. A large December increase is a clear signal that prices will rise even further in the year ahead.

Third-best

According to the official averages, December is Wall Street's third best month. From 1930 to the present, prices have risen at an average rate of +1.44% per year (see Table 26.1). A hypothetical investor, who held shares each December, from 1930 to the present, and converted to cash for the rest of the year would have run a $1,000 investment up to $2,411, not a bad return considering that the money was placed in shares for a just 65 months, a little over five years.

Maybe even better

But, sometimes, averages can mislead and December is a good example. In some respects it is the best month of the year. Prices rise 72% of the time compared with 65% in Number Two-ranked January.

When prices fall, as they do occasionally in even the best of times, the odds of getting hurt badly in December are less than the odds in other good months. Out of 18 down Decembers since 1930, six were less than -1%. In contrast, January had 23 falls during this period. Only three were below 1%. The rest (20) were larger.

Few Big Hits

Big explosions are not a December speciality. Very large price shifts, up or down, occur much less often than you might expect. Shares have risen sharply by +5% or more in December on 10 occasions since records began. In compar-

Table 26.1

DECEMBER PRICE RISES AND DECLINES: 1930–1994

	Average December price change	Up	Down/ no change
1930–39	-1.07%	5	5
1940–49	2.45%	8	2
1950–59	2.46%	8	2
1960–69	0.65%	7	3
1970–79	2.27%	8	2
1980–89	0.90%	6	4
1990–94	3.38%	5	0
Average December price change	1.44%	47	18

Source: Datastream

Table 26.1: December has been a steady money-maker since the 1940s. And even in the money-losing 1930s, most of the damage was due to a -14.53% decline in 1931. The recent record has been incredibly strong: eight rises in a row.

ison, January saw a big rise 16 times. On the down-side, Big Hits of -5% or more have occurred just three times, giving December a lowly rank of 11 on this dimension. January suffered six Big Hits during this period.

Ranking December as Number One or Number Three may be debatable. But on the key issue of profitability, there is little to dispute. December has been a steady money-maker since our records began. While you would not have profited in every single year, your investment would have grown in every completed decade since the 1940s.

Recent trend good
The positive trend continues right up to the present. Prices have risen every December since the 1987 crash, eight times in a row.

INCREASE YOUR PROFIT ODDS

Although the chance of profiting in December is quite good, it is possible to improve the odds by monitoring several historical trends which do a good job of tipping price increases. During election years like 1996, be sure to review the previous chapter for some useful December tips.

November signal

Putting the election issue aside, one of the best tools with which to predict a December up-move is the size of the price shift in the previous month. There have been 15 occasions since our records began when November shifted within a range of +0.12% to -1.89%. December prices rose in every one of those years.

Rose (15)

Fell (0)

December record after a November price shift of +0.12% to -1.89%.

June–November signal

A related trend worth looking for is a small price rise in the six months preceding December. There have been 22 occasions when prices rose from 1 June to 30 November, by +2.49% to +8.65%. December prices rose in each of those years.

Rose (22)

Fell (0)

December record after a June–November price rise of +2.49% to +8.65%

January–November signal

A third signal that does a good job of anticipating December profits is a price shift in the first 11 months of the year within a range of -5.28% to +17.06%. Prices shifted within

370

this range on 31 occasions. December followed with a rise in 30 of those years. The only exception was in 1968 when prices fell by -4.15% despite a favourable 11-month signal. Even with 1968 included, prices rose by an average of +3.13% each time the 11-month signal flashed.

Rose (30)

Fell (1)

December record after a January–November price shift of -5.28% to +17.06%

In the remaining years untouched by any of these three signals, December's prices fall more than half of the time.

LOOKING AHEAD

Rising prices by next December

December price shifts often tip where prices are heading in the next few months. There have been 16 years when December prices rose by at least +3.89%. One year later, prices stood still higher in 15 of those years. The sole exception was in 1983 when a solid December rise was followed by a decline in share prices in the next 12 months.

Rose (15)

Fell (1)

Trend to 30 December (next year) after a December price rise of at least +3.89%

Rising prices by next July

Another good signal to look for is a strong price rise in the period between 1 August to 31 December which is often associated with further price rises in the next seven months. Since our records began, there have been 15 years when the five month trend rose by at least +10.66%. By July 31 of the following year, prices stood still higher in 14 of those years. The sole exception was in 1980.

Rose (14)

Fell (1)

Trend to 31 July (next year) after an August–December price rise of at least +10.66%

Falling prices by next July

On the down-side, here are two indicators that suggest some stormy weather ahead. If prices fall by -4.51% or more from 1 November to 31 December, the odds are good there will be further falls in the seven months ahead. Out of 10 occasions with a two month price drop of this magnitude, prices stood still lower by the following 31 July in eight of those years.

Rose (2)

Fell (8)

Trend to 31 July (next year) after a November–December price fall of at least -4.51%

Falling prices by next March

And finally, there have been 12 occasions when prices shifted slightly within a range of -1.77% to +0.62% in the four months between 1 September and 31 December. They fell in the first quarter of the following year in 10 of those years.

Rose (2)

Fell (10)

Trend to 31 March (next year) after a September–December price shift of -1.77% to +0.62%